Instructor's Resource Manual

for

Siegel's

Criminology

Eighth Edition

Carolyn Dennis
Fayetteville State University

THOMSON
WADSWORTH

Australia • Canada • Mexico • Singapore • Spain • United Kingdom • United States

To Michael
&
Mom and Dad,
With Love

Printed in the United States of America
1 2 3 4 5 6 7   05 04 03 02 01

Printer: Phoenix Color Corporation

0-534-52657-8

For more information about our products, contact us at:
Thomson Learning Academic Resource Center
1-800-423-0563

For permission to use material from this text, contact us by:
Phone: 1-800-730-2214
Fax: 1-800-731-2215
Web: http://www.thomsonrights.com

Asia
Thomson Learning
5 Shenton Way #01-01
UIC Building
Singapore 068808

Australia
Nelson Thomson Learning
102 Dodds Street
South Street
South Melbourne, Victoria 3205
Australia

Canada
Nelson Thomson Learning
1120 Birchmount Road
Toronto, Ontario M1K 5G4
Canada

Europe/Middle East/South Africa
Thomson Learning
High Holborn House
50/51 Bedford Row
London WC1R 4LR
United Kingdom

Latin America
Thomson Learning
Seneca, 53
Colonia Polanco
11560 Mexico D.F.
Mexico

Spain
Paraninfo Thomson Learning
Calle/Magallanes, 25
28015 Madrid, Spain

TABLE OF CONTENTS

Chapter One

Crime and Criminology

Summary

Chapter One provides an overview of criminology. The development of criminology is traced from its conception to today. The various sub-areas of criminology are presented with a discussion of the three perspectives of crime. The chapter concludes by introducing a variety of research methods.

Learning Objectives

After reading this chapter students should be able to:

- Define and describe the study of criminology.
- Review the history of criminology.
- Understand the various components of classical criminology.
- Develop an understanding of the classical school theories and their offspring.
- Realize the distinction between criminology and criminal justice.
- To understand the role of criminologists in our society.
- Explore the various views that criminologist utilize to examine crime.
- Be able to define and measure crime.
- Understand the various types of research.
- Develop an understanding of the ethical issues in criminology.

Chapter Overview

The Study of Criminology
What is Criminology?

A Brief History of Criminology
    Classical Criminology
    Nineteenth Century Positivism
    The Development of Sociological Criminology
        The Foundation of Sociological Criminology
        The Chicago School and Beyond
    Conflict Criminology: Criminology Today
Criminology and Criminal Justice
    The Distinction Between Criminology and Criminal Justice
    The Distinction Between Criminology and Deviance
What Criminologists Do: The Criminological Enterprise
    Criminal Statistics
    Sociology of Law
    Theory Construction
    Victimology
How Criminologists View Crime
    The Consensus View of Crime
    The Conflict View of Crime
    The Interactionist View of Crime
Defining Crime
Survey Research
    Cohort Research
    Aggregate Data Research
    Experimental Research
    Observational and Interview Research
Ethical Issues in Criminology
Summary

Chapter Outline

I.   **Introduction**
    A. Gender, Race and Culture in Criminology, Is Crime an International Phenomenon?
        1. Crime is decreasing in the United States.
        2. Crime is increasing in other countries, such as England, Wales, Russia, the former Soviet Union Republics and Asia.
    B. Concern about crime led to the development of criminology as an academic discipline.
    C. Criminologists use scientific methods to study the nature, extent, cause and control of criminal behavior.

II.   **What is Criminology?**
 A. Criminology is the scientific approach to studying criminal behavior.
   1. Sutherland and Cressey define the important areas of interest to criminologists:
     a. The development of criminal law and its use to define crime.
     b. The cause of law violations.
     c. The methods used to control criminal behavior.
 B. An interdisciplinary science - criminologists have been trained in other fields, most commonly sociology.

III.   **A Brief History of Criminology**
  Prior to the 18th century punishment was cruel, including torture and many were burned, whipped, branded, maimed and executed.
 A. Classical Criminology - Mid 18th century social philosophers rethought the punishment approach.
   1. Punishment should be fair and balanced and related to the crime.
   2. Utilitarianism - behavior occurs when one considers it useful, purposeful and reasonable.
   3. Cesare Beccaria (1738-1794) believed that people want to achieve pleasure and avoid pain.
     a. Therefore, crimes should provide pleasure for the criminal.
     b. To deter crime, pain should counterbalance the pleasure received.
     c. Punishment should be public, prompt, necessary, proportionate to the crime and dictated by the laws.
   4. Classical criminology:
     a. people have free will to choose crime
     b. crime may be more attractive if they have a greater payoff
     c. The more severe, swift and certain the punishment, the better able to control criminal behavior.
 B. Nineteenth-Century Positivism -
   1. August Comte (1798-1857) the founder of sociology, applied scientific methods to the study of society.
     a. People embrace a rational, scientific view of the world - positivists.
     b. Positivism
       1. Human behavior is a function of internal and external forces.
       2. The use of the scientific method to solve problems.
   2. Positivist Criminology - early scientific studies examining human behavior were biologically oriented.
     a. Physiognomists - studied facial features of criminals to determine whether the shape of ears, nose, and eyes and their distance apart were associated with antisocial behavior.
     b. Phrenologists - studied the shape of the skull and bumps on the head to see if these physical traits were linked to criminal behavior.
     c. Phillipe Pinel - coined the term psychopathic personality.
     d. Henry Maudsley (1835-1918) believed that insanity and criminal behavior were strongly linked.

3. Biological Determinism
   a. Cesare Lombroso (1835-1909) studied cadavers of executed criminals to see they were physically different then noncriminals.
   b. Known as the Father of Criminology.
   c. Viewed offenders as "born criminals" that inherited physical problems that impelled them into a life of crime - criminal anthropology.
   d. Held that born criminals suffer from atavistic anomalies - physically, they are throwbacks to more primitive times when people were savages.
   e. Biological Determinism not taken seriously today. Rather, biosocial theory which reflects the assumed link between physical and mental traits, the social environment and behavior.
C. The Development of Sociological Criminology
   1. Foundations of Sociological Criminology can be trace to:
      a. L. A. J. (Adolphe) Quetelet (1796-1974) instigated the use of data and statistics in performing criminological research.
      b. Emile Durkheim (1858-1917) defined crime as a normal and necessary social event. Further argued that crime can be useful and even healthy for society. Without crime, everyone would act the same.
         1. Wrote *The Division of Labor*, which discussed the shift from a small, rural society to the modern large urban population with division of labor and personal isolation.
         2. From this shift flowed anomie, or norm confusion.
      c. The Chicago School and Beyond
         1. Research began at the Sociology Department at the University of Chicago by Robert Ezra Part (1864-1944), Ernest W. Burgess (1886-1966), Louis Wirth (1897-1952) and their colleagues.
         2. They pioneered research on the social ecology of the city.
         3. They concluded that social forces operating in urban areas create criminal interactions; some neighborhoods become "natural areas" for crime.
         4. In the 1930s and 40s, sociologists linked social-psychological to criminality.
         5. Renowned criminologist Edwin Sutherland proposed that people learn criminal attitudes from older, more experienced law violators.
         6. These views linked criminality to the failure of socialization.
         7. By 1950s, most criminologists embraced either the ecological view or the socialization view of crime.
   2. Conflict Criminology - Marx proposed that the character of every civilization is determined by its mode of production - the way its people develop and produce material goods.
      a. Capitalist - Bourgeoisie
      b. People who do the labor - Proletariat

3. Contemporary Criminology
   a. All of the original theories have continued to evolve
   b. Classical theory has evolved into rational choice and deterrence.

IV. **What Criminologists Do: The Criminological Enterprise** - Primarily studying crime and criminal behavior.
   A. The Criminological Enterprise - sub-areas of criminology
      1. Criminal Statistics - involves measuring the amount and trends of criminal activity.
      2. Sociology of Law - Determining the origin of law.
      3. Theory Construction - Predicting individual behavior.
      4. Criminal Behavior Systems - Determining the nature and cause of specific crime patterns.
         a. Crime Typology - the study of criminal behavior involving research on the links between different types of crime and criminals.
      5. Penology - Studying the correction and control of criminal behavior.
      6. Victimology - Studying the nature and cause of victimization.

V. **How Criminologists View Crime**
   A. The Consensus View of Crime - Crimes are behaviors believed to be repugnant to all elements of society.
      1. Substantive criminal law - the written code that defines crimes and their punishments, reflects the values, beliefs, and opinions of society's mainstream.
      2. Social Harm - that which sets strange, unusual or deviant behavior or any other action that departs from social norms, apart from criminal behavior.
   B. The Conflict View of Crime - depicts society as a collection of diverse groups - owners, workers, professionals, and students - who are in constant and continuing conflict.
      1. The definition of crime is controlled by wealth, power, and position and not by moral consensus or the fear of social disruption.
      2. Crime is a political concept designed to protect the power and position of the upper classes at the expense of the poor.
   C. The Interactionist View of Crime
      1. people act according to their own interpretations of reality, through which they assign meaning to things.
      2. They learn the meaning of a thing from the way others react to it, either positively or negatively and
      3. They reevaluate and interpret their own behavior according to the meaning and symbols they have learned from others.
      4. See the law as conforming to the beliefs of "moral crusaders" or moral entrepreneurs, who use their influence to shape the legal process in the way they see fit.

VI. **Defining Crime**
   A. Crime is a violation of societal rules of behavior as interpreted and expressed by a criminal legal code created by people holding social and political power.

5

B. Individuals who violate these rules are subject to sanctions by state authority, social stigma, and loss of status.

VII. Criminology Research Methods

A. Survey Research
1. Surveys involve sampling, which is the process of selecting subjects sharing similar characteristics called populations.
2. A common type of survey is cross-sectional research - simultaneously interviewing or questioning a diverse sample of subjects who represent a cross section of a community.
3. Self-report surveys ask participants to describe their criminal activity.
   a. Pros and Cons of Surveys As Information Gathering Tool
      1. Most widely used method of study
      2. Not foolproof.
   b. Cohort Research: Longitudinal and Retrospective
      1. Longitudinal research involves watching a group of people who share a like characteristic (cohort) over time.
      2. Retrospective Cohort Study - Take an intact cohort of known offenders and look back into their early life by checking their education, family, police and hospital records.
   c. Aggregate Data Research - Explains the social trends and patterns on the crime rate.
      1. Uniform Crime Report complied by FBI - probably the most important source of official crime statistics
   d. Experimental Research
      1. Criminologists manipulate or intervene in the lives of their subjects to see the outcome or effect the intervention has.
      2. True experiments have 3 elements:
         a. random selection of subjects
         b. a control or comparison group
         c. an experimental condition
   a. Time-Series Design - Recording data concerning a particular crime following passage of a law.

B. Observational and Interview Research

VIII. Ethical Issues in Criminological Research

A. What is to be studied.
B. Who is to be studied.
C. How studies are to be conducted.
D. Potential conflicts include
1. When the institution funding research is one of the principal subjects of the project.
2. Who will be the subject?
3. Subjects who are mislead about research purpose.
4. Care must be provided for the subjects.

IX. Summary

Key Terms

Criminal Anthropology - View that individuals inherited criminal traits; born criminal which impelled them into a life of crime.

Criminology - discipline devoted to the development of valid and reliable information that addresses the causes of crime as well as crime patterns.

Atavistic Anomalies - Born criminals who suffer from being thrown back to more primitive times when people were savages.

Criminologists - use scientific methods to study the nature, extent, cause, and control of criminal behavior.

Anomie - A condition produced by normlessness.

Interdisciplinary - Criminology is essentially an interdisciplinary science; criminologists have been trained in diverse fields, most commonly sociology, but also criminal justice, political science, psychology, economics, and the natural sciences.

Chicago School - Sociological positivism secured by research begun in the early 20th century by Robert Ezra Park, Ernest W. Burgess, Louis Wirth and their colleagues in the Sociology Department at the University of Chicago. The scholars who taught at this program created what is still referred to as the Chicago School, in honor of their unique style of doing research.

Criminal Justice System - The agencies of social control that handle criminal offenders.

Bourgeoisie - the owners of the means of production; the capitalist.

Deviant Behavior - strange, unusual or any other action that departs from social norms, apart from criminal behaviors.

Proletariat - the people who do the actual labor.

Legalized - no criminal penalties for a specific act.

Criminological Enterprise - sub-areas of criminology which exist within the broader arena of criminology. These sub-areas include: criminal statistics, sociology of law, theory construction, criminal behavior systems, penology and victimology.

Decriminalized - Reducing the penalty for a criminal act but not actually legalizing it.

White-Collar Crime - economic crime activities.

Utilitarianism - philosophy which emphasized that behavior occurs when the actor considers it useful, purposeful, and reasonable.

Moral Entrepreneurs - Moral crusaders who use their influence to shape the legal process in the way they see fit.

Classical Criminology - has several basic elements: people have free will to choose criminal or lawful solutions to meet their needs; criminal solutions may be more attractive than lawful one; a person's choice of criminal solutions may be controlled by their fear of punishment and the more severe, certain, and swift the punishment, the better able it is to control criminal behavior.

Cohort - a group of people who share a characteristic over time.

Positivist - Followers of Auguste Comte writings.

Discussion Exercise

Some states have higher crime rates than other states. Divide the class into several groups and assign each group a state. Have each group research the crime statistics for their assigned state. Group presentations can include the amount of crime being committed in the various states, who is committing the crime and possible reasons for the crime being committed.

InfoTrac Assignment

This text may come bundled with InfoTrac. This will allow students online access to journal articles. This service is updated daily and provides excellent resources for you and your students.

InfoTrac is very easy to navigate. Have students log on to the web site with their password. Assign various key words from the area to be studied. You will find InfoTrac to be a wonderful resource for discussion and research assignments.

GETTING STARTED: Search term words for subject guide: criminology, Emile Durkheim, victimology, victims, Uniform Crime Report, survey research.

CRITICAL THINKING PROJECT: Using the search term "victims," find articles that explain how statistics of victims are collected. Interestingly, depending on the statistician or the methodology, data may be reflected differently from different reports.

Here are three articles:

Klug, Elizabeth A. "One in four violent crime victims in the United States is physically injured during an attack each year." *Corrections Compendium*.

Newman, Graeme "Counting Victims." *Foreign Policy*.

Crime Data "Injuries from violent crime." *The FBI Law Enforcement Bulletin*.

Test Bank

Essay Questions

1. Define the Consensus View of Crime and the Conflict View of Crime. Compare and contrast these two theories.

2. Describe the difference between Criminology and Criminal Justice. What is the difference between Criminology and Deviance.

3. What is Criminology? Briefly trace the history of Criminology.

3. Describe the various methods of research used by criminologists to measure data. What are the pros and cons of each type of research?

5. List and explain the major perspectives of the Criminological Enterprise.

Fill In the Blank

1. **Criminology** is devoted to the development of valid and reliable information that addresses the causes of crimes as well as crime patterns and trends.

2. **Utilitarianism** emphasizes that behavior occurs when the actor considers it useful, purposeful and reasonable.

3. Criminologists who study the facial features of criminals to determine whether the shape of ears, nose and eyes and the distance between them are associated with antisocial behavior is known as **Physiognomists**.

4. Lombroso held that criminals suffer from **atavistic anomalies.**

5. According to **Durkheim**, crime is part of human nature because it has existed during periods of poverty and prosperity.

6. Interactions people have with various individuals, organizations, institutions and processes of society which help theme mature and develop is known as **socialization**.

7. The most important relationship in industrial culture is between the owners of the means of production, the capitalist **bourgeoisie**, and the people who do the actual labor, the **proletariat**.

8. Studying the correction and control of criminal behavior is known as **penology.**

9. **Victimology** is the study of the nature and cause of victimization.

10. According to the **consensus view**, crimes are behaviors believed to be repugnant to all elements of society.

    11. The consensus view of crime links illegal behavior to the concept of **social harm**

12. The **interactionist view** of crime is similar to the conflict perspective because they both suggest that behavior is outlawed when if offends people who maintain the social, economic and political power necessary to have the law conform to their interests or needs.

13. **Sampling** refers to the process of selecting for study a limited number of subjects who are representative of entire groups sharing similar characteristics.

14. **Self-report surveys** ask participants to describe their recent and lifetime criminal activity.

15. **Longitudinal research** involves observing a group of people who share a like characteristic over time.

Multiple Choice

1. _____ use scientific methods to study the nature, extent, cause and control of criminal behavior.
    a. psychologists
    b. criminologists
    c. physiologists
    d. biologists
    (Answer = b)

2. _____ is the scientific approach to studying criminal behavior.
    a. criminology
    b. police science
    c. political science
    d. psychology
    (Answer = a)

3. The writings of Beccaria and his followers form the core of what today is referred to as:
    a.   survey research
    b.   classical criminology
    c.   criminal statistics
    d.   sociology of law
    (Answer = b)

4. The founder of sociology is:
    a.   Sigmund Freud
    b.   Cesare Beccaria
    c.   Edwin Sutherland
    d.   Auguste Comte
    (Answer = d)

5. Individuals who pioneered the notion that the source of different mental functions is located in different parts of the brain are known as:
    a.   phrenologists
    b.   Physiognomists
    c.   psychologists
    d.   sociologists
    (Answer = a)

6. The father of criminology is:
    a.   Sigmund Freud
    b.   Cesare Lombroso
    c.   Edwin Sutherland
    d.   Phillipe Pinel
    (Answer = b)

7. The theory, which has been coined to reflect the assumed link between physical and mental traits, the social environment, and behavior, is:
    a.   biosocial theory
    b.   the consensus view of crime
    c.   the conflict view of crime
    d.   the interactionist view of crime
    (Answer = a)

8. Which theorist felt that crime is normal because it is virtually impossible to imagine a society in which criminal behavior is totally absent.
    a.   Cesare Becarria
    b.   Phillipe Pinel
    c.   Emile Durkheim
    d.   Auguste Comte
    (Answer = c)

9. Interactions people have with various individuals, organizations, institutions and processes of society which help them mature and develop are known as:
   a. socialization
   b. criminalization
   c. conflict
   d. consensus
   (Answer = a)

10. The capitalist or the owners of the means of production are known as:
    a. proletariat
    b. bourgeoisie
    c. interactionist
    d. positivists
    (Answer = b)

11. The major perspectives of criminology focus on:
    a. Classical/Choice Perspective
    b. Biological/Psychological Perspective
    c. Structural Perspective
    d. All of the above
    (Answer = d)

12. Several sub-areas of criminology exist within the broader areas of criminology. These sub-areas of called the:
    a. the criminological enterprise
    b. criminal statistics
    c. sociology of law
    d. victimology
    (Answer = a)

13. Gathering valid crime data is known as:
    a. theory construction
    b. criminal statistics
    c. sociology of law
    d. penology
    (Answer = b)

14. Studying the correction and control of criminal behavior is:
    a. criminal statistics
    b. sociology of law
    c. theory construction
    d. penology
    (Answer = d)

15. The sub-area of criminology concerned with the role social forces play in shaping criminal law and the role of criminal law in shaping society is known as:
    a.   cohort research
    b.   aggregate data research
    c.   experimental research
    d.   sociology of law
    (Answer = d)

16. Business-related offenses are known as:
    a.   crimes of opportunity
    b.   white-collar crime
    c.   penology
    d.   positivism
    (Answer = b)

17. Research on the links between different types of crime and criminals is known as:
    a.   crime typology
    b.   penology
    c.   victimology
    d.   sociology
    (Answer = a)

18. Victimology involves the study of:
    a.   designing services for the victims of crime
    b.   studying victim culpability
    c.   creating probabilities of victimization risk
    d.   all of the above
    (Answer = d)

19. The written code that defines crimes and their punishments is the:
    a.   substantive criminal law
    b.   procedural criminal law
    c.   civil law
    d.   tort law
    (Answer = a)

20. The consensus view of crime links illegal behavior to the concept of:
    a.   victimology
    b.   sociology
    c.   social harm
    d.   theory construction
    (Answer = c)

21. Society seen as a collection of diverse groups who are in constant and continuing conflict is known as:

    a.   consensus view

    b.   conflict view

    c.   interactionist view

    d.   all of the above

    (Answer = b)

22. The perspective which sees crime as the reflection of the preferences and opinions of people who hold social power in a particular legal jurisdiction is the:

    a.   consensus view

    b.   conflict view

    c.   interactionist view

    d.   all of the above

    (Answer = c)

23. Criminologists conduct research to:

    a.   measure the nature and extent of criminal behavior

    b.   meet other criminologists

    c.   gain recognition as criminologists

    d.   have easy, well-paying positions

    (Answer = a)

24. A common survey of simultaneously interviewing or questioning a diverse sample of subjects who represent a cross section of a community about research topics is:

    a.   sampling

    b.   cross-sectional research

    c.   aggregate data research

    d.   experimental research

    (Answer = b)

25. Asking participants to describe their recent and lifetime criminal activity is:

    a.   sampling

    b.   cross-sectional research

    c.   self-report surveys

    d.   experimental research

    (Answer = c)

26. Observing a group of people who share a like characteristic over time is:

    a.   sampling

    b.   cross-sectional research

    c.   self-report surveys

    d.   longitudinal research

    (Answer = d)

27. A like characteristic is:
   a.   cohort
   b.   anomie
   c.   process perspective
   d.   integrated perspective
   (Answer = a)

28. The Uniform Crime Report is collected by the:
   a.   Federal Bureau of Investigation
   b.   US Congress
   c.   State Agencies
   d.   Local Victim Organizations
   (Answer = a)

29.   The number of crimes reported by citizens to local police departments and the number of arrests made by police agencies in a given year is compiled into the:
   a.   Self-Report Study
   b.   Youth Survey
   c.   National Crime Victimization Survey
   d.   Uniform Crime Report
   (Answer = d)

30.   When criminologists want to see the direct effect of one factor on another, they conduct:
   a.   experimental research
   b.   aggregate data research
   c.   cohort research
   d.   survey research
   (Answer = a)

31. Information, which tells us about the effect of social trends and patterns on the crime rate is known as:
   a.   experimental research
   b.   aggregate data research
   c.   survey research
   d.   cohort research
   (Answer = b)

32. Conflict(s) of interest that may arise in criminological research include:
   a.   when the institution funding research is itself one of the principal subjects
   b.   who will be the subject of inquiries and study
   c.   when subjects are mislead about the purpose of the research
   d.   all of the above
   (Answer = d)

33. Sutherland and Cressey's definition of criminology include the most important areas of interest to criminologists, which include:
   a.   the development of criminal law and its use to define crime
   b.   the cause of law violations
   c.   the methods used to control criminal behavior
   d.   all of the above
   (Answer = d)

34. The theory which believes that people have free will to choose criminal or unlawful solutions to meet their needs or settle their problems:
   a.   classical criminology
   b.   conflict theory
   c.   conflict view
   d.   consensus view
   (Answer = a)

35. Those who follow the writings of Auguste Comte are known as:
   a.   theorists
   b.   positivists
   c.   negativists
   d.   victimologists
   (Answer = b)

36. When people behave abnormally even without being mentally ill, they are:
   a.   criminal
   b.   psychotic
   c.   psychopathic personality
   d.   anomie
   (Answer = c)

37. The Chicago School was developed by a group of Sociologists at:
   a.   the University of North Carolina
   b.   Fayetteville State University
   c.   Harvard University
   d.   University of Chicago
   (Answer = d)

38. The sociologist, which said the people learn criminal attitudes from older, more experienced law violators, is:

   a.   Edwin Sutherland
   b.   Charles Darwin
   c.   Cesare Lombroso
   d.   Reggio Emilia
   (Answer = a)

39. The theorist who observed that the character of every civilization is determined by its mode of production is:
   a.   Sutherland
   b.   Marx
   c.   Lombroso
   d.   Emilia
   (Answer = b)

40. The theory that criminals are rational and use available information to decide if a crime is a worthwhile undertaking is known as:
   a.   conflict theory
   b.   consensus theory
   c.   interactionist theory
   d.   choice theory
   (Answer = d)

   True/False

T   1. Criminologists use scientific methods to study the nature, extent, cause, and control of criminal behavior.

F   2. Criminology is a strict disciplined science; therefore criminologists have only been trained in criminology.

T   3. During the Middle Ages, people who violated social norms or religious practices were believed to be witches or possessed by demons.

T   4. Utilitarianism emphasized that behavior occurs when the actor considers it useful, purposeful and reasonable.

T   5. Physiognomists studied the facial features of criminals to determine whether the shape of ears, nose, and eyes and the distance between them were associated with antisocial behavior.

F   6. Phrenologists studied the intellect of criminals and administered IQ tests.

F   7. Marx felt that the most important relationship in industrial cultures is between the owners of the means of production and other owners.

T   8. The major perspectives of criminology focus on individual, social, political and economic and multiple factors.

T   9. From the structural perspective, crime rates are a function of neighborhood conditions, cultural forces and norm conflict.

F 10. From the process perspective, crime is a function of upbringing, learning and control.

T 11. According to the consensus view of crime, crimes are behaviors believed to be repugnant to all elements of society.

F 12. The procedural criminal law is the written code that defines crimes and their punishments.

T 13. Interactionists see the criminal law as conforming to the beliefs of moral crusaders who use their influence to shape the legal process in the way they see fit.

F 14. Self-report surveys measure the attitudes, beliefs, and values of different groups.

T 15. Longitudinal research involves observing a group of people who share like characteristics.

Chapter Two

The Criminal Law and Its Processes

Summary

Chapter Two examines the origins of the criminal law including the development of the common law. The chapter distinguishes between the various types of laws and the purpose of the criminal law. The chapter concludes with the Legal Definition of A Crime and the various defenses, which a defendant may invoke on their own behalf.

Learning Objectives

After reading this chapter the student should be able to:
- Understand the origins of the common law.
- Define the common law.
- Understand the differences between the common law and statutory law.
- Distinguish between Criminal Law and Tort Law.
- Explain the functions of the Criminal Law.
- Describe the various types of crimes.
- Understand the rationale for enforcing social control.
- Define the legal definition of a crime.
- Understand the various criminal defenses.

Chapter Overview
Introduction
The Origin of Law
The Dark Ages-Origins of Common Law
Crime and Custom
The Norman Conquest
The Common Law

Chapter Outline

I. **Introduction**

    A. All types of interactions must conform to the rules set out by the legal code, which are the specific laws that fall within the scope of "criminal law."

II. **The Origin of Law**

    A. Mores and Folkways - preliterate societies, the equivalents of law

    B. Code of Hammurabi - (1792-1750 B.C.) King Hammurabi of Babylon's first known written laws

    C. Lex Talionis - punishment based on physical retaliation ("an eye for an eye")

    D. Mosaic Code of the Israelites (1200 B.C.) - 2nd of the ancient legal codes - (The 613 laws of the Old Testament, including the Ten Commandments) - the foundation of Judeo-Christian moral teachings and the basis for the US legal system.

E. Twelve Tables - Roman law (451 B.C.) - formulated by 10 noblemen
   1. plebeians - lower classes
   2. patricians - wealthy classes
F. Wergild - Legal systems featuring compensation
   1. Wer - worth of a person
   2. Guilt determined by 2 methods
      a. Compurgation - having the accused swear to an oath of innocence while being backed by a group of "oathhelpers" who would attest to character and innocence.
      b. Ordeal - based on divine intervention; the accused would be subjected to something like placing their hand in boiling water and then it would be seen if God intervened and healed the wounds.
      c. Trial by Combat - one would challenge an accuser to a duel with the outcome determining the legitimacy of the accusation.

III. **Origins of Common Law** - Developed after the Norman Conquest of England in 1066. Helped standardize law and justice.
   A. Shire - County.
   B. Hundreds - Groups of one hundred families.
   C. Tithings -Groups of ten.
   D. Reeve - Head law enforcement official in the shire.
   E. Hundred-gemot - Courts of the hundred group.
   F. Shire-gemot - An assemblage of local landholders.
   G. Hali-gemot - Local nobleman in a manorial court.
   H. Holy-motes or ecclesiastics - Courts held by clergymen and church officials.

IV. **Compensation for Crime**
   A. Criminal law - designed to provide equitable solution in a private dispute.
   B. Before 1066 - crimes considered violation of victim's personal rights and compensation was paid to victim or their family.
   C. No payment resulted in blood feud between families.
   D. Wergild divided into:
      1. bot - paid
      2. wer - part went to the king
      3. wite - remainder went to the victim or kin.

V. **The Norman Conquest** - Justice remained the same as in previous centuries.
   1. Church courts handled acts considered sinful.
   2. Manorial Courts dealt with most secular violations.
   3. Royal Courts established by King William to deal with the most serious breaches of the peace.
   4. Royal Judges looked to previous cases to make decisions.
   5. Stare decisis - Latin for "to stand by decided cases"

VI. **The Common Law** - developed during King Henry II (1154-1189) Law applied to all of the land.
   A. Replaced feudal and county courts.
   B. Used traveling judges, known as circuit judges.
   C. Judges followed a specific route, known as a circuit.

D. Development of juries - local landholders called
   1. To decide the facts of cases
   2. To investigate the crimes
   3. Accuse suspected offenders
   4. Give testimony at trials
E. Royal prosecutors established
   1. Submitted evidence
   2. Brought witnesses to testify before the jury
F. Judicial decisions written and published
   1. Judge-made law or case law - judicial decisions made on a case-by-case basis.

VII. **Common Law and Statutory Law**
   A. Common law - still the law of England
   B. Criminal Attempt Law - also known as inchoate crime
   C. Statutory laws reflect existing social conditions
      1. Deal with morality such as gambling, sexual activity, and drug-related offenses.
      2. Embezzlement - when one takes the possessions of others that have been entrusted to them.
      3. Fraud - when one takes the possessions of another through deception.

VIII. **Common Law and Statutory Law in America**
   A. State legislatures put common law crimes such as murder, burglary, arson and rape into statutory form in criminal codes.

IX. **Classification of Law**
   A. Crimes and Torts
      1. Law divided into criminal law and torts
         a. Civil law - all law other then criminal law
            1. Property law - the law governing transfer/ownership of property.
            2. Contract law - Law of personal agreements.
            3. Tort Law - Law of personal wrongs and damage.
               a. Libel - false and injurious writings
               b. Slander - false and injurious statements
         b. Statute of Limitations - the amount of time by which action must be taken by the state in a criminal matter.
   B. The Differences between Crimes and Torts
      1. Criminal Law - purpose - to give the state the power to protect the public from harm by punishing individuals whose actions threaten social order.
      2. Tort Law - harm or injury is considered a private wrong - main concern to compensate victims for harm that others have inflicted on them.
      3. Criminal Action - state initiates legal proceedings by bringing charges and prosecuting the violator
      4. Civil Action - injured person must file an action to initiate proceedings.
      5. Criminal Matter - Burden of Proof - Beyond A Reasonable Doubt
      6. Civil Matter - Burden of Proof - A Preponderance of the Evidence.

C. Felony and Misdemeanor
   1. Felony - (from the term felonia, an act by which a vassal forfeited his fee) a serious offense such as murder, rape and burglary. Punishable by one year or more up to death in a state prison.
   2. Misdemeanor - a crime punishable by less than a year in a local county facility such as a jail or house of correction; Examples include unarmed assault and battery, petty larceny and disturbing the peace.
D. Mala in Se and Mala Prohibitum
   1. Mala in Se - Rooted in the core values inherent in Western civilization, which is referred to as natural law. Designed to control behaviors such as:
      a. inflicting physical harm on others (assault, rape, murder)
      b. taking possessions that rightfully belong to another (larceny, burglary, robbery)
      c. harming another's property (malicious damage, trespass)
   2. Mala Prohibitum - refer to statutory crimes, violations of laws that reflect current public opinion and social values.
      a. Drug use
      b. Possession of Unlicensed Handguns
X. **Functions of the Criminal Law** - Substantive Criminal Law - a written code defining crimes and their punishments.
   A. Enforcing Social Control - primary purpose of the criminal law - to control the behavior of people within its jurisdiction.
      1. Discouraging Revenge - Enforcement is delegated to the state and therefore prevents individuals from taking revenge.
   B. Expressing Public Opinion and Morality - Criminal law reflects changing public opinions and moral values.
      1. Controlling Public Opinion and Morality is difficult
         a. gauging the will of the majority
         b. respecting the rights of the minority
         c. enforcing laws that many people consider trivial or self-serving
      2. Vagrant - one who goes from place to place without visible means of support and refuses to work
   C. Deterring Criminal Behavior
      1. Social Control Function - to control, restrain and direct human behavior through its ability to punish and correct law violators.
   D. Punishing Wrongdoing - deterrent power of the criminal law
      1. Wrongdoers are subject to physical coercion and punishment.
   E. Maintaining the Social Order
      1. The law promotes activities to sustain an economy based on the accumulation of wealth.
XI. **The Legal Definition of a Crime** - Actus reus + Mens rea (Concurrence)=Crime
   A. Actus reus - the guilty act
   B. Mens rea - the intent to commit an act
   C. Failure to Act can be considered a crime

1. Failure to perform a legally required duty which is based on relationship or status. (Parents taking care of children).
2. Imposition by statute. (Stop and help those in traffic accident).
3. A contractual relationship. (Lifeguards saving swimmers).
   D. Strict Liability - Some crimes do not require mens rea. Strict liability crimes are when one simply does what the statute prohibits such as traffic laws.

XII. Criminal Defenses
   A. Justification - admits committing the criminal act, but maintains that the act was justified and should not be held liable. The justifiable defenses include:
   1. Necessity
   2. Duress
   3. Self-defense
   4. Entrapment
   B. Ignorance or Mistake - can be an excuse if it negates an element of the crime. Usually, ignorance or mistake is no excuse.
   C. The Insanity Plea - the defendant's state of mind at the time of the crime negates their criminal responsibility.

XIII. Changing the Criminal Law
   A. Decriminalized - some states have decriminalized marijuana as a method of giving reduced criminal penalties.
   B. To conform to social issues
   C. Emerging Social issues - such as stalking statutes
   D. Community notification laws - a response to concern about sexual predators moving into neighbors. Usually referred to as "Megan's Law."
   E. Think Like a Criminologist
   1. What would you do with the changing social and economic landscape?

XIV. Summary

Key Terms

Lex Talionis - punishment based on physical retaliation; an eye for an eye.
Wergild - Under medieval law, the money paid by the offender to compensate the victim and the state for a criminal offense.
Ordeal - guilty determined by the belief that divine forces would not let an innocent person to be harmed. Determining guilt by ordeal involved such measures as having the accused place his/her hand in boiling water or holds a hot iron to see if God would intervene and heal the wounds. If the wound healed, the person was not guilty; conversely, if the wounds did not heal, the accused was deemed guilty of the crime for which they were being punished.

Common Law - Early English law, developed by judges that incorporated Anglo-Saxon tribal custom, feudal rules and practices, and the everyday rules of behavior of local villages. Common law became the standardized law of the land in England and eventually formed the basis of the criminal law in the United States.

Stare decisis - Latin for the early courts to determine the outcome of future cases used "to stand by decided cases," Courts were bound to follow the law established in previously decided cases unless a higher authority, such as the king or pope, overruled the law.

Circuit Judges - King Henry II (1154-1189) had judges to travel. These judges followed a specific route known as a circuit and heard cases that previously had been under the jurisdiction of local courts.

Case law - Judge-made law. Judicial decisions made on a case-by-case basis. Cases and decisions filtered through the national court system and eventually produced a fixed body of legal rule and principles.

Embezzlement - when someone takes the possessions of others that have been entrusted to them, such as a bank teller taking the bank deposits.

Civil Law - All law other than criminal law. It includes such legal areas as property law and contract law.

Tort - A civil action in which the individual asks to be compensated for personal harm. The harm may be either physical or mental, and includes such acts as trespassing, assault and battery.

Felony - A serious crime punishable by death or imprisonment for more than one year.

Misdemeanor - A less serious crime punishable by less than a year in a local county facility.

Larceny - Taking and carrying away the personal property of another with the intent to keep and possess the property.

Mala in se - Acts that are outlawed because they violate basic moral values such as rape, murder, assault, and robbery.

Mala Prohibitum - Statutory crimes which involve violations of laws that reflect current public opinion and social values. These crimes are acts that conflict with contemporary standards of morality. Crimes such as these include drug use and possession of unlicensed handguns.

Natural Law - The core values inherent in Western civilization.

Substantive Criminal Law - A written code defining crimes and their punishments.

Actus Reus - An aggressive act, such as taking someone's money, burning a building, or shooting someone.

Mens Rea - The intent to commit the criminal act.

Strict-Liability Crimes - Crimes which do not require the mens rea. In these cases, the person accused is guilty simply by doing what the statute prohibits; mental intent does not enter the picture. Health and safety regulations, traffic laws, and narcotic control laws are strict-liability statutes.

Justification - A type of defense. The individual usually admits committing the criminal act, but maintains that the act was justified and that he/she therefore, should not be held criminal liable. Among the justification defenses are necessity, duress, self-defense, and entrapment.

Exotic Defenses - New, controversial and unusual defenses offered by counsel to defend their clients. Many of these defenses are based on pre-existing conditions or syndromes with which their clients are afflicted. Examples might include "Battered Woman Syndrome," "Vietnam Syndrome," Child Sexual Abuse Syndrome," "Holocaust Survivor Syndrome," and "Adopted Child Syndrome."

Discussion Exercise

Discuss the case of Dr. Jack Kevorkian of Michigan. Dr. Kevorkian has voluntarily participated in several physical-assisted suicides. The State of Michigan has contended that Dr. Kevorkian has murdered these individuals and subsequently convicted him of murder. Debate the issue of physician-assisted suicide or murder.

InfoTrac Assignment

GETTING STARTED: Search term words for subject guide: Law, Common Law, Statutory Law, Felony, Revenge, Criminal Defenses.

CRITICAL THINKING PROJECT: Using the search term "criminal defenses," find articles that discuss the various legal criminal defenses offered by defendants.

Here are three articles:

Skinazi, Heather R. "Not Just A 'Conjured Afterthought': Using Duress as a Defense for Battered Women Who 'Fail to Protect.'" *California Law Review*.

Shain, Martin and Gillian Higgins "The Intoxication Defense and Theories of Criminal Liability: A Praxeological Approach." *Contemporary Drug Problems*.

Allen, Ronald J., Melissa Luttrell and Anne Kreeger "Clarifying Entrapment." *Journal of Criminal Law and Criminology*.

Test Bank

Essay Questions

1. Define the substantive criminal law. Distinguish the differences between the criminal law and the civil law.

2. What is the difference between a misdemeanor and a felony. Identify the specific elements of a crime. Discuss the elements and whether they must be present or not for a crime to have occurred.

3. Compare and contrast the various legal defenses. Which legal defenses are more common and which legal defenses are considered more exotic?

4. Describe the insanity defense. What are the elements of the insanity defense. Identify the various methods of testing the insanity defense.

5. Trace the history of the common law in America.

Fill in the Blank

1. In preliterate societies, common custom and tradition **(mores and folkways)** were the equivalents of law.

2. After the Norman conquest of England, in 1066, a **common law** developed, which helped standardize law and justice.

3. During the Middle Ages, the **reeve** was the head law enforcement official in the shire.

3. **Embezzlement** is when someone takes the possessions of others that have been entrusted to them, such as a bank teller taking the bank deposits.

4. The common-law definition of **arson** is "the malicious burning of the dwelling of another."

5. In a civil case, the defendant is required to pay damages if by a **preponderance of the evidence**, they are found to have committed the wrong.

6. A **felony** is a serious offense punishable by death or imprisonment for more than one year in a state prison.

27

7. A **misdemeanor** is a less serious offense punishable in the community or in a local facility for less than one year.

8. **Substantive criminal law** refers to a written code defining crimes and their punishments.

9. A **vagrant** is a person who goes from place to place without visible means of support and who, though able to work for his or her maintenance, refuses to do so.

10. The **Actus reus** is an aggressive act, such as taking someone's money, burning a building, or shooting someone.

11. Most U.S. jurisdictions have enacted some form of criminal attempt law also known as **inchoate crimes**.

12. **Property law** is the law governing transfer and ownership of property.

13. **Contract law** is the law of personal agreements.

14. **Tort law** is the law of personal wrongs and damage.

15. **Libel** is false and injurious writings.

Multiple Choice

1. Business practices, family life, education, property transfers, inheritance and other common forms of social relations must conform to the rules set out by the:
   - a.   legal code
   - b.   procedural criminal law
   - c.   the Miranda decision
   - d.   criminologists
   (Answer = a)

2. In preliterate societies, common custom and tradition were the equivalents of the law. These were known as:
   - a.   torts and crimes
   - b.   mores and folkways
   - c.   codes and unicodes
   - d.   written and unwritten
   (Answer = b)

3. During the Roman era, the lower class was referred to as:
       a.   patricians
       b.   patriarchs
       c.   plebeians
       d.   pedestrian
       (Answer = c)

4. Some early German and Anglo-Saxon societies developed legal systems featuring compensation known as:
       a.   reeves
       b.   shires
       c.   Lex Talionis
       d.   wergild
       (Answer = d)

5. During the Middle Ages, guilt was determined by two methods:
       a.   compurgation and ordeal
       b.   crime and punishment
       c.   mores and folkways
       d.   all of the above
       (Answer = a)

6. Siding with an enemy in a dispute over terrority or succession is known as:
       a.   assault
       b.   battery
       c.   treason
       d.   Hali-gemot
       (Answer = c)

7. The Latin for "to stand by decided cases" is:
       a.   Actus reus
       b.   stare decisis
       c.   mens rea
       d.   Lex Talionis
       (Answer = b)

8. Traveling judges are commonly referred to as:
       a.   Superior Court Judges
       b.   District Court Judges
       c.   Justices
       d.   Circuit Judges
       (Answer = d)

9. Judge-made law is also referred to as:
   a.   case law
   b.   circuit law
   c.   criminal law
   d.   statute law
   (Answer = a)

10. The malicious burning of the dwelling of another is called:
    a.   larceny
    b.   murder
    c.   arson
    d.   embezzlement
    (Answer = c)

11. Law can be divided into two broad categories:
    a.   property and contract law
    b.   criminal and civil law
    c.   embezzlement and fraud
    d.   all of the above
    (Answer = b)

12. The law governing transfer and ownership of property is called:
    a.   contract law
    b.   civil law
    c.   criminal law
    d.   property law
    (Answer = d)

13. The law of personal agreements is called:
    a.   contract law
    b.   civil law
    c.   criminal law
    d.   property law
    (Answer = a)

14. The law of personal wrongs and damage is:
    a.   criminal law
    b.   contract law
    c.   property law
    d.   tort law
    (Answer = d)

15. A civil action in which an individual asks to be compensated for personal harm is a:
     a.   tart
     b.   tort
     c.   port
     d.   court
     (Answer = b)

16. In criminal matters, the defendant's guilty must be proven:
     a.   beyond a reasonable doubt
     b.   by a preponderance of the evidence
     c.   beyond a shadow of a doubt
     d.   none of the above
     (Answer = a)

17. In a civil case, the defendant is required to pay damages if by a:
     a.   beyond a reasonable doubt
     b.   by a preponderance of the evidence
     c.   beyond a shadow of a doubt
     d.   none of the above
     (Answer = b)

18. A crime punishable by death or imprisonment for more than one year in a state prison is a:
     a.   ordinance
     b.   misdemeanor
     c.   felony
     d.   all of the above
     (Answer = c)

19. A crime punishable by less than a year in a local county facility usually called a jail or house or correction is a:
     a.   ordinance
     b.   misdemeanor
     c.   felony
     d.   all of the above
     (Answer = b)

20. Statutory crimes refer to:
     a.   Mala in se
     b.   Mala Prohibitum
     c.   Actus reus
     d.   mens rea
     (Answer = b)

20. A person who goes from place to place without visible means of support and who, though able to work for his or her maintenance, refuses to do so is a:
      a.   sociologist
      b.   criminologist
      c.   alien
      d.   vagrant
      (Answer = d)

22. Functions of the criminal law include:
      a.   social control
      b.   deterrence
      c.   discouraging revenge
      d.   all of the above
      (Answer = d)

23. The ability to control, restrain and direct human behavior through its ability to punish and correct law violators is:
      a.   social control function
      b.   deterrence
      c.   discouraging revenge
      d.   all of the above
      (Answer = a)

24. The aggressive act of the crime is the:
      a.   mens rea
      b.   Actus reus
      c.   strict liability
      d.   concurrence
      (Answer = b)

25. The intent to commit the act is the:
      a.   mens rea
      b.   Actus reus
      c.   strict liability
      d.   concurrence
      (Answer = a)

26. Failure to act can be considered a crime under which of the following circumstances?
      a.   Failure to perform a legally required duty based on relation or status
      b.   Imposition by statute
      c.   A contractual relationship
      d.   all of the above
      (Answer = d)

27. Public-welfare offenses are known as:
    a.   limited liability crimes
    b.   strict liability crimes
    c.   unlimited liability crimes
    d.   none of the above
    (Answer = b)

28. When the individual admits committing the criminal act, but maintains that the act
    was justified and that he or she, therefore, should not be held criminally liable, it is
    known as:
    a.   unjustification
    b.   no justification
    c.   justification
    d.   none of the above
    (Answer = c)

29. In some states, crimes such as possession of marijuana have been given reduced
    penalties or:
    a.   decriminalized
    b.   justification
    c.   legalization
    d.   standardization
    (Answer = a)

30. The willful, malicious and repeated following and harassing of another person is:
    a.   murder
    b.   stalking
    c.   carjacking
    d.   larceny
    (Answer = b)

31. Sexual offenders who target children are:
    a.   terrorists
    b.   stalkers
    c.   pedophiles
    d.   none of the above
    (Answer = c)

32. Wergild was divided into:
    a.   bot
    b.   wer
    c.   wite
    d.   all of the above
    (Answer = d)

33. Church courts handled acts that might be considered sinful and the local hundred or
    _____ death with most secular violations.
     a.   manorial courts
     b.   state courts
     c.   legal courts
     d.   appellate courts
     (Answer = a)

34. The English system of law came into existence during the reign of:
     a.   Henry VIII
     b.   Elizabeth II
     c.   Victoria
     d.   Henry II
     (Answer = d)

34. Representatives who submitted evidence and brought witnesses to testify before the
    jury was originally known as:
     a.   district attorneys
     b.   royal prosecutors
     c.   defense attorneys
     d.   public defenders
     (Answer = b)

36. Judicial decisions made on a case-by-case basis is known as:
     a.   case law
     b.   property law
     c.   contract law
     d.   all of the above
     (Answer = a)

37. In a criminal action, the legal proceedings are initiated by the:
     a.   defendant
     b.   victim
     c.   state
     d.   defense attorney
     (Answer = c)

38. In a civil action, the legal proceedings are initiated by the:
     a.   defendant
     b.   injured party
     c.   state
     d.   defense attorney
     (Answer = b)

39. An institution where felony defendants is held is called a:
        a.   jail
        b.   juvenile detention center
        c.   state prison
        d.   house of correction
        (Answer = c)

40. Examples of crimes against property include:
        a.   burglary
        b.   arson
        c.   larceny
        d.   all of the above
        (Answer = d)

True/False

T   1. Punishment based on physical retaliation was known as lex talionis.

F   2. The Ten Commandments was the original written code of laws.

T   3. In the Middle Ages, guilty was determined by two methods: compurgation and ordeal.

F   4. The common law was developed in Switzerland after the Norman Conquest in 1066.

F   5. The head law enforcement official in Middle Age England was called the shire.

T   6. Judge-made law is also known as case law.

T   7. Most U.S. jurisdictions have enacted some form of criminal attempt law also known as inchoate crimes.

F   8. Law can be divided into three categories: civil, criminal and tort.

T   9. Property law is the law governing transfer of property.

T   10. A statute of limitations specifies the amount of time by which action must be taken by the state in a criminal matter.

F   11. The main purpose of the criminal law is to compensate victims for harm that others have inflicted on them.

T   12. In a criminal action, the state initiates the legal proceedings by bringing charges and prosecuting the violator.

F   13. Procedural criminal law refers to a written code defining crimes and their punishments.

T   14. A vagrant is a person who goes from place to place without visible means of support and who, though able to work for his or her maintenance, refuses to do so.

F   15. Less than 20 states have enacted stalking statutes since it is a rare occurrence in criminal justice.

Chapter Three

The Nature and Extent of Crime

Summary

Chapter Three introduces the methods of measuring crime in our society. Crime data is collected from official crime data, victim surveys and self-report surveys. The chapter looks at the various trends in crime and what the future holds. Chapter Three concludes with a thorough analysis of crime patterns.

Learning Objectives

After reading this chapter the student should be able to:

- Be familiar with the various methods of measuring crime.
- Develop an understanding of the Uniform Crime Report.
- Describe the National Crime Victimization Survey.
- Examine Self-Report Studies.
- Explore the compatibility of these data resources.
- Discuss the validity of each of these measurements of crime.
- Recognize the trends of violent crime.
- Understand the trends of property crime.
- Describe the trends in the victimization data.
- Examine the trends in the Self-Report data.
- Explore what the future holds for measuring crime.
- Identify specific crime patterns as related to race, age, gender and social class.

Chapter Overview

Introduction
Measuring Crime
      Official Crime Data: The Uniform Crime Report
      Victim Surveys: The National Crime Victimization Survey
      Self-Report Surveys
      Are the Crime Data Sources Compatible?
Crime Trends
      Trends in Violent Crime
      Trends in Property Crime
      Trends in Victimization Data
      Trends in Self-Report Data
      What the Future Holds
Crime Patterns
      The Ecology of Crime
      Use of Firearms
      Social Class and Crime
      Age and Crime
      Gender and Crime
      Race and Crime
      Criminal Careers
Summary

Chapter Outline

I.   **Introduction**
II.   **Measuring Crime**
      A. Official Data: The Uniform Crime Report - best known, most widely cited source of official criminal statistics - generated by the FBI
          1. Collecting the Uniform Crime Report
               a. Law enforcement agencies report the number of index crimes known to FBI
               b. Law enforcement also report crimes cleared
                    1. by at least one person being arrested

         2. by exceptional means, such as, offender leaving area

     2. How Accurate are the Uniform Crime Reports? - suspect, at least

        a. Report Practices - many victims do not report victimization to police

        b. Law Enforcement Practices - method used by police to record crime are not always accurate

        c. Methodological Problems

           1. No federal crimes are reported

           2. Reports are voluntary and vary in accuracy and completeness.

           3. Not all police departments submit reports.

           4. The FBI uses estimates in its total crime projections.

           5. If offender commits multiple crimes, only most serious is recorded.

           6. Each act is listed as single offense for some crimes, but not others.

           7. Incomplete acts are lumped together with completed ones.

           8. Differences between FBI's definition of crimes and those of states.

     3. The Future of the Uniform Crime Report

        a. Expanded crime categories

        b. More accounting by local law enforcement

B. Victim Surveys: The National Crime Victimization Survey (NCVS)

     1. Surveys which ask crime victims about their encounters with criminals.

     2. Considered a relatively, unbiased, valid estimate of all victimizations

C. Unreported Crimes - NCVS showed many unreported crimes to police in its data.

     1. Is the NCVS Valid? - Use with caution

        a. Over-reporting by victims misinterpretation of events

        b. Underreporting by victims due to possible embarrassment or memory loss

        c. Inability to record the personal criminal activity of those interviewed

        d. Sampling errors

        e. Inadequate question format that invalidates responses

D. Self-Report Surveys - Administered to groups of subjects through a mass distribution of questionnaires

     1. Are Self-Reports Accurate? Some feel that their accuracy is questionable.

        a. Will respondents actually admit criminal activity?

     2. Questioning Self-Report Accuracy

        a. Cannot guarantee that the sample is accurate

E. Are Crime Statistics Sources Compatible?

     1. FBI - Uniform Crime Report omits many crimes

     2. NCVS - has unreported crime, but limited samples

     3. Self-report surveys provide demographic of offenders, but accuracy is questionable

III.   **Crime Trends**

  A. Trends in Violent Crime - trending downward

     1. Year 2000 - violent crime at low since 1985.

     2. Decrease in the number of murders.

  B. Trends in Property Crime - declining, but possibly stabilizing.

1. Victimization Trends - Year 2000, 26 million recorded victimizations - a decline from 1999.
2. Self-Report Findings
   a. the number of lawbreakers is greater than the number projected by official statistics
   b. most common offense - truancy, alcohol abuse, use of a fake ID, shoplifting or larceny under $50, fighting, marijuana use and damage to the property of others
C. What the Future Holds
1. Criminologist James A. Fox predicts increased youth violence
2. Criminologists Steffensmeier and Harer predict a more moderate increase in crime

IV. **Crime Patterns** - Criminologists look for stable crime rate patterns to gain insight into the nature of crime.
A. The Ecology of Crime - Patterns in the crime rate seem to be linked to ecological factors.
   1. Day, Season and Climate - most reported crimes occur during the warm months of July and August. Crime rates are higher on the first day of the month when government checks arrive.
   2. Temperature - crime rates increase with rising temperatures and then decline at some point (85 degrees) when it may be too hot for physical exertion.
   3. Population Density - large urban areas have higher rates of violence
   4. Region - southern states consistently have higher rates of crime.
B. Use of Firearms - firearms are involved in 20% of robberies, 10% of assaults, 6% of rapes and 70% of murders in 1998.
C. Social Class and Crime - lower class people have the greatest incentive to commit crime
   1. Instrumental crimes - resorting to theft and other illegal activities to obtain desired goods and services
   2. Expressive crimes - crimes such as rape and assault
   3. Class and Self-Reports - Self-Reports do not show a direct relationship between crime and class
      a. The Class-Crime Controversy
      b. if class is related to crime, then economic and social factors, such as poverty and neighborhood disorganization, cause criminal behavior
      c. truly hard to determine the relationship between class and crime
   4. Does Class Matter?
      a. If crime is directly related to the lower class then crime would be worse.
      b. There are many other factors to consider in the equation such as income inequality, social opportunities.
D. Age and Crime - general agreement that age is related to crime - youth commit more of the crime
   1. The Age and Crime Controversy

a. All people commit less crime as they age.

b. Adults develop the ability to delay gratification and forgo the immediate gains that law violations bring.

c. Others argue that most people age out of crime

d. Early age criminals are more likely to become chronic offenders.

E. Gender and Crime - male crime rates are higher than females

1. Explaining Gender Differences: Biological Views

a. emotional

b. physical

c. psychological

d. female criminals viewed as sexually controlling or sexually naïve

1. chivalry hypothesis - much female criminality is hidden because our culture's generally protective and benevolent attitudes toward women. (Less likely to arrest, etc.).

2. Explaining Gender Differences: Socialization - girls and boys are socialized differently

a. girls - socialized to be less aggressive; to respond to provocation by feeling anxious and depressed

b. boys - encouraged to retaliate with aggression

3. Explaining Gender Differences: Feminist Views

a. Liberal Feminist Theory - the traditionally lower crime rate for women could be explained by women's second-class economic and social position

4. Is Convergence Likely? - some theorist do not think that female criminality will rise despite the emancipation of women; while others feel differently

F. Race and Crime - Official crime data indicates that minority group members are involved in a disproportionate share of criminal activity - African-Americans comprise 12% of the population and account for 40% of the Part I violent crime arrests and 34% of property crime arrests.

1. Racism and Discrimination - some criminologists view black crime as a function of socialization in a society where black families were torn apart and black cultured destroyed due to slavery.

2. Institutional Racism - an element of daily life in the African-American community

a. some jurisdictions treat young African-American males me harshly

b. unemployed or indigent African-Americans receive longer prison sentences than like Caucasians

c. African-American victims receive less public concern and media attention then white victims

3. Economic and Social Disparity - Blacks and whites face different economic and social realities

a. African-Americans have higher unemployment rates and lower incomes than whites

b. African-Americans face a higher degree of social isolation and economic deprivation

4. Family Dissolution - tied to low employment rates among African-American males, which places a strain on marriages

5. Is Convergence Possible? Convergence in crime rates will occur if economic and social obstacles can be removed.

G. Criminal Careers - most offenders commit a single criminal act and upon arrest, discontinue their antisocial activity; a small group of criminal offenders account for a majority of all criminal offenders

1. Who are Chronic Offenders? - Research by Schumacher and Kurt found certain traits may characterize the chronic offender

a. problems in the home

b. problems at school

c. substance abuse problems

d. delinquency factor

2. Persistence: The Continuity of Crime - persistent juvenile offenders are the ones most likely to continue their criminal careers into adulthood

3. Implications of the Chronic Offender Concept - since few become chronic offenders then there is a common trait

XV. Summary

Key Terms

Uniform Crime Report - The best-known and most widely cited source of official criminal statistics. Complied by the FBI from over 17,000 police departments. Its major analysis involved the index crimes or Part I crimes: murder and nonnegligent manslaughter, forcible rape, robbery, aggravated assault, burglary, larceny, arson, and motor vehicle theft.

Index Crimes - The eight crimes that, because of their seriousness and frequency, the FBI reports the incidence of the annual Uniform Crime Reports. Index crimes include murder, rape, assault, robbery, burglary, arson, larceny, and motor vehicle theft.

Part I Crimes - The major unit of analysis of the Uniform Crime Report. Part I crimes include murder and nonnegligent manslaughter, forcible rape, robbery aggravated assault, burglary, larceny, arson, and motor vehicle theft.

Part II Crimes - All other crimes that are not included in the Part I offenses of the Uniform Crime Report.

National Incident Based Reporting System - a new program that is attempting to provide more detailed information on individual criminal incidents by using a uniform, comprehensive program. This program requires local police agencies to provide at least a brief account of each incident and arrest within 22 crime patterns, including the incident, victim, and offender information.

National Crime Victimization Survey - A national survey sponsored by the Bureau of Justice Statistics of the U.S. Department of Justice. Households are asked to report on the frequency, characteristics and consequences of criminal victimization for such crimes as rape, sexual assault, robbery, assault, theft, household burglary, and motor vehicle theft.

Self-Report Survey - A research approach that requires subjects to reveal their own participation in delinquent or criminal acts.

Aging Out - The process by which individuals reduce the frequency of their offending behavior as they age.

Early Onset - A term that refers to the assumption that a criminal career begins early in life and that people who are deviant at a very young age are the ones most likely to persist in crime.

Desistance - The process in which crime rate declines with the perpetrator's age; synonymous with the aging-out process.

Masculinity Hypothesis - The view that women who commit crimes have biological and psychological traits similar to men.

Chivalry Hypothesis - Female criminality is hidden because of our culture's generally protective and benevolent attitudes toward women.

Career criminal - persistent or chronic offenders.

Chronic Offender - According to Wolfgang, a delinquent offender who is arrested five or more times before he/she is 18 and who stands a good chance of becoming an adult criminal.

Continuity of Crime - The view that crime begins early in life and continues throughout the life course. Thus, the best predictor of future criminality is past criminality.

Three Strikes and You're Out - Policy of giving people convicted of three violent offenses a mandatory life term without parole.

Discussion Exercise

Gun Control is a hot topic in the United States. Poll the class as to their views on gun control. Divide the class into two groups. One group will be pro gun control and the second group will be anti-gun control. Have each group prepare a presentation for their side. Poll the class again to see if the results changed after the presentations.

InfoTrac Assignment

GETTING STARTED: Search term words for subject guide: Uniform Crime Report, National Crime Victimization Survey, Self-Report Survey, Violent Crime, Crime Patterns.

CRITICAL THINKING PROJECT: Using the search term "National Crime Victimization Survey," find articles that examine the reporting behavior of rape victims. Discuss the differences in the National Crime Victimization Survey and the Uniform Crime Report 's data on the crime of rape.

Here are three articles:

Bachman, Ronet "The Factors Related to Rape Reporting Behavior and Arrest: New Evidence from the National Crime Victimization Survey." *Criminal Justice and Behavior.*

Transcript. "Statement on the National Crime Victimization Survey." *Weekly Compilation of Presidential Documents.*

Bachman, Ronet and Raymond Paternoster "A Contemporary Look at the Effects of Rape Law Reform: How Far Have We Really Come?" *Journal of Criminal Law and Criminology.*

Test Bank

Essay Questions

1. Describe the accepted methods of measuring crime in the United States. What are the positive and negative aspects of each method?
2. Discuss the crime trend in the United States. Which area of crime are on the decline and which areas are on the rise?
3. What is Self-Report Data? Is it useful and is it accurate. Discuss the pros and cons of self-report data.
4. What are crime patterns? Do certain aspects of society or individuals predispose one to antisocial behavior?
5. What is the Uniform Crime Report? How is it complied? What are the pros and cons of this method of data collection? Describe the predicted future of the Uniform Crime Report.

Fill In The Blank

1. The Federal Bureau of Investigation's **Uniform Crime Report** is the best known and most widely cited source of official criminal statistics.

2. The most important and widely used victim survey, **The National Crime Victimization Survey** is sponsored by the Bureau of Justice Statistics of the U.S. Department of Justice.

3. The property crimes reported in the **Uniform Crime Report** include burglary, larceny, and motor vehicle theft.

4. Property crimes may be **stabilizing**.

5. **Urban** areas have by far the highest violence rates.

6. **Southern** states have had consistently high crime rates in almost all crime categories.

7. All people regardless of their demographic characteristics commit **less** crime as they age.

8. Female's criminality is often masked because criminal justice authorities were reluctant to take action against a woman is known as the **chivalry hypothesis**.

9. Persistent offenders are referred to as **career criminals (or chronic offenders).**

10. The policy of giving people convicted of three violent offenses a mandatory life term without parole is known as **three strikes and you're out.**

11. The view that women who commit crimes have biological and psychological traits similar to men is known as **masculinity hypothesis**.

12. **Part II Crimes** are all other crimes that are not included in the Part I offenses of the Uniform Crime Report.

13. **Aging Out** is the process by which individuals reduce the frequency of their offending behavior as they age.

14. **Continuity of Crime** is the view that crime begins early in life and continues throughout the life course.

15. **Desistance** is the process in which the crime rate declines with the perpetrator's age.

Multiple Choice

1. The best known and most widely cited source of official criminal statistics is:
   a. the Uniform Crime Report
   b. the National Crime Victimization Survey
   c. Self-Report Studies
   d. None of the above
   (Answer = a)

2. The Uniform Crime Report is compiled by the:
   a. State Bureau of Investigation
   b. The office of the President
   c. The White House
   d. Federal Bureau of Investigation
   (Answer = d)

3. The Part I crimes of the Uniform Crime Report contain ____ crimes:
   a. 12
   b. 7
   c. 4
   d. 9
   (Answer = b)

4. Problems with the Uniform Crime Report include:
   a. reporting practices
   b. law enforcement practices
   c. methodological problems
   d. all of the above
   (Answer = d)

5. Crimes that the police do not know about are considered:
   a. unreported
   b. reported
   c. detailed
   d. systematic
   (Answer = a)

6. The NCVS has been cited with which of the following problems?
   a. over-reporting
   b. underreporting
   c. sampling errors
   d. all of the above
   (Answer = d)

7. A research approach that requires subjects to reveal their own participation in delinquent or criminal acts is known as:
   a. Uniform Crime Report
   b. Self-Report Survey
   c. NCVS
   d. FBI
   (Answer = b)

8. Most reported crimes occur during:
   a. summer
   b. winter
   c. fall
   d. spring
   (Answer = a)

9. The highest violence rates occur in:
   a. rural areas
   b. scenic areas
   c. urban areas
   d. Disney World
   (Answer = c)

10. The highest crime rate is found in which region of the country?
    a. north
    b. south
    c. east
    d. west
    (Answer = b)

11. Traditionally, crime has been thought of a _____-class phenomenon.
    a. upper
    b. middle
    c. upper-middle
    d. lower
    (Answer = d)

12. Those unable to obtain desired goods and services through conventional means may consequently resort to theft and other illegal activities. These activities are known as:
    a. instrumental crimes
    b. expressive crimes
    c. index crimes
    d. crimes of passion
    (Answer = a)

13. _____ are associated with those living in poverty who engage in disproportionate amounts of rape and assault as a means of expressing their rage, frustration, and anger against society.
    a. instrumental crimes
    b. expressive crimes
    c. index crimes
    d. crimes of passion
    (Answer = b)

14. Characteristics which predict chronic offending are:
    a. school behavior
    b. family problems
    c. delinquency factors
    d. all of the above
    (Answer = d)

15. Examples of school behavior problems are:
    a. poor parental supervision
    b. criminal family members
    c. documented child abuse
    d. none of the above
    (Answer = d)

16. Examples of delinquency factors include:
    a. stealing pattern
    b. runaway pattern
    c. gang member
    d. all of the above
    (Answer = d)

17. The continuity of crime is also known as:
    a. Desistance
    b. persistence
    c. resistance
    d. none of the above
    (Answer = b)

18. A repeat offender is also known as a:
    a. chronic offender
    b. career criminal
    c. all of the above
    d. none of the above
    (Answer = c)

19. Chronic offenders begin their criminal careers:
    a. early in life
    b. late in life
    c. in their 30's
    d. in their 40's
    (Answer = a)

20. The process by which individuals reduce the frequency of their offending behavior as they age is known as:
    a. continuity of crime
    b. aging out
    c. chronic offender
    d. career criminal
    (Answer = b)

21. The taking or attempting to take anything of value from the care, custody, or control of a person by force or threat of force or violence is known as:
    a. murder
    b. forcible rape
    c. robbery
    d. arson
    (Answer = c)

22. An unlawful attack by one person upon another for the purpose of inflicting severe or aggravated bodily injury is called:
    a. murder
    b. forcible rape
    c. robbery
    d. aggravated assault
    (Answer = d)

23. The unlawful entry of a structure to commit a felony or a theft is called:
    a. murder
    b. burglary
    c. forcible rape
    d. robbery
    (Answer = b)

24. The unlawful taking, carrying, leading or riding away of property from the possession or constructive possession of another is called:
    a. murder
    b. burglary
    c. larceny
    d. robbery
    (Answer = c)

25. The theft or attempted theft of a motor vehicle is called:
    a. murder
    b. burglary
    c. larceny
    d. motor vehicle theft
    (Answer = d)

26. Any willful or malicious burning or attempt to burn, with or without intent to defraud, a dwelling house, public building, motor vehicle or aircraft, personal property of another or the like, is called:
    a. murder
    b. theft
    c. larceny
    d. arson
    (Answer = d)

27. Crimes are cleared by law enforcement officers by:
    a. when at least one person is arrested, charged, and turned over to the court for prosecution
    b. by exceptional means
    c. all of the above
    d. none of the above
    (Answer = c)

28. Which crimes are more likely to be solved by the police?
    a. violent crimes
    b. property crimes
    c. larceny crimes
    d. theft crimes
    (Answer = a)

29. Which of the following methods does the UCR use to express crime data?
    a. number of crimes reported to the police and arrests made
    b. crime rates per 100,000 people
    c. changes in the number and rate of crime over time
    d. all of the above
    (Answer = d)

30. Which of the following are considered to be methodological problems for the UCR?
    a. no federal crimes reported
    b. reports are involuntary
    c. all of the above
    d. none of the above
    (Answer = a)

31. A victim's misinterpretation of events is known as:
    a. sampling error
    b. inability
    c. underreporting
    d. over-reporting
    (Answer = d)

32. Embarrassment of reporting crime to interviewers may be a reason for:
    a. sampling error
    b. inability
    c. underreporting
    d. over-reporting
    (Answer = c)

33. A group of respondents who do not represent the nation as a whole is can produce:
    a. sampling error
    b. inability
    c. underreporting
    d. over-reporting
    (Answer = a)

34. The UCR omits data about:
    a. victims
    b. number of murders
    c. people arrested
    d. all of the above
    (Answer = a)

35. Self-report studies can include offender information that includes:
    a. attitudes
    b. values
    c. beliefs
    d. all of the above
    (Answer = d)

36. In the year 2000, _____ crimes were reported to police.
    a. 20 million
    b. 100 million
    c. 11.6 million
    d. 1 million
    (Answer = c)

37. Crime rates drop when:
    a. market conditions change
    b. an alternative criminal opportunity develops
    c. all of the above
    d. none of the above
    (Answer = c)

38. In the year 2000 there were an estimated _____ victimizations recorded in the US.
    a. 26 million
    b. 100 million
    c. 50 million
    d. 1 million
    (Answer = a)

39. According to a self-report study, about ____ of all high school students engaged in theft within the last year.
   a. 1/2
   b. 3/4
   c. 1/4
   d. 1/3
   (Answer = d)

40. According to a self-report study, about _____ of all high school students engaged in a serious violent act within the last year.
   a. 10%
   b. 20%
   c. 30%
   d. 70%
   (Answer = b)

True/False

T   1. Today, there are three significant methods used to measure the nature and extent of crime: Official data; victim data; and self-report data.

F   2. The Bureau of Justice Statistics compiles the Uniform Crime report.

F   3. The Uniform Crime Report is a survey complied by victims.

T   4. Self-report surveys are administered to groups of subjects through a mass distribution of questionnaires.

T   5. Self-report surveys can provide information on the personal characteristics of offenders, such as their attitudes, values, beliefs, and psychological profiles.

F   6. Studies have indicated that a gradual increase in the crime rate, especially in violent crime, occurred from 1830 to 1860.

F   7. Self-report surveys indicate that the most common offense is murder and arson.

T   8. Most reported crimes occur during the warm summer months of July and August.

T   9. Large urban areas have by far the highest violence rates.

F   10. For many years, northern states have had consistently high crime rates in almost all crime categories.

T   11.   Firearms play a dominant role in criminal activity.

T   12.   Instrumental crimes are those who are unable to obtain desired goods and services through conventional means may resort to, such as, theft and other illegal activities.

F   13.   Victims report that the assailant was female in more than 80% of all violent personal crimes.

T   14.   In the 1970s liberal feminist theory focused attention on the social and economic role of women in society and its relationship to female crime rates.

T   15.   Official crime data indicate that minority group members are involved in a disproportionate share of criminal activity.

Chapter Four

Victims and Victimization

Summary

Chapter Four begins with a discussion of the problems that victim's face after the crime has occurred. The chapter then focuses on the nature of victimization. This discussion introduces the various demographics, which may predispose one to victimization. Theories of Victimization are defined and explained with a conclusion of how society should care for the victim.

Learning Objectives

After reading this chapter the student should be able to:
- Develop an understanding for the problems suffered by crime victims.
- Be familiar with the concepts of loss, suffering, fear and antisocial behavior.
- Understand the nature of victimization.
- Describe the typical victim.
- Differentiate between the victim and their perpetrator.
- Discuss the various theories of victimization.
- Examine the Victim Precipitation Theory.
- Recognize the relevance of Lifestyle Theories in regards to victimology.
- Become familiar with Routine Activities Theory.
- Examine the Government's Response as to caring for the Victim.
- Explore the various Victim Service Programs.
- Identify specific rights for victims.

Chapter Overview
Introduction
Problems of Crime Victims
      Loss
      Suffering
      Fear
      Antisocial Behavior
The Nature of Victimization
      The Social Ecology of Victimization
      The Victim's Household
      Victim Characteristics
      The Victims and Their Criminals
Theories of Victimization
      Victim Precipitation Theory
      Lifestyle Theories
      Routine Activities Theory
Caring for the Victim
      The Government's Response
      Victim Service Programs
      Victims' Rights
      self-protection
      Community Organization
      Summary

Chapter Outline

I.   **Introduction**
      A. Victimologists - Criminologists who focus their attention on crime victims
II.   **Problems of Crime Victims**
      A. Loss - What it costs the Victim
          1. Money
          2. Property
          3. Time
          4. Security
          5. Long-term Suffering

6. Trauma
7. Injury
8. Death

B. Suffering
1. Pain
2. Injury
3. Loss of Limbs, Teeth, Mobility
4. Stress and Anxiety
5. Victimization by the Justice System

C. Fear
1. Fundamental Life Change
2. Less secure
3. Fear for the safety of others - altruistic fear (fear for others)

D. Antisocial Behavior
1. Strong evidences that people who are crime victims seem more likely to commit crime themselves.
2. Cycle of Violence
   a. Abuse-crime phenomenon - boys and girls more likely to engage in violent behavior if they were:
      1. the target of physical abuse
      2. Exposed to violent behavior among the adults they knew or lived with; and/or exposed to weapons.

III.   The Nature of Victimization
A. The Social Ecology of Victimization
1. Violent crimes are more likely to take place in open, public areas
2. During the daytime or early evening
3. More serious crimes usually take place after 6 p.m.

B. The Victim's Household
1. Larger, low-income, African-American, western, and urban areas are most vulnerable to crime
2. Rural, affluent, white, northeast are less likely to contain crime victims

C. Victim Characteristics
1. Gender - except for rape and sexual assault, males are more often victims
2. Age - young people face a greater victimization risk
3. Social Status - lower income individuals are more likely to be victims
4. Martial Status - divorce and never-married are victimized more than married people
5. Race and Ethnicity - African-Americans are more likely to be victims of robbery and violent crime than Whites
6. Repeat Victimization - prior victims have a higher chance of future victimization than nonvictims

D. The Victims and Their Criminals
1. Most crimes committed by a single offender over age 20.
2. Crime tends to be intraracial.
3. Substance abuse involved in about 1/3 of violent crime.

4. Relatives or acquaintances commit about 40% of violent crimes.
5. Victimization is common among family.

IV. **Theories of Victimization**

A. Victim Precipitation Theory - some people may actually initiate the confrontation that eventually leads to their injury or death.
   1. Active Precipitation - occurs when victims act provocatively, use threats or fighting words, or even attack first.
   2. Passive Precipitation - occurs when the victim exhibits some personal characteristic that unknowingly either threatens or encourages the attacker.

B. Lifestyle Theory - Some criminologists believe that people may become crime victims because their lifestyle increases their exposure to criminal offenders.
   1. High-Risk Lifestyles
      a. Drinking
      b. Taking drugs
      c. Getting involved in crime
      d. Runaways
   2. Victims and Criminals - a career as a criminal may predispose one to be victimized
   3. Deviant Place Theory - Victims do not encourage crime, but are victim prone because they reside in socially disorganized high-crime areas
      a. Poor
      b. Densely populated
      c. Highly transient neighborhoods

C. Routine Activities Theory - articulated by Lawrence Cohen and Marcus Felson - the volume and distribution of predatory crime are closely related to the interaction of three variables that reflect the routine activities of the typical American lifestyle.
   1. The availability of suitable targets - easy access homes
      The absence of capable guardians - police, homeowners
      The presence of motivated offenders - such as a large number of unemployed teens.
      a. Hot Spots - A place where potentially motivated criminals congregate which makes the location a hot spot for crime.
   2. Moral Guardianship - moral beliefs and socialization may influence the routine activities that produce crime
   3. Lifestyle, Opportunity and Routine Activities
      a. A person's living arrangement can affect their risk; those who live in unguarded areas are at the mercy of motivated offenders.
      b. Lifestyle effects the opportunity for crime because it controls a persons
         1. proximity to criminals
         2. time of exposure to criminals
         3. their attractiveness as a target
         4. their ability to be protected

4. Empirical Support
    a. Cohen and Felson argue that crime increased between 1960 and 1980 due to fewer guardians in the home (women in the workforce)
    b. Skyrocketing drug use in the 1980s created motivated offenders

V. Caring for the Victim
A. The Government's Response
    1. President Reagan created Task Force on Victims of Crime in 1982
        a. Suggested recognizing victim's rights
        b. Providing the defendant with due process
    2. Omnibus Victim and Witness Protection Act passed
        a. Required the use of victim impact statements at federal criminal case sentencing
    3. 1984 - Comprehensive Crime Control Act and Victims of Crime Act
        a. Authorized federal funding for state victim compensation and assistance projects
B. Victim Service Programs - estimated 2000 victim-witness assistance programs have developed in U.S.
    1. Victim Compensation - victim may receive compensation from the state for losses incurred during the crime
        a. most states have a lack of funding
        b. compensation made for: medical bills, loss of wages, loss of future earning, and counseling
    2. Court Services
        a. Prepare victims and witnesses by explaining court procedures
        b. Explain how to be a witness
        c. Explain how bail works
        d. Explain what to do if the defendant makes a threat
        e. Provide transportation to and from court
        f. Provide escort to court
    3. Public Education
        a. familiarize the public with their services and with other victim agencies
        b. teach methods of dealing with conflict
    4. Crisis Intervention
        a. Clients referred to area agencies to aid in dealing with their ordeal
    5. Victim-Offender Reconciliation Programs (VORP)
        a. Mediators to facilitate face-to-face encounters between victims and their attackers.
        b. Goal - to agree on restitution and possibly reconciliation
C. Victims' Rights - Scholar Carrington suggests that crime victims have legal rights that should allow them basic rights from the government.
    1. Victim Advocacy - those wanting to lobby for victims
D. Self-Protection - many have invoked self-protection by taking matters into their own hands, building fences, surveillance cameras and many more
    1. Fighting Back - some victims fight back their assailant

      a. May get others around to help

      b. May cause assailant to flee

      c. May cause assailant to attack in a more violent way

  E. Community Organization - communities organizing on the neighborhood level against crime

    1. Block Watches

    2. Neighborhood Patrols

    3. Little evidence they affect the crime rate

VI.   Summary

Key Terms

Victimology - The study of the victim's role in criminal transactions.

Victimologists - Criminologists who focus their attention on crime victims.

Cycle of Violence - Abuse-crime phenomenon.

Chronic Victims - Individuals who are repeatedly crime victims.

Parricide - The killing of a close relative by a child.

Patricide - The murder of a father by his son or daughter.

Matricide - The murder of a mother by her son or daughter.

Victim Precipitation - View that some people may actually initiate the confrontation that eventually leads to their injury or death.

Active Precipitation - occurs when victims act provocatively, use threats or fighting words, or even attack first.

Victim-Precipitated Crime - A crime in which the victim's behavior was the spark that ignited the subsequent offense, as when the victim abused the offender verbally or physically.

Passive Precipitation - occurs when the victim exhibits some personal characteristic that unknowingly either threatens or encourages the attacker.

Deviant Place Hypothesis - Victims do not encourage crime, but are victim prone because they reside in socially disorganized high-crime areas where they have the greatest risk of coming into contact with criminal offenders, irrespective of their own behavior or lifestyle.

Routine Activities Theory - Cohen and Felson concluded that the volume and distribution of predatory crime (violent crimes against a person and crimes in which an offender attempts to steal an object directly) are closely related to the interaction of three variable that reflect the routine activities of the typical American lifestyle: the availability of suitable targets, the absence of capable guardians and the presence of motivated offenders.

Suitable Targets - A variable of routine activities theory. An example would be a home that contained easily salable goods.

Capable Guardians - A variable of routine activities theory. An example would be police, homeowners, neighbors, friends and relatives.

Motivated Offenders - A variable of routine activities theory. An example would be a large number of teenagers.

Proximity Hypothesis - The view that people become crime victims because they live or work in areas with large criminal populations.

Victim-Witness Assistance Program - Local program to assist victim/witnesses with medical bills, transportation, loss of wages, counseling and other needs caused by the crime.

Victim Compensation - Money paid to the victim, usually from a state victim compensation program, to assist in the loss of wages, medical bills, loss of future earnings, and counseling.

Crisis Intervention - A local network of public and private social service agencies that can provide emergency and long-term assistance with transportation, medical care, shelter, food, and clothing.

Exclusionary Rule - The principle that prohibits using evidence illegally obtained in a trial. Based on the Fourth Amendment "right of the people to be secure in their persons, houses, papers, and effects, against unreasonable searches and seizures," the rule is not a bar to prosecution, as legally obtained evidence may be available that may be used in a trial.

Preventive Detention - The practice of holding dangerous suspects before trial without bail.

Discussion Exercise

There are three main theories as to why individuals are victimized. Divide the class into three groups and have each group discuss one of the theories: victim precipitation theory, lifestyle theory and routine activities theory. Have each group explain the theory to the class and cite examples of known cases.

InfoTrac Assignment

GETTING STARTED: Search term words for subject guide: Crime Victims, Loss, Fear.

CRITICAL THINKING PROJECT: Using the search term "Fear," find articles that discuss the fear that is being generated in our society. Look at how levels of fear have risen since the September 11th terrorist attacks on the United States and the fear of urbanites.

Here are three articles:

Levi, Michael "Business, Cities and Fears About Crimes." *Urban Studies*.

Bannister, Jon and Nick Fyfe "Introduction: Fear and the City." *Urban Studies*.

Schmidt, Brad and Jeffrey Winters "Fear Not: Americans Have Been Very Jittery Lately. As We Cautiously Open Our Mail, Terror is Ever Present. Here, We Take a Look at Fear Itself." *Psychology Today*.

Test Bank

Essay Questions

1. Describe the problems, which most crime victims suffer. What are some of the remedies that a victim can use to help their plight?
2. Compare and contrast the various theories of victimization. Give examples of sensational crimes in which the theory applies.
3. Define the nature of victimization. Are there certain characteristics, which predispose one to becoming a victim? Are victims and criminals similar in their characteristics?
4. Should society participate in the care of victims? What has been the government's response to caring for victims? In your opinion, is this sufficient?
5. Describe Victim Service Programs. Are they effective? If they are not effective, how can they be improved?

Fill In The Blank

1. Criminologists who focus their attention on crime victims refer to themselves **victimologists**.

2. The abuse-crime phenomenon is referred to as **the cycle of violence.**

3. The practice of holding dangerous suspects before trial without bail is **preventive detention.**

4. Concerning Routine Activities Theory, police and homeowners would be considered **capable guardians**.

5. The study of the victim's role in criminal transactions is known as **victimology**.

6. **Victim compensation** is money paid to the victim, usually from a state victim compensation program.

7. The **Exclusionary Rule** is the principle that prohibits using evidence illegally obtained in a trial.

8. The murder of a mother by her son or daughter is **matricide**.

9. **Parricide** is the killing of a close relative by a child.

10. As a variable of Routine Activities Theory, a large number of teenagers would be **motivated offenders.**

11. In **Routine Activities Theory**, Cohen and Felson concluded that the volume and distribution of predatory crime are closely related to the interaction of three variables that reflect the routine activities of the typical American lifestyle: the availability of suitable targets, the absence of capable guardians and the presence of motivated offenders.

12. Local programs designed to assist victim/witnesses with medical bills, transportation, loss of wages, counseling and other needs caused by the crime are called **Victim-Witness Assistance Program**.

13. Individuals who are repeatedly crime victims are **chronic victims**.

14. **Victim Precipitation** is the view that some people may actually initiate the confrontation that eventually leads to their injury or death.

15. A variable of Routine Activities Theory, an example of **Suitable Targets** would be a home that contained easily salable goods.

Multiple Choice

1. Criminologists who focus their attention on crime victims refer to themselves:
   a. Victimologists
   b. Sociologists
   c. Psychologists
   d. None of the above
   (Answer = a)

2. Victims of crime suffer which of the following:
   a. Loss
   b. Suffering
   c. Fear
   d. All of the above
   (Answer = d)

3. The abuse-crime phenomenon is referred to as:
   a. Self-protection
   b. The cycle of violence
   c. Antisocial behavior
   d. All of the above
   (Answer = b)

4. Some characteristics increase risk because they arouse anger, jealousy, or destructive impulses in potential offenders. This is known as:
   a. Target vulnerability
   b. Target gratifiability
   c. Target victims
   d. Target antagonism
   (Answer = d)

5. Sibling homicide is known as:
   a. Siblicide
   b. Genocide
   c. Brothericide
   d. Sistercide
   (Answer = a)

6. Some people may actually initiate the confrontation that eventually leads to their injury or death. This is known as:
   a. Lifestyle Theory
   b. High-Risk Lifestyle
   c. Deviant Place Theory
   d. Victim Precipitation Theory
   (Answer = d)

7. When victims act provocatively, use threats or fighting words, or even attack first, it is known as:
   a. Passive Precipitation
   b. Active Precipitation
   c. Deviant Place Theory
   d. Lifestyle Theory
   (Answer = b)

8. When the victim exhibits some personal characteristic that unknowingly either threatens or encourages the attacker it is known as:
   a. Passive Precipitation
   b. Active Precipitation
   c. Deviant Place Theory
   d. Lifestyle Theory
   (Answer = a)

9. In Routine Activities Theory, police and homeowners would be an example of:
    a. Suitable targets
    b. Motivated offenders
    c. Capable guardians
    d. All of the above
    (Answer = c)

10. In Routine Activities Theory, a large number of unemployed teenagers would be and example of:
    a. Suitable targets
    b. Motivated offenders
    c. Capable guardians
    d. All of the above
    (Answer = b)

11. Lifestyle effects the opportunity for crime because it controls a persons:
    a. Proximity to criminals
    b. Time of exposure to criminals
    c. Their attractiveness as a target
    d. All of the above
    (Answer = d)

12. Criminologists who focus their attention on crime victims are known as:
    a. Victimologists
    b. Sociologists
    c. Typologists
    d. Psychologists
    (Answer = a)

13. A local program to assist victim/witnesses with medical bills, transportation, loss of wages, counseling and other needs caused by the crime is:
    a. Social services
    b. Victim-Witness Assistance Program
    c. Rape crisis center
    d. Guardian Ad Litem Program
    (Answer = b)

14. The practice of holding dangerous suspects before trial without bail is:
    a. Probation
    b. Parole
    c. House arrest
    d. Preventive detention
    (Answer = d)

15. The view that people become crime victims because they live or work in areas with large criminal populations is:
    a. Routine activities theory
    b. Victim precipitation
    c. Suitable targets
    d. Proximity Hypothesis
    (Answer = d)

16. The murder of a father by his son or daughter is:
    a. Matricide
    b. Siblicide
    c. Friendicide
    d. Patricide
    (Answer = d)

17. When victims act provocatively, use threats or fighting words, or even attack first, the following may occur:
    a. Passive precipitation
    b. Active precipitation
    c. Desistance
    d. persistence
    (Answer = b)

18. This occurs when the victim exhibits some personal characteristic that unknowingly either threatens or encourages the attacker:
    a. Persistence
    b. Desistance
    c. Passive precipitation
    d. Active precipitation
    (Answer = c)

19. The killing of a close relative by a child is:
    a. Parricide
    b. Patricide
    c. Matricide
    d. Friendicide
    (Answer = a)

20. The mother of a mother by her son or daughter is known as:
    a. Parricide
    b. Matricide
    c. Patricide
    d. Friendicide
    (Answer = b)

21. As an example of routine activities theory, an example would be a large number of teenagers:
    a. Chronic victims
    b. Capable guardians
    c. Motivated offenders
    d. Unmotivated offenders
    (Answer = c)

22. The view that some people may actually initiate the confrontation that eventually leads to their injury or death is called:
    a. Victim compensation
    b. Proximity hypothesis
    c. Preventive detention
    d. Victim precipitation
    (Answer = d)

23. As a variable of routine activities theory, an example would be a home that contained easily salable:
    a. Motivated offenders
    b. Suitable targets
    c. Victimologists
    d. Chronic offenders
    (Answer = b)

24. Individuals who are repeatedly crime victims are called:
    a. Motivated offenders
    b. Capable guardians
    c. Chronic victims
    d. None of the above
    (Answer = c)

25. The total cost of victimization is estimated to be over _____ annually.
    a. $100
    b. $1000
    c. $1 million
    d. $100 billion
    (Answer = d)

26. Each heroin addict is estimated to cost society about _____ per year.
    a. $135
    b. $1350
    c. $13500
    d. $135000
    (Answer = d)

27. According to the Bureau of Justice Statistics, there are on average _____ victims of violent crime in the U.S. each year.
    a. 10
    b. 100
    c. 10 million
    d. 1 million
    (Answer = c)

28. Many people fear for the safety of others in their lives. This is called:
    a. Altruistic fear
    b. Self-protection
    c. Fear for your life
    d. Cycle of violence
    (Answer = a)

29. The current leading source of information about the nature and extent of victimization is the:
    a. Uniform Crime Report
    b. Self-report Surveys
    c. Youth Surveys
    d. National Crime Victimization Survey
    (Answer = d)

30. The group most vulnerable to crime is:
    a. Low-income, African-American, western and urban
    b. Affluent, rural, White, Northeastern
    c. All of the above
    d. None of the above
    (Answer = a)

31. Which age group has more violent crime committed against them?
    a. 65+
    b. 35-49
    c. 25-35
    d. 16-19
    (Answer = d)

32. Which income level has more violent crime committed against them?
    a. $75,000 or more
    b. $2500-$34000
    c. Less than $7,500
    d. None of the above
    (Answer = c)

33. Which of the following are less likely to become a victim?
    a. Married
    b. Single
    c. Divorced
    d. None of the above
    (Answer = a)

34. Which ethnic group members are more likely to become a victim of a crime?
    a. African- Americans
    b. Whites
    c. Hispanics
    d. Asians
    (Answer = a)

35. The median age of sibling homicide offenders is _____ years old.
    a. 6
    b. 20
    c. 65
    d. 23
    (Answer = d)

36. Which theorists suggested female victims often contribute to their attacks by dressing provocatively or pursuing a relationship with the rapist?
    a. Sigmund Freud
    b. Edwin Sutherland
    c. Menachem Amir
    d. Charles Darwin
    (Answer = c)

37. Males who carry weapons are approximately _____ times more likely to be victimized than those who did not carry weapons.
    a. 1
    b. 2
    c. 3
    d. 4
    (Answer = c)

38. Deviant places are:
    a. Poor
    b. Densely populated
    c. Highly transient neighborhoods
    d. All of the above
    (Answer = d)

39. Cohen and Felson argue that crime rates _____ between 1960-1980 because the number of adult caretakers at home during the day decreased as a result of increased female participation in the workforce.
   a. Decreased
   b. Stayed the same
   c. Did not change
   d. Increased
   (Answer = d)

40. Skyrocketing drug use in the _____ created an excess of motivated offenders, and the rates of some crimes, such as robbery, increased dramatically.
   a. 1960s
   b. 1980s
   c. 1990s
   d. 2000s
   (Answer = b)

True/False

T   1.   The National Crime Victimization Survey indicates that in 2000, U.S. residents' age 12 or older experienced approximately 25.9 million crimes.

F   2.   Based on estimates of property taken during larcenies, burglaries and other reported crimes, the FBI estimates victims lose about $12 per year.

F   3.   Very few crime victims suffer injury each year, ranging from a scratch to a gun shot.

T   4.   Research shows that both boys and girls are more likely to engage in violent behavior if they were (1) the target of physical abuse and (2) exposed to violent behavior among adults they know or live with; exposed to weapons.

T   5.   In 2000, an estimated 25.9 million victimizations occurred, a decline from 28.8 million property and violent crimes experienced in 1999.

F   6.   The NCVS shows that violent crimes are slightly more likely to take place in dark, closed places in the middle of the night.

F   7.   The NCVS tells us that affluent, rural, white homes in the Northeast are the most likely to contain crime victims or be the target of theft offenses, such as burglary or larceny.

T   8.   Individuals who have been crime victims maintain a significantly higher chance of future victimization than people who have remained nonvictims.

T	9. Victims reported that a single offender committed most crimes over age 20.

F	10. Crime tends to be interracial.

T	11. Victimization commonly occurs within families and involves parents, children, and extended family.

T	12. According to the victim precipitation view, some people may actually initiate the confrontation that eventually leads to their injury or death.

F	13. According to deviant place theory, victims encourage crime and are victim prone because they live in safe, nice neighborhoods.

T	14. Motivated people such as teenage males, drug users, and unemployed adults, are the ones most likely to commit crime.

T	15. Some criminologists believe that moral beliefs and socialization may influence the routine activities that produce crime.

Chapter Five

The Development of Rational Choice Theory

Summary

Chapter Five examines the development of rational choice theory. Particular attention is paid to the issue of whether crime is rational or irrational. Methods of eliminating crime are introduced and the chapter concludes with a discussion of the policy implications of rational choice theory.

Learning Objectives

After reading this chapter the student should be able to:
- Define the Classical Theory of Crime.
- Develop an understanding of how Choice Theory emerged.
- Describe Rational Choice and Routine Activities Theory.
- Discuss the rationale of crime, specifically street crimes, drug use, and violence.
- Identify methods of eliminating crime.
- Describe methods of situation crime prevention.
- Define Deterrence.
- Identify the various types of deterrence.
- Determine the effectiveness of incapacitation.
- Discuss the policy implications of Choice Theory.
- Cite examples of Just Deserts.

Chapter Overview
The Classical Theory of Crime: Choice Theory Emerges
The Concepts of Rational Choice

Chapter Outline

I. Introduction
  A. The Development of Rational Choice Theory - the view that crime is a decision to violate any law and is made for a variety of reasons, including greed, revenge, need, anger, lust, jealousy, thrill-seeking or vanity.
  B. Rooted in the classical school developed by Cesare Beccaria

II. The Classical Theory of Crime
  A. Beccaria influenced thinkers that criminal chose to commit crime
  B. Jeremy Bentham (1748-1833) popularized Beccaria's views
   1. Utilitarianism - people chose actions whether they receive pleasure and to avoid pain
   2. Punishment - has four objectives
      a. To prevent all criminal offenses.
      b. When it does not prevent, to convince offenders to commit lesser offenses
      c. To ensure that a criminal uses no more force than is necessary
      d. To prevent crime as cheaply as possible

III. Choice Theory Emerges - 1970's
  A. Thinking About Crime
   1. In the 1970s, thinking began to reflect that criminals are rational actors who plan their crimes, fear punishment and deserve to be penalized for their misdeeds.
   2. James Q. Wilson wrote *Thinking About Crime* and said that unless we react forcefully to crime, those "sitting on the fence" will decide that crime pays.
  B. Impact on Crime Control - shift in U.S. Public Policy
   1. Tougher laws passed

73

2. Stiffer penalties enacted

IV. The Concepts of Rational Choice - law-violating behavior occurs when an offender decides to risk breaking the law after considering both personal factors and situation factors.

    A. Offense and Offender
        1. Offense-specific - offenders will react selectively to the characteristics of particular offenses.
        2. Offender-specific - criminals are not simply automatons who, for one reason or another, engage in random acts of antisocial behavior.
        3. Crime is an event.
        4. Criminality is a personal trait.
    B. Structuring Criminality - a number of personal factors condition people to choose criminality.
        1. Economic Opportunity - crime occurs when one feels they will profit
        2. Learning and Experience - career criminal learn their limits; when to chance and when to be cautious
        3. Learning Criminal Techniques - to avoid detection
        4. Structuring Crime - criminals choose where and when to commit crime
        5. Choosing the Type of Crime - some criminals are specialists such as thieves
        6. Choosing the Time and Place of Crime - criminals select times that are better and are selective in the location of the crime
        7. Choosing the Target of Crime - select more vulnerable targets

V.   **Is Crime Rational?** - crimes are the product of rational, objective thought
    A. Are Street Crimes Rational? - Seems more random acts of criminal opportunity than well-thought out conspiracies.
    B. Is Drug Use Rational? - at the onset, drug use is controlled by rational decision making
    C. Can Violence Be Rational? - there are cases of rational, thought-out violence
    D. Rational Killers? - many homicides are the result of careful planning
    E. Rational Rapists? - serial rapists show rationality to avoid detection
        1. Edgework - the exhilarating, momentary integration of danger, risk, and skill that motivates people to try a variety of dangerous criminal and non-criminal behavior.
    F. The Seductions of Crime - immediate benefits to criminality

VI.   **Eliminating Crime** - if crime is rational, then offenders should be able to be convinced to make different choices.
    A. Situational Crime Prevention - Criminal acts will be avoided if:
- potential targets are carefully guarded
- the means to commit crime are controlled
- potential offenders are carefully monitored.

        1. Targeting Specific Crimes
- Increase the effort needed to commit crime
- Increase the risks of committing crime
- Reduce the rewards for committing crime

- Induce guilt or shame for committing crime.
2. Crime Discouragers
   a. Guardians - Monitor targets (security guards)
   b. Handlers - Monitor potential offenders (parole officers and parents)
   c. Managers - Monitor places (homeowners and doorway attendants)
3. Diffusion and Discouragement
   a. Diffusion occurs when:
      1. efforts to prevent one crime unintentionally prevent another
      2. and crime control efforts in one locale reduce crime in other nontarget areas.
   b. Discouragement - when efforts to eliminate one type of crime convinces would-be lawbreakers to forgo other criminal activity because crime no longer pays.
4. Displacement, Extinction and Fear
   a. Displacement - doing something in one area which may place the crime in another area
   b. Extinction - crime reduction programs may produce a short-term positive effect, but benefits as criminals adjust to new conditions.
   c. Fear - situational crime prevention efforts may be compromised in a climate where fear and social disorganization are overwhelming.
B. General Deterrence - crime rates are influence and controlled by the threat of punishment. If people fear punishment, they will not break the law.
   1. Certainty of Punishment - The crime rate should decrease with the certainty of punishment. However, crime continues because criminals believe:
      a. there is only a small chance they will get arrested even if they are aware of the crime
      b. that police officers are sometimes reluctant to make arrests even if they are aware of the crime
      c. that even if apprehended there is a good chance of receiving a lenient punishment.
   2. Does Increasing Police Activity Deter Crime?
      a. little evidence that increasing officers decrease crime rates
      b. Crackdowns - sudden changes in police activity designed to increase the communicated threat or actual certainty of punishment-to-lower crime.
   3. Severity of Punishment and Deterrence - increasing the punishment for specific crimes can reduce their occurrence
   4. Capital Punishment
      a. Immediate impact - studies show that the overall impact of executions might actually increase the incidence of homicide
      b. Comparative Research - states with and without the death penalty show no difference in their murder rates

    c. Time-Series Studies - look at the long-term association between capital sentencing and murder. Studies show no relationship between the deterrence of capital sentencing and the murder rate.

5. Rethinking the Deterrent Effect of Capital Punishment - some found that increasing the number of executions has helped reduce the murder rate

6. Informal Sanctions
    a. may have a greater deterrent impact than formal legal punishment
    b. Occur when significant others, such as parents, peers, neighbors and teachers direct their disapproval, stigma, anger, and indignation toward an offender.

7. Shame and Humiliation - can be a powerful deterrent to crime

8. Critique of General Deterrence
    a. Rationality - deterrence theory assumes a rational offender weighs the costs and decides on their course of action
    b. Need - many offenders are members of the underclass
        1. People cut off from society, lacking the education and skills they need to be in demand in the modern economy
    c. Greed - some immune to deterrence because they feel the profits are worth the risk
    d. Severity and Speed - Beccaria said punishment should be severe and swift; ours is not.

C. Specific Deterrence - criminal sanctions should be so powerful that known criminals will never repeat their criminal acts.
    1. Does Specific Deterrence Deter Crime? - Chronic offenders continue to offend.

D. Incapacitation - some feel that sending more to prison would reduce crime
    1. Can Incapacitation Reduce Crime? - studies show the results would be minimal
    2. The Logic Behind Incarceration - may not work as a deterrent
        a. Little evidence that incapacitating criminals will deter them from future criminality
        b. First time offenders are exposed to more experienced inmates
        c. Older offenders are usually sentenced and may be kept beyond the time they are a threat to society
        d. Very expensive to incarcerate everyone
    3. Selective Incapacitation: Three Strives and You're Out
        a. Discovering the chronic offender and incarcerate them for life

VII. **Policy Implications of Choice Theory**
A. Just Desert - Andrew Von Hirsch in his book *Doing Justice*
    1. Those who violate others' rights deserve to be punished.
    2. We should not deliberately add to human suffering; punishment makes those punished suffer.

3. Punishment may prevent more misery than it inflicts.

VIII. Summary

Key Terms

Choice Theory - The belief that criminals choose to commit crime.

Classical Theory - The theoretical perspective suggesting that (1) people have free will to choose criminal or conventional behaviors; (2) people choose to commit crime for reasons of greed or personal need; and (3) crime can be controlled only by the fear of criminal sanctions.

Utilitarianism - philosophy which emphasized that behavior occurs when the actor considers it useful, purposeful, and reasonable

Rational Choice - The view that crime is a matter of rational choice. The decision to violate any law is made for a variety of personal reasons, including greed, revenge, need, anger, lust, jealously, thrill-seeking or vanity.

Crime Displacement - Preventing crime in one location, but the crime may be relocated to another location.

Suitable Targets - According to routine activities, a target for crime that is relatively valuable, easily transportable, and not capably guarded.

Capable Guardians- A variable of routine activities theory. An example would be police, homeowners, neighbors, friends and relatives.

Motivated Criminals - The potential criminals in a population. According to rational choice theory, crime rates will vary according to the number of motivated criminals.

Edgework - the "exhilarating, momentary integration of danger, risk and skill" that motivates people to try a variety of dangerous criminal and non-criminal behavior.

Seductions of Crime - Immediate benefits to criminality.

Situational Crime Prevention - Policies that convince potential criminals to desist from criminal activities, delay their actions, or avoid a particular target.

Defensible Space - The principle that crime prevention can be achieved through modifying the physical environment to reduce the opportunity individuals have to commit crime.

Crime Discouragers - People whose behavior directly influences crime prevention. Discouragers may be grouped into three categories: guardians, handlers and managers.

Extinction - Crime reduction programs may produce a short-term positive effect, but benefits dissipate as criminals adjust to new conditions.

Diffusion of Benefits - A hidden benefit to situation crime prevention. Diffusion occurs when (1) efforts to prevent one crime unintentionally prevent another and (2) crime control efforts in one locale reduce crime in other nontarget areas.

Discouragement - A hidden benefit to situation crime prevention. Discouragement occurs when efforts to eliminate one type of crime convince would-be lawbreakers to forgo other criminal activity because crime no longer pays.

General Deterrence - Crime rates are influenced and controlled by the threat of punishment.

Deterrence Theory - The severity of punishment is inversely proportional to the level of crime rates.

Crackdowns - Sudden changes in police activity designed to increase the communicated threat or actual certainty of punishment to lower crime rates.

Informal Sanctions - Occur when significant others, such as parents, peers, neighbors and teachers direct their disapproval, stigma, anger and indignation toward an offender.

Stigmatization - The labeling that taints a person's identity and changes him/her in the eyes of others.

Reintegrative Shaming - A method of correction that encourages offenders to confront their misdeeds, experience shame because of the harm they caused, and then be reincluded in society.

Selective Incapacitation - This model proposes that if a small number of people account for a relatively large percentage of the nation's crime, then an effort to incapacitate these few troublemakers might have a significant payoff.

Three Strikes and You're Out - Policy of giving people convicted of three violent offenses a mandatory life term without parole.

Just Desert - The philosophy of justice that asserts that those who violate the rights of others deserve to be punished. The severity of punishment should be commensurate with the seriousness of the crime.

Blameworthy - The amount of culpability or guilt a person maintains for participating in a particular criminal offense.

Discussion Exercise

Discuss recent films such as *Natural Born Killers, Hannibal* and *Blow.* Were these criminals rational? Did they make a choice to be a criminal or were there other contributing elements to their criminality? Could any of these individuals avoided criminal behaviors or was it beyond their control?

InfoTrac Assignment

GETTING STARTED: Search term words for subject guide: Rational Choice Theory, Street Crimes, Drug Use, Situation Crime, Deterrence, Incapacitation, Just Desert.

CRITICAL THINKING PROJECT: Using the search term "Street Crimes," find articles that discuss this aspect of crime.

Here are three articles:

Bresnick, Jan "Get Street-Smart! Today's Guide to Personal Safety and Crime Prevention." *Prevention*.

Young, Thomas J. "Parricide Rates and Criminal Street Violence in the United States: Is There a Correlation." *Adolescence*.

Lowe, Jennifer "Street Crimes are Moving Into Malls, But Officials Say They're Still Safe." *Knight-Ridder/Tribune News Service*.

Test Bank

Essay Questions

1. Describe deterrence. What is the difference between general and specific deterrence. Does deterrence strategies work in eliminated crime?
2. What are the policy implication of choice theory? Define choice theory and how it emerged.
3. Is crime a rational choice? Give specific examples for your discussion.
4. Describe the seduction of crime. What makes crime alluring to some and not as alluring to others?
5. Describe the concepts of rational choice theory. Trace the origin of this theory and its implications on our policies today.

Fill In The Blank

1. **Utilitarianism** is the philosophy, which emphasized that behavior, occurs when the actor considered it useful, purposeful, and reasonable.

2. Crime reduction programs which may produce a short-term positive effect, but the benefits dissipate as criminals adjust to new conditions is known as **extinction**.

3. **General Deterrence** says that crime rates are influenced and controlled by the threat of punishment.

4. The policy of giving individuals convicted of three violent offenses a mandatory life term without parole is known as **Three Strikes and You're Out**.

5. A method of correction that encourages offenders to confront their misdeeds, experience shame because of the harm they caused, and then be reincluded in society is known as **Reintegrative Shaming**.

6. __Motivated criminals__ are the potential criminals in a population.

7. __Just Desert__ is the philosophy of justice that asserts that those who violate the rights of others deserve to be punished.

8. __Informal sanctions__ occur when significant others, such as parents, peer, neighbors and teachers direct their disapproval, stigma, anger and indignation toward the offender.

9. __Rational Choice Theory__ views that criminal make a rational choice to commit crime.

10. Immediate benefits to criminality are known as the __Seductions of Crime.__

11. __Selective Incapacitation__ is the model that proposes that if a small number of people account for a relatively large percentage of the nation's crime, then an effort to incapacitate these few troublemakers might have a significant payoff.

12. __Situational Crime Prevention__ are policies that convince potential criminals to desist from criminal activities, delay their actions, or avoid a particular target.

13. __Stigmatization__ is the labeling that taints a person's identity and changes him or her in the eyes of others.

14. According to routine activities, a target for crime that is relatively valuable, easily transportable, and not capably guarded is a __Suitable Target.__

15. __Blameworthy__ is the amount of culpability or guilt a person maintains for participating in a particular criminal offense.

Multiple Choice

1. The philosophy, which emphasized that behavior, occurs when the actor considered it useful, purposeful, and reasonable.
    a. Utilitarianism
    b. Rational Choice
    c. Deterrence Theory
    d. Discouragement
    (Answer = a)

2. Crime reduction programs which may produce a short-term positive effect, but the benefits dissipate as criminals adjust to new conditions is known as: Crime displacement
   a. Crackdowns
   b. Loss
   c. Deterrence
   d. Extinction
   (Answer = d)

3. Crime rates are influenced and controlled by the threat of punishment.
   a. Specific Deterrence
   b. General Deterrence
   c. Diffusion of Benefits
   d. Crime Displacement
   (Answer = b)

4. The policy of giving individuals convicted of three violent offenses a mandatory life term without parole is known as:
   a. the death penalty
   b. probation
   c. parole
   e. Three Strikes and You're Out
   (Answer = d)

5. A method of correction that encourages offenders to confront their misdeeds, experience shame because of the harm they caused, and then be reincluded in society is known as:
   a. Reintegrative Shaming
   b. Crackdowns
   c. Blameworthy
   d. Edgework
   (Answer = a)

6. The potential criminals in a population are known as:
   a. Victims
   b. Defendants
   c. Law enforcement
   e. Motivated criminals
   (Answer = d)

7. The philosophy of justice that asserts that those who violate the rights of others deserve to be punished is known as:
    a. Crime discouragers
    b. Just Desert
    c. Crackdowns
    d. None of the above
    (Answer = b)

8. These occur when significant others, such as parents, peer, neighbors and teachers direct their disapproval, stigma, anger and indignation toward the offender:
    a. Informal sanctions
    b. Formal sanctions
    c. Delayed sanctions
    d. Reactive sanctions
    (Answer = a)

9. The view that criminal make a rational choice to commit crime:
    a. Deterrence theory
    b. Crime displacement
    c. Rational Choice Theory
    d. Classical theory
    (Answer = c)

10. Immediate benefits to criminality are known as:
    a. Diffusion of benefits
    b. Seductions of Crime
    c. Suitable targets
    d. Motivated offenders
    (Answer = b)

11. The model that proposes that if a small number of people account for a relatively large percentage of the nation's crime, then an effort to incapacitate these few troublemakers might have a significant payoff.
    a. Deterrence theory
    b. Classical theory
    c. Rational choice theory
    d. Selective Incapacitation
    (Answer = d)

12. Policies that convince potential criminals to desist from criminal activities, delay their actions, or avoid a particular target are known as:
   a. Situational Crime Prevention
   b. Crime displacement
   c. Crime discouragers
   d. Deterrence
   (Answer = a)

13. The labeling that taints a person's identity and changes him or her in the eyes of others:
   a. Extinction
   b. Stigmatization
   c. Reintegrative shaming
   d. Informal sanctions
   (Answer = b)

14. According to routine activities, a target for crime that is relatively valuable, easily transportable, and not capably guarded is a:
   a. Motivated criminal
   b. Just desert
   c. Crackdown
   d. Suitable Target
   (Answer = d)

15. The amount of culpability or guilt a person maintains for participating in a particular criminal offense is:
   a. Utilitarianism
   b. Selective incapacitation
   c. Extinction
   e. Blameworthy
   (Answer = d)

16. A variable of routine activities theory and an example would be police or homeowners is:
   a. Discouragers
   b. Suitable targets
   c. Victims
   d. Capable guardians
   (Answer = d)

17. The exhilarating, momentary integration of danger, risk and skill that motivates people to try a variety of dangerous criminal and non-criminal behaviors is known as:
    a. discouragers
    b. edgework
    c. suitable targets
    d. defensible space
    (Answer = b)

18. This occurs when efforts to eliminate one type of crime convince would-be lawbreakers to forgo other criminal activity because crime no longer pays:
    a. Persistence
    b. Desistance
    c. discouragement
    d. Passive precipitation
    (Answer = c)

19. The belief that criminals choose to commit crimes is:
    a. Choice theory
    b. Deterrence theory
    c. Classical theory
    d. Crime displacement
    (Answer = a)

20. When (1) effort to prevent one crime unintentionally prevent another and (2) crime control efforts in one locale reduce crime in other nontarget areas it is known as:
    a. Choice theory
    b. Diffusion of benefits
    c. Crackdowns
    d. Discouragement
    (Answer = b)

21. Preventing crime in one location, but the crime may be relocated to another location is:
    a. Crime discouragers
    b. Edgework
    c. Crime displacement
    d. Deterrence theory
    (Answer = c)

22. The principle that crime prevention can be achieved through modifying the physical environment to reduce the opportunity individuals have to commit crime is called:
   a. Crime displacement
   b. Edgework
   c. Crime discouragers
   d. Defensible space
   (Answer = d)

23. The severity of punishment is inversely proportional to the level of crime benefits is known as:
   a. Defensible space
   b. Deterrence theory
   c. Discouragement
   d. Diffusion of benefits
   (Answer = b)

24. Sudden changes in police activity designed to increase the communicated threat or actual certainty of punishment to lower crime rates is:
   a. Crime discouragers
   b. Edgework
   c. Crackdowns
   d. Crime displacement
   (Answer = c)

25. People whose behavior directly influences crime prevention are known as:
   a. Capable guardians
   b. Legal guardians
   c. Chronic offenders
   d. Crime discouragers
   (Answer = d)

26. Rational choice theory has its roots in the classical school of criminology developed by:
   a. Sigmund Freud
   b. Karl Marx
   c. Mark Martin
   d. Cesare Beccaria
   (Answer = d)

27. Who wrote *Thinking About Crime?*
    a. Charles Murray
    b. Louis Cox
    c. James Q. Wilson
    d. Mark Twain
    (Answer = c)

28. Offenders reacting selectively to the characteristics of particular offenses is known as:
    a. Offense specific
    b. Offender specific
    c. Rational choice
    d. Altruistic fear
    (Answer = a)

29. The notion that criminals are not simply automatons who, for one reason or another, engage in random acts of antisocial behavior is known as:
    a. Altruistic fear
    b. Rational choice
    c. Offense specific
    d. Offender specific
    (Answer = d)

30. Personal factors which may influence people to commit crime are:
    a. Economic opportunity
    b. Learning and experience
    c. Learning criminal techniques
    d. All of the above
    (Answer = d)

31. Reducing anticipated rewards may include which of the following?
    a. Target removal
    b. Identifying property
    c. All of the above
    d. None of the above
    (Answer = c)

32. Examples of inducing guilt or shame may be which of the following?
    a. Rule setting
    b. Strengthening moral condemnation
    c. All of the above
    d. None of the above
    (Answer = c)

33. Crime persists because most offenders believe that:
    a. There is only a small chance they will be arrested for committing a particular crime
    b. That police officers are sometimes reluctant to make arrests even if they are aware of crime
    c. That even if apprehended there is a good chance of receiving a lenient punishment
    d. All of the above
    (Answer = d)

34. The most famous police experiment was conducted where?
    a. Kansas City, Missouri
    b. Kansas City, Kansas
    c. Fayetteville, North Carolina
    d. Las Cruces, New Mexico
    (Answer = a)

35. Between 1993-97 the probability of going to prison for murder increased:
    a. 6%
    b. 20%
    c. 65%
    d. 17%
    (Answer = d)

36. Between 1993-97 the murder rate dropped:
    a. 6%
    b. 20%
    c. 23%
    d. 65%
    (Answer = c)

37. Between 1993-97 robbery declined:
    a. 1%
    b. 2%
    c. 21%
    d. 4%
    (Answer = c)

38. Between 1993-97 the probability of going prison after a conviction increased:
    a. 2%
    b. 4%
    c. 10%
    d. 14%
    (Answer = d)

39. The type of study which has been conducted on the impact of capital punishment is called:
   a. Immediate impact
   b. Comparative research
   c. Time series analysis
   d. All of the above
   (Answer = d)

40. Research which compares the murder rates in jurisdictions that have abolished the death penalty with the rates of those that employ the death penalty are called:
   a. Immediate impact
   b. Comparative research
   c. Time series analysis
   d. Discouragement
   (Answer = b)

True/False

T   1. The view that crime is a matter of rational choice is held by a number of criminologists who believe that the decision to violate any law is made for a variety of personal reasons including greed, revenge, need, anger, lust, jealousy, thrill-seeking or vanity.

F   2. Rational choice theory has root in the Chicago School of Sociology developed by the Italian social thinker Cesare Beccaria.

F   3. To deter people from committing more serious offenses, Beccaria believed punishment should be lenient.

T   4. Britain philosopher Jeremy Bentham helped popularize Beccaria's views in his writings on utilitarianism.

T   5. The purpose of law is to produce and support the total happiness of the community it serves.

F   6. Selling hours means learning how to hide drugs on their person, in the street or home.

F   7. Stashing means that drug dealers are aware of not selling drugs at the wrong time of day.

T   8. Routine activities means that dealers camouflaged their activities within the bustle of their daily lives.

T   9. The peep game is scooping out the terrority to make sure the turf is free from anything out of place that may be potential threat.

F   10. Most burglars commit crime in impermeable neighborhoods.

T   11. Mutual societies involve drugs shared among friends at parties or teenage hangouts.

T   12. Periodic markets are drug sites that provide relatively low incomes because sales can be made only at limited times during the day.

F   13. Fixed-site neighborhoods are so drug-infested that law-abiding citizens have moved out.

T   14. Edgework is the exhilarating, momentary integration of danger, risk and skill that motivates people to try a variety of dangerous criminal and non-criminal behavior.

T   15. Sociologist Jack Katz argues that there are immediate benefits to criminality, which he labels the seductions of crime.

Chapter Six

Trait Theories

Summary

Chapter Six examines the trait theories of criminology. A discussion of the foundations and explanations of the various biological trait theories is key. This chapter also looks at the psychological trait theories and their implications. The chapter concludes with the social policy implications that these theories have had in our society.

Learning Objectives
After reading this chapter the student should be able to:
- Understand the foundations of Biological Trait Theory.
- Explore the impact of Sociobiology.
- Define the Modern Trait Theories.
- Describe the various Biological Trait Theories.
- Distinguish between Biochemical Conditions and Neurophysiological Conditions and their relationship to crime.
- Discuss genetics in regards to their cause and effect on crime.
- Evaluate the Biological Branch of Trait Theory.
- Describe the Psychological Trait Theories.
- Define the Theory of Imitation.
- Understand the Psychodynamic Perspective.
- Discuss the Behavioral Theories.
- Describe the relationship between mental illness and crime.
- Evaluate any correlation between personality and crime.
- Understand the Social Policy implications of the Trait Theories.

Chapter Overview
Introduction
Foundations of Biological Trait Theory

Chapter Outline

I. Introduction

    A. Trait theory - all people are aware and fear the sanctioning power of the law, but some are unable to control their urges and passions. Divided into two sub-divisions:

        1. biological make-up

        2. psychological make-up

II. Foundations of Biological Trait Theory

    A. The inheritance school traced the activities of several generations of families believed to have an especially large number of criminal members

    B. William Sheldon, 50 years ago, of the somatotype school, held that criminals manifest distinct physiques that makes them susceptible to particular types of delinquent behavior.

        1. Mesomorphs - have well-developed muscles and an athletic appearance; active aggressive and the most likely to be criminals

        2. Endomorphs - heavy builds and is slow moving; less likely to commit violent crime, possibly engage in less strenuous crimes

        3. Ectomorphs - tall, thin, less social and more intellectual than other types

    C. Impact of Sociobiology

        1. Biological explanations of crime fell out of favor in the early 20th century

        2. Biophobia - the belief that no serious consideration should be given to biological factors when attempting to understand human nature

3. Early 1970s criminologist Edmund O. Wilson published *Sociobiology* and the biological basis for crime reemerged.
4. Sociobiologists view the gene as ultimate unit of life that controls all human destiny.
5. People are controlled by the need to have their genetics survive and dominate others.
6. Reciprocal altruism - people are motivated by believing that their actions will be reciprocated and that their gene survival will be enhanced.

D. Modern Trait Theories - each offender is unique, physically and mentally
1. Social Interaction - trait theorist are not overly concerned with legal definitions of crime
2. Trait theorist focus on basic human behavior and drives-aggression, violence and the tendency to act on impulse
3. Trait theorist argue that chronic offenders suffer some biological/psychological condition that renders them incapable of resisting social pressures and problems

III. Biosocial Theories - believe that physical, environmental, and social conditions work together to produce human behavior

A. Learning Potential and Its Effect on Individual Behavior Patterns -
1. Social behavior is learned
2. Each individual organism has a unique potential for learning
3. People learn through a process involving the brain and central nervous system
4. Learning takes place when physical changes occur in the brain
   a. Instinct - some believe that learning is influenced by instinctual drives
   b. Instincts are inherited, natural and unlearned dispositions that activate specific behavior patterns designed to reach certain goals.

B. BioChemical Conditions and Crime
1. Chemical and Mineral Influences - minimum levels of minerals and chemicals are needed for normal brain functioning and growth
2. Diet and Crime - malnourished or those lacking in certain vitamins may be predisposed to learning and behavior disorders
3. Sugar and Crime - diets high in sugar and carbohydrates have been linked to violence and aggression
4. Glucose Metabolism/Hypoglycemia
   a. Research indicates that persistent abnormality in the way the brain metabolizes glucose (sugar) can be linked to antisocial behaviors, such as substance abuse
   b. Hypoglycemia - when glucose in the blood falls below levels necessary for normal and efficient brain functioning. Linked to outburst of antisocial behavior and violence.
5. Hormonal Influences - James Q. Wilson feels that hormones may be the key to understanding human behavior.
   a. Androgens - abnormal levels of male sex hormones which may produce aggressive behavior

b. How Hormones May Influence Behavior - hormones cause areas of the brain to become less sensitive to environmental stimuli.

    1. neocortex - part of the brain that controls sympathetic feelings toward others

c. Premenstrual Syndrome - PMS - the onset of the menstrual cycle triggers excessive amounts of the female sex hormones, which affects antisocial, aggressive behavior.

d. Allergies - unusual or excessive reactions of the body to foreign substances

    1. Cerebral allergies - cause an excessive reaction of the brain

    2. Neuroallergies - affect the nervous system

e. Environmental contaminants - dangerous amounts of copper, cadmium, mercury and inorganic gases, such as chlorine and nitrogen dioxide are found in the ecosystem and can influence behavior.

f. Lead Levels - studies have shown that lead ingestion can cause aggressive behavior.

C. Neurophysiological Conditions and Crime - neurophysiology is the study of brain activity

  1. Neurological Impairments and Crime - numerous ways to test neurological functioning

    a. Electroencephalograph (EEG) - the most important measure of neurophysiological functioning

  2. Minimal Brain Dysfunction (MBD)

    a. related to an abnormality in cerebral structure

    .b. Linked to serious antisocial acts

    c. Dyslexia

    d. Visual Perception Problems

    e. Hyperactivity

    f. Poor Attention Span

    g. Temper Tantrums

    h. Aggressiveness

  3. Attention Deficit/Hyperactivity Disorder (ADHD)

    a. Attention Deficit - a child shows a developmentally inappropriate lack of attention, impulsivity and hyperactivity

    b. Conduct Disorder - many ADHD children continually engage I aggressive and antisocial behavior in early childhood and disorders are sustained over the life course

  4. Other Brain Dysfunctions - have been related to violent crime

    a. Tumors, Injury and Disease

      1. Tumors - linked to wide variety of psychological problems, including personality changes, hallucinations, and psychotic episodes

      2. Head injuries - linked to personality reversals marked by outbursts of antisocial and violent behavior

3. Disease - cerebral arteriosclerosis, epilepsy, senile dementia, Korsakoff's syndrome and Huntington's chorea

   b. Brain Chemistry - neurotransmitters are chemical compounds that influence or activate brain functions

     1. Abnormal levels of chemicals lead to aggression

     2. Low supply of enzymes linked to violence and property crime

     3. Violent prone people often treated with Haldol, Stelazine, Prolizin and Risperdal - they help control levels of neurotransmitters and are often referred to as chemical restraints or chemical straightjackets.

  5. Arousal Theory - some people's brains function differently in response to environmental stimuli.

   a. Sensation seekers - those seeking out stimulating activities, which may include aggressive, violent behavior patterns.

D. Genetics and Crime - data, which suggests that human traits associated with criminality, have a genetic basis.

  1. Psychopathy - personality conditions linked to aggression, impulsivity, and neuroticism.

  2. Psychopathology - an example would be schizophrenia.

  3. Parental Deviance - idea that if criminal tendencies are inherited, then criminal parents will produce criminal children

  4. Twin Behavior - if criminal behavior is inherited, it would reason that both twins would be either criminal or not

   a. Studies found that similarities between twins due to genes, not the environment; twins reared apart are so similar, the environment, if anything makes them different.

  5. Evaluating Genetic Research

   a. Contagion effect - the genetic predisposition and early experiences which make some people, including twins, susceptible to deviant behavior which is transmitted by the presence of antisocial siblings in the household.

  6. Adoption Studies - if adopted children behave more like their biological parents, then their adopted parents it would show an a biological basis for crime and vice versa an environmental basis for crime

E. Evolutionary Theory - some believe that human traits that produce violence and aggression are produced through the long process of human evolution.

  1. The Evolution of Gender and Crime - aggressive males tend to mate with more partners thus producing more aggressive individuals.

  2. Violence and Evolution - some believe that violent offenses are often drive by evolutionary and reproductive factors

  3. Evolution and Female Criminality - females are forced into a position of high dependence and limited power and must compete to secure partners who can provide necessary resources.

F. Evaluation of the Biosocial Branch of Trait Theory

1. Behavior is a product of interacting biological and environmental events.
2. Most significant criticism is the lack of adequate empirical testing.

III. **Psychological Trait Theories** - focuses on the psychological aspects of crime including the association between intelligence, personality, learning and criminal behavior.

A. Charles Goring (1870-1919) uncovered a relationship between crime and defective intelligence - involves such traits as feeblemindedness, epilepsy, insanity and defective social instinct.

B. Psychodynamic Perspective - or Psychoanalytic psychology - originated by Viennese psychiatrist Sigmund Freud (1856-1939)

1. Human personality contains a three part structure
   a. Id - the primitive part of people's mental makeup present at birth
      1. Represents unconscious biological drives for sex, food, and other life-sustaining necessities
      2. Follows the pleasure principle: it requires instant gratification without concern for the rights of others.
   b. Ego - develops early in life, when a child learns that their wishes cannot be instantly gratified
      1. Part of the personality that compensates for the demands of the id
      2. Guided by the reality principle: it takes into account what is practical and conventional by societal standards
   c. Superego - develops as a result of incorporating within the personality the moral standards and values of parents, community and significant others.
      1. The moral aspect of people's personality; passes judgment on behavior.
      2. Divided into 2 parts: conscience and ego ideal.
      3. Conscience deals with right and wrong.
      4. Ego ideal is forced to control the id and force people into morally acceptable and responsible behaviors.

C. Psychosexual Stages of Human Development
   1. Eros - most basic human drive present at birth; expressed sexually by seeking pleasure for the body
      a. Oral stage - first year of life, a child attains pleasure by sucking and biting
      b. Anal stage - second and third years of life, the focus of sexual attention is on bodily wastes
      c. Phallic stage - third year when children focus their attention on their genitals.
         1. Oedipus complex - males begin to have sexual feelings for their mother
         2. The Electra complex - girls begin to have sexual feelings for their father
      d. Latency - age six when children repress their feelings of sexuality until the genital stage begins at puberty.
         3. If conflicts are encountered during any of the psychosexual stages, a person can become fixated at that point and trouble could arise later.

D. Psychodynamics of Abnormal Behavior
   1. Neurotics - originally referred to people who experience feelings of mental anguish are afraid that they are losing control of their personalities.
   2. Psychotics - people who had lost total control and who are dominated by their primitive id.
   3. Today these terms are referred to as disorders.
   4. Schizophrenics - exhibit illogical and incoherent thought processes and a lack of insight into their behavior.
   5. Paranoid schizophrenics - suffer complex behavior delusions involving wrongdoing or persecution - they think everyone is out to get them.
   6. Alfred Adler (1870-1937), founder of individual psychology, - inferiority complex - peoples whom has feelings of inferiority and compensates for them with a drive for superiority.
   7. Erik Erikson (1902-1984) - the identity crisis - a period of serious personal questioning people undertake in an effort to determine their own values and sense of direction.
   8. August Aichorn - latent delinquency found in youth whose personality (1) seeks immediate gratification (2) satisfying their personal needs more important than relating to others and (3) satisfy instinctive urges.
E. Psychodyamics of Criminal Behavior
   1. Depicts an aggressive, frustrated person dominated by events that occurred early in childhood.
   2. Bi-polar disorder - moods alternate between periods of wild elation and deep depression
   3. Crime - manifestation of feelings of oppression and an inability to develop proper psychological defenses and rationales to control feelings.
F. Behavior Theories - human actions are developed through learning experiences.
   1. Social Learning Theory - branch of behavior theory.
      a. Social Learning and Violence - violence as learned through a process - behavior modeling after three principal sources:
         1. Family members
         2. Environmental experiences
         3. Mass Media
      b. Four factors may contribute to violent and/or aggressive behavior
         1. An event that heightens arousal
         2. Aggressive skills
         3. Expected outcomes
         4. Consistency of behavior with values
G. Cognitive Theory
   1. Psychologists focus on mental processes and how people perceive and mentally represent the world around them and solve problems.
   2. Moral Development Branch - concerned with the way people morally represent and reason around the world.
   3. Humanistic Psychology - stresses self-awareness and getting in touch with feelings.

4. Information Processing Branch - focuses on the way people process, store, encode, retrieve, and manipulate information to make decisions and solve problems.
5. Moral and Intellectual Development Theory
   a. Founder Jean Piaget (1896-1980)
   b. Hypothesized that people's reasoning processes develop in an orderly fashion, beginning at birth and continuing until they are 12 years old.
   c. Lawrence Kohlberg applied the concept of moral development to issues in criminology.
   d. He found people travel through stages of moral development.
6. Information Processing
   a. When people make decisions, they engage in a sequence of cognitive thought processes:
   b. They encode information
   c. They search for a proper response
   d. Finally, they act on their decision
   e. People who use information properly, who are better conditioned to make reasoned judgments and can make quick and reasoned decisions are better able to avoid antisocial behavior choices.
H. Crime and Mental Illness - research indicates that many offenders who engage in serious, violent crimes suffer from some sort of mental disturbance.
   1. Is the Link Valid - some studies show those with prior mental disorders did not reoffend.
I. Personality and Crime - reasonably stable patterns of behavior, including thoughts and emotions that distinguish one from another.
   1. Hans Eysenck identified 2 antisocial personality traits
      a. Extraversion-introversion
      b. Stability-instability
   2. Anti-Social Personality/Psychopathy/Sociopathy- terms used interchangeably
   3. Research on Personality
      a. Minnesota Multiphasic Personality Inventory (MMPI) - measures different personality traits
      b. California Personality Inventory (CPI) - distinguish deviant from nondeviant groups
      c. Multidimensional Personality Questionnaire (MPQ) - assesses personality traits as control, aggression, alienation and well-being
J. Intelligence and Crime - testing to determine if correlation between IQ and crime
   1. Nature Theory - intelligence is largely determined genetically and low IQ or intelligence is linked to criminal behavior.
   2. Nuture Theory - Nuture School of Intelligence - intelligence viewed as partly biological, but primarily sociological
   3. Rediscovering IQ and Criminality - Hirschi and Hindelang published in 1977 a paper linking the two
   4. Cross-National Studies

     a. Weschsler Adult Intelligence Scale - standard IQ test
    5. IQ and Crime Reconsidered

V. Social Policy Implications - biological and psychological views of criminality have influenced crime control and prevention policy
    1. Biologically Oriented Therapy - programs altered diet, changed lighting, compensated for learning disabilities, treated allergies and more.

VI. Summary

Key Terms

Trait Theories - The view of crime causation that some individuals are unable to control their urges and passions.

Inheritance School - The activities of several generations of families believed to have an especially large number of criminal members.

Somatotype - The view developed by William Sheldon that criminals manifest distinct physiques that make them susceptible to particular types of delinquent behavior.

Biophobia - The belief that no serious consideration should be given to biological factors when attempting to understand human nature.

Equipotentiality - Not all humans are born with equal potential to learn and achieve.

Hypoglycemia - A condition that occurs when glucose (sugar) in the blood falls below levels necessary for normal and efficient brain functioning.

Androgens - Abnormal levels of male sex hormones.

Testosterone - The principal male steroid hormone. Testosterone levels decline during the life cycle and may explain why violence rates diminish over time.

Premenstrual Syndrome (PMS) - The condition which at the onset of the menstrual cycle triggers excessive amounts of the female sex hormones which affect antisocial, aggressive behavior.

Electroencephalograph (EEG) - The most important measure of neurophysiological functioning. An EEG records the electrical impulses given off by the brain.

Neurophysiology - The study of brain activity.

Attention Deficit Disorder - Disorder in which a child shows a developmentally inappropriate lack of attention, impulsivity, and hyperactivity.

Conduct Disorder - Many children continually engage in aggressive and anti-social behavior in early childhood.

Arousal Theory - Some individuals may engage in crime due to the attraction of "getting away with it"; from this perspective, delinquency is a thrilling demonstration of personal competence.

Psychopathy - Personality conditions linked to aggression, impulsivity and neuroticism.

Psychopathy - Personality conditions linked to aggression, impulsivity and neuroticism.

Schizophrenia - A type of psychosis often marked by bizarre behavior, hallucinations, loss of thought control, and inappropriate emotional responses.

Cognitive - The mental processes and how people perceive and mentally represent the world around them and solve problems.

Eros - The most basic human drive present at birth; the instinct to preserve and create life.

Anal Stage - During the second and third years of life, the focus of sexual attention is on the elimination of bodily wastes.

Oral Stage - According to Freud, during the first year of life, a child attains pleasure by sucking and biting.

Phallic Stage - According to Freud, during the third year when children focus their attention on their genitals.

Latency - According to Freud, at age six, children develop feelings of sexuality, which are repressed until the genital stage begins at puberty.

Oedipus Complex - During the phallic stage, males begin to have sexual feelings for their mother.

Electra Complex - During the phallic, girls develop sexual feelings for their fathers.

Fixate - If conflict is encountered during any of the psychosexual stages of development, an adult will exhibit behavior traits characteristic of those encountered during infantile sexual development.

Neurotic - People who experience feelings of mental anguish and are afraid that they are losing control of their personalities.

Paranoid Schizophrenic - Suffer complex behavior delusions involving wrongdoing or persecution - they think that everyone is out to get them.

Inferiority Complex - Alfred Adler (1870-1937) described people who have feelings of inferiority and compensate for them with a drive for superiority.

Identity Crisis - Erik Erikson (1902-1984) identified a period of serious personal questioning people undertake in an effort to determine their own values and sense of direction.

Minnesota Multiphasic Personality Inventory (MMPI) - One of the most widely used psychological tests. The MMPI has subscales designed to measure many different personality traits, including psychopathic deviation, schizophrenia and hypomania.

California Personality Inventory (CPI) - Frequently administered personality test, which has been used to distinguish deviants from nondeviant groups.

Multidimensional Personality Questionnaire (MPQ) - Questionnaire which allows researchers to assess such personality traits as control, aggression, alienation and well-being.

Nature Theory - Argues that intelligence is largely determined genetically, that ancestry determines IQ, and that low intelligence, as demonstrated by low IQ, is linked to criminal behavior.

Nurture Theory - Intelligence must be viewed as partly biological, but primarily sociological.

Wechsler Adult Intelligence Scale - An IQ test.

Discussion Exercise

Can personality traits predispose an individual to commit crimes? Divide the class into groups. One group is to describe a successful individual. Another group is to describe a not so successful individual. A third group is to describe a criminal. Are there distinct traits for the successful individual, the not so successful individual and the criminal individual?

InfoTrac Assignment

GETTING STARTED: Search term words for subject guide: Sociobiology, Genetics, Psychodynamic Perspective, Behavioral Theories, Cognitive Theory, Mental Illness, Personality, Intelligence.

CRITICAL THINKING PROJECT: Using the search term "Psychodynamic Perspective," find articles that discuss this psychological trait theory. Examine this theory and compare it to other theories of crime.

Here are three articles:

Jarrett, Michael and Kamil Kellner "Coping With Uncertainty: A Psychodynamic Perspective on the Work of Top Teams." *Journal of Management Development.*

Muskin, Philip R. "The Request to Die: Role for a Psychodynamic Perspective on Physician-Assisted Suicide." *The Journal of the American Medical Association.*

Allan, Philip "The Psychodynamic Perspective." *Psychology Review.*

Test Bank

Essay Questions

1. Describe sociobiology and its impact on criminal justice, social policy and society.

2. Compare and contrast Biochemical/Neurophysiological conditions and their relationship to crime in our society.
3. What is the Psychodynamic Perspective of the Psychological Trait Theories? Who wrote this theory and what is its implication for us?
4. Describe Cognitive Theory. Compare Cognitive Theory to the Behavioral Theories. Is there a relationship?
5. What have researchers found in regards to the effect of mental illness and crime? Which area of the Psychological Trait Theories seems more likely to be the cause of crime?

Fill In The Blank

1. During the second and third years of life, the focus of sexual attention is on the elimination of bodily wastes and is known as the **Anal Stage.**

2. The view of crime causation that some individuals are unable to control their urges and passions is known as **Trait Theories**.

3. Individuals who suffer complex behavior delusions involving wrongdoing or persecution are known as **Paranoid Schizophrenic**.

4. The view developed by William Sheldon that criminals manifest distinct physiques that make them susceptible to particular types of delinquent behavior is known as **Somatotype**.

5. Personality conditions linked to aggression, impulsivity and neuroticism are called **Psychopathy**.

6. During the phallic stage, a male begin to have sexual feelings for their mother and is known as the **Oedipus Complex**.

7. **Equipotentiality** is the ideal that not all humans are born with equal potential to learn and achieve.

8. **Hypoglycemia** is a condition that occurs when glucose (sugar) in the blood falls below levels necessary for normal and efficient brain functioning.

9. **Eros** is the most basic human drive present at birth; the instinct to preserve and create life.

10. **Conduct Disorder** is when many children continually engage in aggressive and anti-social behavior in early childhood.

11. The study of brain activity is **Neurophysiology**.

12. The principal male steroid hormone is **Testosterone**.

13. **Cognitive** is the mental processes and how people perceive and mentally represent the world around them and solve problems.

14. According to Freud, at age six, children develop feelings of sexuality, which are repressed until the genital stage begins at puberty and is known as **Latency.**

15. **Schizophrenia** is a type of psychosis often marked by bizarre behavior, hallucinations, loss of thought control, and inappropriate emotional responses.

Multiple Choice

1. The most basic human drive present at birth is:
   a. Eros
   b. Biophobia
   c. Electra complex
   d. Testosterone
   (Answer = a)

2. During the second and third years of life, the focus of sexual attention is on the elimination of bodily wastes and is known as:
   a. Oral stage
   b. Premenstrual syndrome
   c. Eros
   d. Anal stage
   (Answer = d)

3. The mental processes and how people perceive and mentally represent the world around them and solve problems is known as:
   a. Conduct disorder
   b. Cognitive
   c. Biophobia
   d. Arousal theory
   (Answer = b)

4. The view of crime causation that some individuals are unable to control their urges and passions is known as:
   a. Arousal theory
   b. Electra Complex
   c. Nature theory
   d. Trait theory
   (Answer = d)

5. One of the most widely used psychological test which is designed to measure many different personality traits, including psychopathic deviation, schizophrenia and hypomania is known as:
   a. Minnesota Mutiphasic Personality Inventory
   b. Multidimensional Personality Questionnaire
   c. California Personality Inventory
   d. Wechsler Adult Intelligence Scale
   (Answer = a)

6. According to Freud, during the first year of life, a child attains pleasure by sucking and biting, which is known as:
   a. Anal stage
   b. Electra Complex
   c. Latency
   d. Oral stage
   (Answer = d)

7. Not all humans are born with equal potential to learn and achieve and this is known as:
   a. Eros
   b. Equipotentiality
   c. Electra Complex
   d. Androgens
   (Answer = b)

8.Abnormal levels of male sex hormones are:
   a. Androgens
   b. Eros
   c. Testosterone
   d. Hypoglycemia
   (Answer = a)

9. Many children continually engage in aggressive and anti-social behavior in early childhood and this is called:
   a. Arousal theory
   b. Attention deficit disorder
   c. Conduct disorder
   d. Neurophysiology
   (Answer = c)

10. A common IQ test is:
    a. California Personality Inventory
    b. Wechsler Adult Intelligence Scale
    c. Minnesota Multiphasic Personality Inventory
    d. Multidimensional Personality Questionnaire
    (Answer = b)

11. During the phallic stage, males begin to have sexual feelings for their mother and this is called:
    a. Electra Complex
    b. Oral stage
    c. Anal stage
    d. Oedipus Complex
    (Answer = d)

12. Personality conditions linked to aggression, impulsivity and neuroticism are known as:
    a. Psychopathy
    b. Equipotentiality
    c. Biophobia
    d. Neurotic
    (Answer = a)

13. The notion that some individuals may engage in crime due to the attraction of "getting away with it":
    a. Biophobia
    b. Arousal theory
    c. Nature theory
    d. Nurture theory
    (Answer = b)

14. The most important measure of neurophysiological functions is an:
    a. Identity crisis
    b. Inferiority complex
    c. Eros
    d. Electroencephalograph
    (Answer = d)

15. The principal male steroid hormone is:
    a. Hypoglycemia
    b. Somatotype
    c. Neurophysiology
    d. Testosterone
    (Answer = d)

16. If conflict is encountered during any of the psychosexual stages of development, an adult will exhibit behavior traits characteristic of those encountered during infantile sexual development and this is known as:
   a. Anal stage
   b. Oral stage
   c. Electra complex
   d. Discouragers
   (Answer = d)

17. A condition that occurs when glucose in the blood falls below levels necessary for normal and efficient brain functioning is known as:
   a. Conduct disorder
   b. Hypoglycemia
   c. Phallic stage
   d. Testosterone
   (Answer = b)

18. A frequently administered personality test, which has been used to distinguish deviants from nondeviant groups is the:
   a. Minnesota Multiphasic Personality Inventory
   b. Multidimensional Personality Questionnaire
   c. California Personality Inventory
   d. Weschler Adult Intelligence Scale
   (Answer = c)

19. Disorder in which a child shows a developmentally inappropriate lack of attention, impulsivity and hyperactivity is:
   a. Attention deficit disorder
   b. Oedipus Complex
   c. Hypoglycemia
   d. Psychopathy
   (Answer = a)

20. The belief that no serious consideration should be given to biological factors when attempting to understand human nature is known as:
   a. Choice theory
   b. Biophobia
   c. Nature theory
   d. Nurture theory
   (Answer = b)

21. Programs which alter diet, change lighting, compensate for learning disabilities and treat allergies are known as:
    a. Biophobia
    b. Equipotentiality
    c. Biologically oriented therapy
    d. Neurophysiology
    (Answer = c)

22. When individuals experience a serious personal questions they are having an:
    a. Eros
    b. Inferiority complex
    c. Oedipus complex
    d. Identity crisis
    (Answer = d)

23. View developed by William Sheldon that criminals manifest distinct physiques that make them susceptible to particular types of delinquent behavior is known as:
    a. Psychopathy
    b. Somatotype
    c. Nurture theory
    d. Nature theory
    (Answer = b)

24. The study of the activities of several generations of families believed to have an especially large number of criminal members is the:
    a. Nature theory
    b. Nurture theory
    c. Inheritance school
    d. Classical school
    (Answer = c)

25. A type of psychosis often marked by bizarre behavior, hallucinations, loss of thought control, and inappropriate emotional responses is known as:
    a. Psychopathy
    b. Testosterone
    c. Hypoglycemia
    d. Schizophrenia
    (Answer = d)

26. The concept used to describe people who have feelings of inferiority and compensate for them with a drive for superiority is:
    a. Identity crisis
    b. Phallic stage
    c. Psychopathy
    d. Inferiority complex
    (Answer = d)

27. According to Freud, at age six, children develop feelings of sexuality, which are repressed until the genital stage begins at puberty and this is known as:
    a. Phallic stage
    b. Oral stage
    c. Latency
    d. Anal stage
    (Answer = c)

28. The condition which at the onset of the menstrual cycle triggers excessive amounts of the female sex hormones which affect antisocial, aggressive behavior is known as:
    a. Premenstrual syndrome
    b. Oedipus complex
    c. Neurophysiology
    d. Latency
    (Answer = a)

29. The questionnaire which allows researchers to assess such personality traits as control, aggression, alienation and well-being is known as:
    a. Minnesota Multiphasic Personality Inventory
    b. California Personality Inventory
    c. Wechsler Adult Intelligence Scale
    d. Multidimensional Personality Questionnaire
    (Answer = d)

30. According to Freud, during the third year when children focus their attention on their genitals is known as:
    a. Latency
    b. Oral stage
    c. Anal stage
    d. Phallic stage
    (Answer = d)

31. Individuals who suffer complex behavior delusions involving wrongdoing or persecution are:
    a. Psychopathy
    b. Neurophysiology
    c. Paranoid schizophrenic
    d. Hypoglycemia
    (Answer = c)

32. Intelligence must be viewed as partly biological, but primarily sociological is:
    a. Nature theory
    b. Inheritance school
    c. Nuture theory
    d. Classical school
    (Answer = c)

33. Theory which argues that intelligence is largely determined genetically is:
    a. Nurture theory
    b. Inheritance school
    c. Classical school
    d. Nature theory
    (Answer = d)

34. Individuals that have well-developed muscles and an athletic appearance are:
    a. Mesomorphs
    b. Endomorphs
    c. Ectomorphs
    d. Somatotypes
    (Answer = a)

35. Individuals that have heavy builds and are slow-moving are:
    a. Mesomorphs
    b. Ectomorphs
    c. Somatotypes
    d. Endomorphs
    (Answer = d)

36. Individuals that are tall, thin, less social and more intellectual are:
    a. Mesomorphs
    b. Somatotypes
    c. Ectomorphs
    d. Endomorphs
    (Answer = c)

37. The belief that when we come to the aid of others that our actions will be reciprocated and that our gene survival capability will be enhanced is known as:
    a. Biochemical
    b. Arousal theory
    c. Reciprocal altruism
    d. All of the above
    (Answer = c)

38. The Biosocial perspectives on Criminality are:
    a. Biochemical
    b. Neurophysiological
    c. Genetic
    d. All of the above
    (Answer = d)

39. The part of the brain that controls sympathetic feelings towards others is called:
    a. Hormones
    b. Androgens
    c. Testosterone
    d. Neocortex
    (Answer = d)

40. The study of brain activity is:
    a. Nature theory
    b. Neurophysiology
    c. Nuture theory
    d. Somatotype
    (Answer = b)

True/False

T   1. Trait theories can be divided into two major sub-divisions: one that stresses psychological functioning and the other that stresses biological make-up.

F   2. Cesare Lombroso's work on the dead criminal was a direct offshoot of applying the scientific method to the study of crime.

F   3. Memsomorphs have heavy builds and are slow-moving.

T   4. Biophobia is the belief that no serious consideration should be given to biological factors when attempting to understand human nature.

T   5. Biosocial criminologists maintain that minimum level of minerals and chemicals are needed for normal brain functioning and growth, especially in the early years of life.

F   6. Neuroallergies cause an excessive reaction of the brain.

F   7. The study of brain activity is nitrophysiology.

T   8. Traditionally, the most important measure of neurophysiological functioning is the electroencephalograph.

T   9. Minimal Brain Dysfunction is related to an abnormality in the cerebral structure.

F   10. The biosocial view is that behavior is a product of interacting social and environmental events.

T   11. Individuals who have feelings of inferiority and compensate for them with a drive for superiority have an inferiority complex.

T   12. Latent delinquency is found in youngsters whose personality requires them to seek immediate gratification, consider satisfying their personal needs more important than relating to others and satisfy instinctive urges without considering right and wrong.

F   13. Strong egos are associated with immaturity, poor social skills, and excessive dependence on others.

T   14. Behavior theory maintains that human actions are developed through learning experiences.

T   15. Social learning is the branch of behavior theory most relevant to criminology.

Chapter Seven

Social Structure Theories

Summary

Chapter Seven explains in detail the social structure theories. The chapter begins with an analysis of the socio-economic structure and crime and then examines the various components of each of the theories. Particular emphasis is devoted to the strain theories and the cultural deviance theories. The chapter concludes with an evaluation of the social structure theories and their implication on social policy.

Learning Objectives
After reading this chapter the student should be able to:
- Understand the relationship of the socioeconomic structure and crime.
- Explore the relevance of being lower class and the probability of criminal behavior.
- Define the Social Structure Theories.
- Describe the various branches of Social Structure Theory.
- Distinguish between the various Strain Theories.
- Discuss Social Disorganization Theory.
- Evaluate Cultural Deviance Theory.
- Describe the impact of Social Structure Theory on social policy.

Chapter Overview
Introduction
Socio-economic Structure and Crime
      Lower-Class Culture
Social Structure Theories
      Branches of Social Structure Theory
Social Disorganization Theory
      The Work of Shaw and McKay
      The Social Ecology School

Strain Theories
    Anomie
    Theory of Anomie
    Institutional Anomie Theory
    Relative Deprivation Theory
    General Strain Theory (GST)
Cultural Deviance Theory
    Conduct Norms
    Focal Concerns
    Theory of Delinquent Subcultures
    Theory of Differential Opportunity
Evaluation of Social Structure Theories
    Is the Structural Approach Valid?
Social Structure Theory and Social Policy
Summary

Chapter Outline

I. Introduction

II. Socioeconomic Structure and Crime
- A. People in U.S. live in a stratified society
  1. Social strata - created by unequal distribution of wealth, power and prestige
  2. Social classes - segments of population that have similar portions of things and share attitudes, values, norms and lifestyles
- B. Problems of the Lower Class
  1. Inadequate housing and healthcare
  2. Disrupted family lives
  3. Underemployment
  4. Despair
  5. More prone to depression
  6. Less likely to have achievement motivation
  7. Less likely to put off immediate gratification
  8. Less willing to stay in school
- C. Child Poverty
  1. 25% of children under six live in poverty
  2. 6% of white children are extremely poor
  3. 50% of black children live in extreme poverty
  4. More likely to suffer physical illness
  5. Greater risk of dropping out of school
- D. The Underclass - a culture of poverty passed from one generation to the next
  1. Cut off from society, members lacking education and skills to be effective

III. Social Structure Theories - view that the disadvantaged economic class position is a primary cause of crime

A. Branches of Social Structure Theory
   1. Social Disorganization Theory - focuses on the urban environmental conditions that affect crime
      a. High unemployment
      b. School dropout rates
      c. Deteriorated housing
      d. Low income levels
      e. Large numbers of single-parent households
   2. Strain Theory - crime is a function of the conflict between goals people have and their means to legally obtain them.
      a. Social and economic goals are common
      b. Ability to obtain these goals is class-dependent
      c. Consequently, lower class feels anger, frustration and resentment: strain
   3. Cultural Deviance Theory - combines strain and social disorganization
      a. Subculture - unique lower-class culture develops in disorganized neighbors.
      b. Unique set of values and beliefs
      c. Criminal behavior is an expression of conformity to unique values
      d. Cultural transmission - process where subcultural values handed down from one generation to the next

IV. **Social Disorganization Theory** - links crime rates to neighborhood ecological characteristics.
   A. The Work of Shaw and McKay - Chicago sociologists who linked life in transitional slum areas to the inclination to commit crime.
      1. Transitional Neighborhoods - poverty ridden, suffered high rates of population turnover and were incapable of inducing people to stay and defend the neighborhood against criminals.
      2. Concentric Zones - the interzone areas exhibited higher rates of crime (central city and a transitional area).
      3. The Legacy of Shaw and McKay
         a. Crime rates correspond to neighborhood structure.
         b. Crime is a constant fixture of poverty areas.
   B. The Social Ecology School - emphasizes the association of community deterioration and economic decline to criminality and less emphasis on value conflict.
      1. Community Deterioration - deserted houses, abandoned buildings are magnets for crime; poor, needing repair houses have the highest rates of violence.
      2. Poverty Concentration - in the same area
         a. Concentration effect - when working and middle-class families flee inner-city poverty areas it results in the most disadvantaged population being consolidated in urban ghettos.
      3. Employment Opportunities - lack of opportunity perpetuates higher crime rates.
      4. Community Fear
         a. Race and Fear

b. Gangs and Fear

c. Mistrust and Fear

    1. Siege Mentality - residents become suspicious of authority that the outside world is considered the enemy out to destroy the neighborhood.

5. Community Change - as areas decline, residents flee to more stable locales.

    a. The Cycles of Community Change - infra-structure may change

6. Collective Efficacy - cohesive communities with high levels of social control develop mutual trust and shared responsibilities

    a. Informal Social Control - direct criticism, ridicule, ostracism, desertion or physical punishment

    b. Institutional Social Control - businesses, stores, schools, churches and social service and volunteer organizations

    c. Public Social Control - policing

    d. The Effects of Collective Efficacy - if sufficient, children less likely to engage in problem behaviors.

7. Social Support/Altruism

    a. Neighborhoods providing strong social supports help young people cope with life's stressors.

    b. Social Altruism - indications of generosity such as the ratio of contributions given to a charity by area income levels has been linked to crime rates.

    c. Crime rates are lower in altruistic areas.

V. Strain Theories

A. The Definition of Anomie - Emile Durkheim - an anomic society is one where rules, or norms, have broken down or become inoperative due to rapid social change.

B. Theory of Anomie - Applied by Robert Merton - found two culture elements interact to produce anomic conditions: culturally defined goals and socially approved means of obtaining them.

1. Social Adaptations - each has own concept of the goals of society and how to attain them.

    a. Conformity - individuals embrace conventional social goals and have the means to attain them.

    b. Innovation - individual accepts social goals, but rejects or is incapable of attaining them through legitimate means.

    c. Ritualism - those that receive pleasure from practicing traditional ceremonies regardless of whether they have a goal.

    d. Retreatism - reject both the goals and means of society.

    e. Rebellion - substituting an alternative set of goals and means for conventional ones.

2. Evaluation of Anomie Theory - number of questions unanswered by Merton

    a. No explanation as to why people choose to commit certain crimes

    b. Anomie assumes all share same goals; which everyone does not.

3. Anomie Reconsidered - many Americans may feel anomic due to economic displacement in a shifting economy.

C. Institutional Anomie Theory - anomie theory view antisocial behavior as a function of cultural and institutional influences in American society.
   1. Impact of Anomie - social institutions have been rendered powerless
      a. Non-economic functions and roles have been devalued.
      b. When conflict emerges, non-economic roles become subordinate to economic roles
      c. Economics penetrates into non-economic realms.
      d. According to Messner and Rosenfield, high crime rates are due to the relationship between culture and institutions.
   2. Supporting Research
      a. Chamlin and Cochran found high church membership, lower divorce rates, high voter turnout and lower crime rate.
D. Relative Deprivation Theory
   1. Lower-class people may feel deprived as they compare their life to the affluent
   2. Frustration increases and the likelihood increases that the poor will choose illegitimate life enhancing activities
   3. Affluent may feel deprived if they fail to achieve lofty and unlimited goals.
E. General Strain Theory - (GST) - Sociologist Robert Agnew explains individuals who feel stress and strain are more likely to commit crime.
   1. Multiple Sources of Stress - Criminality is the result of:
      a. Negative affective states - - anger, frustration and adverse emotions
      b. Strain caused by failure to achieve positively valued goals.
      c. Strain caused by disjunction of expectations and achievements.
      d. Stain as the removal of positively valued stimuli from the individual.
      e. Strain as the presentation of negative stimuli.
   2. Sources of Strain
      a. Many different sources
      b. Target - something to blame problems on
   3. Social Sources
      a. May feel strain due to groups one associates with.
   4. Community Sources of Strain
      a. They influence the goals people pursue and the ability to achieve.
      b. They influence feelings of relative deprivation and exposure to adverse stimuli.
      c. They influence the likelihood of angry, strain-filled individuals will interact with one another.
   5. Coping With Strain
      a. Not all that experience strain will commit crime.
      b. Crime may provide relief and satisfaction for one living in stressful life.
   6. Strain and Career Criminals
   7. Evaluating General Strain Theory
      a. Adds to literature describing how social and life history influence offending patterns.
      b. Empirical support for GST.

8. Gender Issues
    a. Evidence indicates that females under strain commit less crime than like men.
    b. Criminal behavior more prevalent with men than women.

VI.   **Cultural Deviance Theory** - Combines social disorganization and strain to explain how people living in deteriorated neighborhoods react to social isolation and economic deprivation.

    A.   Conduct Norms - rules governing daily living conditions within subcultures.

        1. Culture conflict - occurs when rules expressed in the criminal law clash with the demands of group conduct norms.

    B.   Focal Concern - Unique value system that dominates lower-class culture.

        1. Miller's Lower Class Focal Concerns
           a. Trouble
           b. Toughness
           c. Smartness
           d. Excitement
           e. Fate
           f. Autonomy

    C.   Theory of Delinquent Subcultures - Albert Cohen

        1.   Status frustration - lower-class youth experience culture conflict because social conditions make them incapable of achieving success legitimately.

        2.   The development of the delinquent subculture is a consequence of socialization practices found in the ghetto or slum environment.

        3.   Middle-Class Measuring Rods - standards set by authority figures

        4.   The Formation of Deviant Subcultures - lower-class boys suffer rejection by middle-class decision makers leading boys to join one of these subcultures:

           a. Corner Boy - not a chronic offender, but a truant engaging in petty or status offenses.

           b. College Boy - embraces the cultural and social values of the middle class and actively strives to be successful by those standards.

           c. Delinquent Boy - adopts norms and principles in direct opposition to middle-class values.

               1. Reaction formation - frustrated by their inability to succeed, individuals develop overly intense responses that seem disproportionate to the stimuli that trigger them.

    D.   Theory of Differential Opportunity - Richard Cloward and Lloyd Ohlin wrote *Delinquency and Opportunity* - combining strain and social disorganization principles into a portrayal of a gang-sustaining criminal subculture.

1.   Differential Opportunities - people in all strata of society share the same success goals; however, those in the lower class have limited means of achieving them.
2.   Because of differential opportunity, kids are likely to join a gang:
      a.   Criminal Gangs - in slum areas where close connections between adolescent and adult offenders create an environment for successful criminal enterprise.
      b.   Conflict Gangs - develop in communities unable to provide either legitimate or illegitimate opportunities. Crime in this area is individualistic, unorganized, petty, poorly paid, and unprotected.
      c.   Retreatist Gangs - double failures, unable to gain success through legitimate means and unwilling to do so through illegal ones.
3.   Analysis of Differential Opportunity - important because it integrates cultural deviance and social disorganization variables and it recognizes different modes of criminal adaptation.

VII.   **Evaluation of Social Structure Theories** - influenced criminological theory and crime prevention strategies.
       A.   Is the Structural Approach Valid? Questionable.

VIII. **Social Structure Theory and Social Policy**
       A.   Social structure theory has a significant influence on social policy.
             1. Provide welfare and AFDC.
             2. Chicago Area Project - Crime prevention effort
             3. Kennedy and Johnson's Administrations - War on Poverty

IX.   **Summary**

<u>**Key Terms**</u>

Culture of Poverty - Marked by apathy, cynicism, helplessness, and mistrust of social institutions, such as schools, government agencies, and the police.

At-risk - Children and adults who are more likely to be a part of the culture of poverty.

Cultural Deviance Theory - The third variation of structural theory, combines elements of both strain and social disorganization. According to this view, because of strain and

Siege Mentality - View that the outside world is considered the enemy out to destroy the neighborhood. This view leads to a mistrust of critical social institutions, including business, government and schools.

Anomie - According to Durkheim, an anomic society is one in which rules of behavior - norms- have broken down or become inoperative during periods of rapid social change or social crisis such as war or famine.

Relative Deprivation - The condition that exists when people of wealth and poverty live in close proximity to one another. Some criminologists attribute crime rate differentials to relative deprivation.

General Strain Theory - According to Robert Agnew, individuals who feel stress and stain are more likely to commit crimes.

Negative Affective States - The anger, frustration, and adverse emotions that emerge in the wake of negative and destructive social relationships. These states are produced by a variety of sources of strain.

Culture Conflict - Occurs when the rules expressed in the criminal law clash with the demands of group conduct norms.

Conduct Norms - Rules governing the day-to-day living conditions with a culture, group or political structure.

social isolation, a unique lower-class culture develops in disorganized neighborhoods.

Focal Concerns - Unique value system that dominates life among the lower class.

Middle-Class Measuring Rods - Standards set by authority figures such as teachers, employers or supervisors.

Discussion Exercise

Examine the Los Angeles Riot of April 29, 1992. What components of strain theory are evident in this devastating event? Would other theories such as differential opportunity be relevant to this riot?

InfoTrac Assignment

GETTING STARTED: Search term words for subject guide: Social Structure Theory, Social Disorganization Theory, Social Ecology School, Anomie Theory, Relative Deprivation Theory, Strain Theory, Social Norms.

CRITICAL THINKING PROJECT: Using the search term "Anomie Theory," find articles that discuss this important Social Structure Theory. Examine this theory and compare it to other theories of crime.

Here are three articles:

Arts, Wil, Piet Hermkens and Peter Van Wijck "Anomie, Distributive Injustice and Dissatisfaction with Material Well-Being in Eastern Europe: A Comparative Study." *International Journal of Comparative Sociology.*

Einstadter, Werner "The Legacy of Anomie Theory: Advances in Criminological Theory, vol. 6." *Social Forces.*

Messner, Steven F. and Richard Rosenfeld "Political Restraint of the Market and Levels of Criminal Homicide: A Cross-National Application of Institutional-Anomie Theory." *Social Forces.*

Test Bank

Essay Questions

1. Describe the Socio-economic structure and its relationship to crime. If one is a member of the lower class, does it predispose them to a life of crime?
2. Define the Social Structure theories. What are the various branches of Social Structure theory? What is their impact on criminal justice, social policy and society?
3. What is the Social Ecology School? Describe the work of Shaw and McKay. What influence has their study had on social policy?
4. Describe Strain Theory. Which theorists developed the most important variations of Strain Theory? Give current 20th and 21st century examples of Strain Theory in our society.
5. Compare and contrast Relative Deprivation Theory and General Strain Theory. What are the differences? What are the similarities? Are these theories important to social policy making?

Fill In The Blank

1. The view that the outside world is considered the enemy out to destroy the neighborhood is **Siege Mentality.**

2. According to Durkheim, an **anomic** society is one in which rules of behavior have broken down or become inoperative during periods of rapid social change or social crisis such as war or famine.

3. **Relative Deprivation** is the condition that exists when people of wealth poverty live in close proximity to one another.

4. Children and adults who are more likely to be a part of the culture of poverty are considered **At-risk**.

5. The anger, frustration, and adverse emotions that emerge in the wake of negative and destructive social relationships are known as **Negative Affective States**.

6. Standards set by authority figures such as teachers, employers or supervisors are called **Middle-Class Measuring Rods**.

7. **Conduct Norms** are the rules governing day-to-day living conditions with a culture, group or political structure.

8. The third variation of structural theory, **Cultural Deviance Theory** combines elements of both strain and social disorganization.

9. According to Robert Agnew, **General Strain Theory** says that individuals who feel stress and stain are more likely to commit crimes.

10. **Focal Concerns** are the unique value system that dominates life among the lower class.

11. **Culture Conflict** occurs when the rules expressed in the criminal law clash with the demands of group conduct norms.

12. Apathy, cynicism, helplessness, and mistrust of social institutions, such as schools, government agencies, and the police mark the **Culture of Poverty**.

13. **Social Classes** are segments of the population whose members have a relatively similar portion of desirable things and who share attitudes, values, norms, and an identifiable lifestyle.

14. **Social Strata** are created by the unequal distribution of wealth, power, and prestige.

15. Gunnar Myrdal described a worldwide **Underclass** that was cut off from society, its members lacking the education and skills needed to be effectively in demand in modern society.

Multiple Choice

1. According to Durkheim, a society in which rules of behavior have broken down or become inoperative during periods of rapid social change or social crisis such as war or famine is:
   a. Anomie
   b. At-risk
   c. Pathologic
   d. All of the above
   (Answer = a)

2. The view that the outside world is considered the enemy out to destroy the neighborhood is known as:
   a. Anomie
   b. Culture conflict
   c. Middle-class measuring rods
   d. Siege mentality
   (Answer = d)

3. Children and adults who are more likely to be a part of the culture of poverty are:
   a. Focal concerns
   b. At-risk
   c. Middle-class measuring rods
   d. Negative affective states
   (Answer = b)

4. The condition that exists when people of wealth and poverty live in close proximity to one another is:
   a. General strain theory
   b. Anomie
   c. Siege mentality
   d. Relative deprivation
   (Answer = d)

5. The anger, frustration, and adverse emotions that emerge in the wake of negative and destructive social relationships is:
   a. Negative affective states
   b. Positive affective states
   c. Anomie
   d. Siege mentality
   (Answer = a)

6. The rules, which govern day-to-day living conditions with a culture, group or political structure, are known as:
   a. Policy
   b. Social policy
   c. Middle-class measuring rods
   d. Conduct norms
   (Answer = d)

7. The third variation of structural theory, combines elements of both strain and social disorganization is known as:
   a. Anomie
   b. Cultural deviance theory
   c. Culture of poverty
   d. Social structure theory
   (Answer = b)

8. This occurs when the rules expressed in the criminal law clash with the demands of group conduct norms:
   a. Culture conflict
   b. Culture of poverty
   c. Cultural deviance theory
   d. Relative deprivation
   (Answer = a)

9. The anger, frustration and adverse emotions that emerge in the wake of negative and destructive social relationships is called:
   a. Conduct disorder
   b. Relative deprivation
   c. Negative affective states
   d. Culture conflict
   (Answer = c)

10. Standards set by authority figures such as teachers, employers, or supervisors are:
    a. Anomie
    b. Middle-class measuring rods
    c. Conduct norms
    d. Focal concerns
    (Answer = b)

11. The view according to Robert Agnew, that individuals who feel stress and strain are more likely to commit crimes is called:
   a. Electra Complex
   b. Negative affective states
   c. Relative deprivation
   d. General strain theory
   (Answer = d)

12. The unique value system that dominates life among the lower classes is known as:
   a. focal concerns
   b. middle-class measuring rods
   c. culture of poverty
   d. culture conflict
   (Answer = a)

13. The view that apathy, cynicism, helplessness, and mistrust of social institutions, such as schools, government agencies and the police is termed:
   a. Culture conflict
   b. Culture of poverty
   c. Focal concerns
   d. Negative affective states
   (Answer = b)

14. People in the United States live in what type of society?
   a. Unified
   b. Verified
   c. Unstratified
   d. Stratified
   (Answer = d)

15. The unequal distribution of wealth, power and prestige create:
   a. Social harmony
   b. Social peace
   c. Social joy
   d. Social strata
   (Answer = d)

16. Segments of the population whose members have a relatively similar portion of desirable things and who share attitudes, values, norms and an identifiable lifestyle are known as:
   a. Social strata
   b. Social harmony
   c. Social joy
   d. Social classes
   (Answer = d)

17. What percent of children now live in poverty?
    a. 5%
    b. 25%
    c. 50%
    d. 75%
    (Answer = b)

18. What percentages of white children live in poverty?
    a. 25%
    b. 50%
    c. 6%
    d. 75%
    (Answer = c)

19. What percentages of black children live in poverty?
    a. 50%
    b. 25%
    c. 6%
    d. 75%
    (Answer = a)

20. Members of the underclass who are socially isolated, live in urban inner cities and occupy the bottom rung of the social ladder are known as:
    a. Business people
    b. Truly disadvantaged
    c. Truly advantaged
    d. Successful
    (Answer = b)

21. The branches within the social structure perspective are:
    a. Social disorganization
    b. Strain theory
    c. Cultural deviance theory
    d. All of the above
    (Answer = d)

22. The theory which holds that crime is a function of the conflict between the goals people have and the means they can use to legally obtain them is:
    a. Cultural conflict
    b. Cultural deviance theory
    c. Social disorganization
    d. Strain theory
    (Answer = d)

23. Social disorganization theory focuses on which of the following conditions in the environment?
    a. Unequal distribution of wealth
    b. Deteriorated neighborhoods
    c. Frustration
    d. All of the above
    (Answer = b)

24. Strain theory focuses on which of the following conflict between goals and means?
    a. Inadequate social control
    b. Deteriorated neighborhoods
    c. Frustration
    d. All of the above
    (Answer = c)

25. Cultural deviance theory focuses on which of the following factors?
    a. Development of subcultures as a result of disorganization and stress
    b. Subcultural values in opposition to conventional values
    c. All of the above
    d. None of the above
    (Answer = d)

26. Social disorganization theory was popularized by:
    a. Martin and Gordon
    b. Winfree and Mays
    c. Sutherland and Durkeim
    d. McKay and Shaw
    (Answer = d)

27. Poverty-ridden neighborhoods which suffer high rates of population turnover and are incapable of inducing residents to remain are known as:
    a. Suburbs
    b. Gated communities
    c. Transitional neighborhoods
    d. College campuses
    (Answer = c)

28. A renewal stage in which obsolete housing is replace and upgraded is known as:
    a. Gentrification
    b. Turnover
    c. Transitional neighborhoods
    d. None of the above
    (Answer = a)

29. Informal control mechanisms include which of the following:
    a. Direct criticism
    b. Ridicule
    c. Ostracism
    d. All of the above
    (Answer = d)

30. Institutional social control includes which of the following:
    a. Schools
    b. Gangs
    c. MTV
    d. Nightclubs
    (Answer = a)

31. Public social control includes which of the following:
    a. Schools
    b. Churches
    c. Police
    d. Gangs
    (Answer = c)

32. A characteristic of pre-industrial society, held together by traditions, shared values and unquestioned beliefs is known as:
    a. Organic solidarity
    b. Solidarity
    c. Mechanic solidarity
    d. None of the above
    (Answer = c)

33. The basic components of Strain Theory include which of the following?
    a. Poverty
    b. Crime and delinquency
    c. Criminal careers
    d. All of the above
    (Answer = d)

34. Development of isolated slum culture, lack of conventional social opportunities and racial and ethnic discrimination are elements of:
    a. Poverty
    b. Strain
    c. Crime and delinquency
    d. Criminal careers
    (Answer = a)

35. Which of the following are means to attaining goals according to Merton?
   a. Conformity
   b. Innovation
   c. Ritualism
   d. All of the above
   (Answer = d)

36. When individuals embrace conventional social goals and have to means at their disposal to attain them is known as:
   a. Innovation
   b. Ritualism
   c. Conformity
   d. Rebellion
   (Answer = c)

37. When an individual accepts the goals of society, but rejects or is incapable of attaining them through legitimate means, it is called:
   a. Conformity
   b. Ritualism
   c. Innovation
   d. Rebellion
   (Answer = c)

38. Those who gain pleasure from practicing traditional ceremonies regardless of whether they have a real purpose or a goal are:
   a. Conformists
   b. Ritualist
   c. Retreatist
   d. Rebels
   (Answer = b)

39. Those who reject both the goals and the means of society are:
   a. Conformists
   b. Ritualists
   c. Rebels
   d. Retreatists
   (Answer = d)

40. Substituting an alternative set of goals and means for conventional ones is:
   a. Ritualism
   b. Rebellion
   c. Retreatism
   d. Realism
   (Answer = b)

True/False

T   1. People in the United States live in a stratified society.

F   2. Social strata are segments of the population whose members have a relatively similar portion of desirable things and who share attitudes, values, norms, and an identifiable lifestyle.

F   3. In the year 2000, the poverty rate rose to 22.3 percent, the highest since 1979.

T   4. Lower-class areas are scenes of inadequate housing and health care, disrupted family lives, underemployment and despair.

T   5. Children who grow up in low-income homes are less likely to achieve in school and are less likely to complete their schooling than children with more affluent parents.

F   6. Strain theory holds that the conditions within the urban environment affect crime rates.

F   7. Cultural deviance theory links crime rates to neighborhood ecological characteristics.

T   8. Subcultural values are handed down from one generation to the next in a process called cultural transmission.

T   9. Crime rates have been associated with community deterioration: disorder, poverty, alienation, disassociation, and fear of crime.

F   10. Areas in which houses are in poor repair, boarded-up and burned out and whose owners are best described as "slumlords" are also the location of the lowest violence rates.

T   11. Sources of institutional social control include businesses, stores, schools, churches and social service and volunteer organizations.

T   12. When social control is weak, there may be an over-reliance on formal punishment, such as arrest and prosecution, to control offenders, a situation, which helps destabilize neighborhoods by putting many of its residents behind bars.

F   13. When incarcerated adults are typically under-employed, they do not engage in any legitimate work.

T   14. Prisoners have significantly more medical and mental health problems than the general population, due to lifestyles that often include crowded or itinerant living conditions.

T   15. As the prison population has grown, the negative impact of incarceration may be lessened.

Chapter Eight

Social Process Theories
Learning, Control and Reaction

Summary

Chapter Eight examines the Social Process Theories: Learning, Control and Reaction. The chapter begins with a discussion of socialization and crime and then shifts to describing the various social process theories. Chapter Eight concludes with an evaluation of social process theory and the impact of these theories on social policy.

Learning Objectives

After reading this chapter the student should be able to:
- Develop an understanding of the effects of socialization and crime.
- Define and describe the Social Learning Theories.
- Review Differential Association Theory.
- Understand Differential Reinforcement Theory.
- Develop an understanding of Neutralization Theory.
- To understand the Social Control Theories.
- Explore the elements of the Social Bond.
- Be able to define Social Reaction Theory.
- Understand the correlation between crime and Labeling Theory.
- Develop an understanding of primary and secondary deviance.

Chapter Overview

Introduction
Socialization and Crime
      Family Relations
      Educational Experience

Chapter Outline

I.   **Introduction**
II. **Socialization and Crime**
     A. Social process theories
        1. Criminality is a function of individual socialization.
        2. People are influenced by interactions with various organizations, institutions, and processes of society such as education, employment, and family life and peer relations.
        3. All people have the potential to become delinquents or criminals.
     B. Family Relations
        1. Youth from home with conflict and tension more likely to become criminal.
        2. Lack of love can lead to criminality.
        3. Children with strong, positive role models less likely to become criminal.

131

4. Parental efficacy - supportive parents who effectively control their children are more likely to raise children who refrain from delinquency.
5. Child Abuse and Crime - link between child abuse, neglect, sexual abuse and crime.
C. Educational Experience
1. Children who do poorly in school, lack educational motivation and feel alienated are more likely to engage in criminality.
2. Schools label problem youth, which contributes to criminality.
3. Many crimes occur on school grounds.
D. Peer Relations
1. Peer groups influence decision making and behavior choices.
2. Cliques - small groups of friends who share activities and confidences
3. Crowds - loosely organized groups of children who share interests and activities.
4. Adolescents feel pressure to conform to group values.
E. Institutional Involvement and Belief
1. Studies show that participation in institutions such as religion eschew crime and anti-social behavior.
F. The Effects of Socialization on Crime
1. Anyone with a positive self-image, learned moral values, support of their parents, peers, teachers and neighbors can resist inducement to crime.
2. Social process approach - an individual's socialization determines the likelihood of criminality.
   a. Social learning theory - crime is a learned behavior.
   b. Social control theory - everyone has the potential to become a criminal, but most are controlled by his or her bond to society.
   c. Social reaction theory - people become criminal when significant members of society label them as such and they accept those labels as a personal identity.

III. **Social Learning Theories** - crime is a product of learning the norms, values and behaviors associated with criminal activity.
A. Differential Association Theory - Edwin H. Sutherland published in 1939 *Principles of Criminality*
1. Principles of Differential Association
   a. Criminal behavior is learned.
   b. Criminal behavior is learned as a byproduct of interacting with others.
   c. Learning criminal behavior occurs within intimate personal groups.
   d. Learning criminal behavior involves learning the techniques of committing the crime, which are sometimes very complicated and sometimes very simple.
   e. The specific direction of motives and drives is learned from perceptions of various aspects of the legal code as being favorable or unfavorable.
   f. Differential Associations may vary in frequency, duration, priority and intensity.

2. Testing Differential Association - research has been fairly sparse, however, some testing has some that there is a correlation between :
    a. having deviant friends
    b. holding deviant attitudes
    c. and committing deviant acts.
3. Analysis of Differential Association Theory
    a. Cultural deviance critique - differential association is invalid because it suggests that criminals are people properly socialized into a deviant subculture.
    b. Fails to explain why one exposed to delinquency succumbs and another does not.
B. Differential Reinforcement Theory - Akers and Burgess (1966)
    1. Also known as direct conditioning - occurs when behavior is reinforced either by being rewarded or punished while interacting with others.
    2. When behavior is punished, this is known as negative reinforcement.
    3. Testing Differential Reinforcement - testing showed that learning deviant behavior is not static.
C. Neutralization Theory - Matza and Sykes
    1. View the process of becoming a criminal as a learning experience, in which potential delinquents and criminals master techniques that enable them to counterbalance or neutralize conventional values and drift back and forth between illegitimate and conventional behavior.
    2. Subterranean value - morally tinged influences, which have become entrenched in the culture but are publicly condemned.
    3. Drift - the movement from one extreme of behavior to another.
    4. Model based on:
        a. Criminals sometimes voice a sense of guilt over their illegal acts.
        b. Offenders frequently respect and admire honest, law-abiding persons.
        c. Criminals draw a line between those whom they can victimize and those whom they cannot.
        d. Criminals are not immune to the demands of conformity.
    5. Techniques of Neutralization
        a. Denial of Responsibility
        b. Denial of injury
        c. Denial of Victim
        d. Condemnation of the condemners
        e. Appeal to higher loyalties
    6. Testing Neutralization Theory - attempts have been made to test, but the results have been inconclusive.
D. Are Learning Theories Valid?
    1. Little evident to substantiate that people learn the techniques that enable them to become criminals before they actually commit criminal acts.

IV. **Social Control Theories**
   A. Maintain that people have the potential to violate the law and that modern society presents many opportunities for illegal activity.
      1. Some have self-control, which keeps them from hurting others violating social norms.
      2. Others develop a commitment to conformity - adhered to because of a real, present and logical reason to obey the rules of society.
      3. Their attachment and commitment to conventional institutions, individuals and processes control people's behavior.
   B. Self-Concept and Crime
      1. Containment Theory - Walter Reckless - argued that a strong self-image insulates a youth from the pressures and pulls of criminogenic influences in the environment.
      2. Self-enhancement Theory - Sociologist Howard Kaplan
         a. Youth with poor self-concepts are most likely to engage in delinquent behavior, successful participation in criminality actually helps raise their self-esteem.
   C. Social Control Theory - Travis Hirschi (1969) *Causes of Delinquency*
      1. Links the onset of criminality to the weakening of the ties that bind people to society.
   D. Elements of the Social Bond
      1. Attachment - a person's sensitivity to and interest in others.
      2. Commitment - the time, energy, and effort expended in conventional lines of action such as getting an education and saving money for the future.
      3. Involvement - when individuals are involved in school, recreation and family, they are insulated from the lure of criminal behavior.
      4. Belief - Those who live in the same social setting often share common moral beliefs.
   E. Testing Social Control Theory - Hirschi tested youth in self-report survey.
      1. Found youth strongly attached to parents are less likely to commit criminal acts.
      2. Commitment to conventional values were indicative of conventional behavior.
      3. Youth involved in conventional behavior were less likely to commit crime.
      4. Youth involved in nonconventional behavior were more delinquency-prone.
      5. Youth who had poor relationships with people tended toward delinquency.
      6. Those who shunned unconventional acts were attached to their peers.
      7. Delinquents and nondelinquents shared similar beliefs about society.
      8. Supporting Research - corroborated by numerous research studies showing that delinquent youth often feel detached from society.
         a. Opposing Views - some question some or all of the elements of the theory. Some have questioned the relationship of the following to the theory:

134

1. Friendship
2. Not all elements of the bond are equal.
3. Deviant Peers and Parents.
4. Restricted in Scope.
5. Changing Bonds.
6. Crime and Social Bonds.

V. **Social Reaction Theory** - commonly called labeling theory
   A. Explains how criminal career form based on destructive social interactions and encounters.
   B. Roots found in symbolic interaction theory - people communicate via symbols-gestures, signs, words, or images that stand for or represent something else.
   C. Crime and Labeling Theory
      1. Crime and deviance are defined by the social audience's reaction to people and their behavior and the subsequent effects of that reaction; they are not defined by the moral content of the illegal act itself.
      2. Moral entrepreneurs - people who create rules.
   D. Differential Enforcement - the law is differentially applied, benefiting those who hold economic and social power and penalizing the powerless.
   E. Becoming Labeled - the less personal power and fewer resources a person has, the greater the chance he or she will become labeled.
   F. Consequences of Labeling
      1. Creation of stigma - labeled deviant becomes a social outcast who may be prevented from enjoying higher education, well-paying jobs, and other social benefits.
      2. Such alienation leads to a low self-image.
      3. Differential Social Control
         a. The process of labeling may produce a re-evaluation of the self, which reflects actual or perceived appraisals made by others.
         b. Reflective role-taking - informal and institutional social control processes.
      4. Joining Deviant Cliques - when children are labeled as deviant, they may join similarly outcast delinquent peers.
      5. Retrospective Reading - process of the past of the labeled person being reviewed and reevaluated to fit his or her current status.
      6. Dramatization of Evil - the person becomes the thing he or she is labeled.
   G. Primary and Secondary Deviance
      1. Primary deviance - involves norm violations or crimes that have very little influence on the actor and can be quickly forgotten.
      2. Secondary deviance - occurs when a deviant event comes to the attention of significant others or social control agents who apply a negative label.
      3. Deviance amplification effect - offenders feel isolated from the mainstream of society and become firmly locked within their deviant role.
   H. Research on Social Reaction Theory - divided into two categories:
      1. Research on who gets labeled

a. The poor and powerless are victimized by the law and justice system; labels are not equally distributed across class and racial lines.

b. Contextual discrimination - refers to judges' practices in some jurisdictions to impose harsher sentences on African-Americans only in some instances such as when they victimize whites and not other African-Americans.

2. The Effects of Labeling - empirical evidence that negative labels actually have a dramatic influence on the self-image of offenders.

3. Labeling and Career Criminals - evidence that labeling plays an important role in persistent offending.

I. Is Labeling Theory Valid? - some found little to support the theory

1. Labeling Reexamined - others found supporting evidence of the theory

a. Labeling perspective identifies the role played by social control agents in the process of crime causation.

b. Labeling theory recognizes that criminality is not a disease or pathological behavior.

c. It distinguishes between criminal acts and criminal careers and shows that these concepts are interrelated and treated differently.

VI. **An Evaluation of Social Process Theory**

A. The three branches are compatible because they suggest that criminal behavior is part of the socialization process.

VII. **Social Process Theory and Social Policy**

A. Major influence on social policy-making since 1950's.

B. Head Start Program

C. Diversion Programs - designed to remove both juvenile and adult offenders from the normal channels of the criminal justice process by placing them in programs designed for rehabilitation.

D. Restitution - an offender is asked to either pay back the victim of the crime for any loss incurred, or do some useful work in the community in lieu of receiving court-ordered sentence.

VIII. **Summary**

<u>**Key Terms**</u>

Socialization - Process of human development and enculturation. Socialization is influenced by key social processes and institutions.

Cliques - Small groups of friends who share activities and confidences.

Crowds - Loosely organized groups of children who share interests and activities.

Social Learning Theory - A branch of the Social Process Approach. Social Learning Theory suggests that people learn the techniques and attitudes of crime from close and intimate relationships with criminal peers; crime is a learned behavior.

Social Control Theory - A branch of the Social Process Approach. Social Control Theory maintains that everyone has the potential to become a criminal, but that their bond to society controls most people. Crime occurs when the forces that bind people to society are weakened or broken.

Social Reaction Theory - A branch of the Social Process Approach. Also known as Labeling Theory. Social Reaction Theory says people become criminals when significant members of society label them as such and they accept those labels as a personal identity.

Labeling Theory - See Social Reaction Theory.

Differential Association - According to Sutherland, the principle that criminal acts are related to a person's exposure to an excess amount of antisocial attitudes and values.

Differential Reinforcement - According to Akers, the principal that both deviant and conventional behavior is learned. Whether deviant or criminal behavior has been initiated or persists depends on the degree to which it has been rewards or punished.

Neutralize - According to Matza and Sykes, the principle that becoming a criminal is a learning process in which potential delinquents and criminals master techniques that enable them to counterbalance or neutralize conventional value and drift back and forth between illegitimate and conventional behavior.

Drift - The movement from one extreme of behavior to another, resulting in behavior that is sometimes conventional, free, or deviant and at other times constrained and sober.

Subterranean Behaviors - The morally tinged influences, which have become entrenched in the culture but are publicly, condemned. They exist side by side with conventional values and while condemned in public may be admired or practiced in private.

Techniques of Neutralization - According to neutralization theory, the ability of delinquent youth to neutralize moral constraints so they may drift into criminal acts.

Commitment to Conformity - People's behavior, including criminal activity, is controlled by people's attachment and commitment to conventional institutions, individuals, and processes. If the commitment is absent, they are free to violate the law and engage in deviant behavior.

Symbolic Interaction - People communicate via symbols - gestures, signs, words, or images that stand for or represent something else.

Stigma - An enduring label that taints a person's identity and changes him/her in the eyes of others.

Moral Entrepreneurs - People who create rules.

Primary and Secondary Deviance - According to Lemert, primary deviance involves norm violations or crimes that have very little influence on the actor and can be quickly forgotten. In contrast, secondary deviance occurs when a deviant event comes to the attention of significant others or social control agents who apply a negative label.

Reflective role-taking - When one believes that others view them as antisocial or troublemakers, they take on attitudes and roles that reflect this assumption; they expect to become suspects and then to be rejected.

Reflected appraisal - According to Matsueda and Heimer, a youth's self-evaluation based on his/her perceptions of how others evaluate him/her.

Discussion Exercise

Examine the career and life of Robert Downey, Jr. Downey, a renowned actor, has a serious addiction to drugs. Has Downey been labeled as an addict or a criminal? Has labeling theory been a factor in the treatment of Downey? What elements of social process theory apply to the Downey situation?

InfoTrac Assignment

GETTING STARTED: Search term words for subject guide: Differential Association Theory, Neutralization Theory, Social Control Theory, Labeling Theory.

CRITICAL THINKING PROJECT: Using the search term "Social Control Theory," find articles that discuss this important Social Process Theory. Examine this theory and compare it to other theories of crime.

Here are three articles:

Brezina, Timothy "Adolescent Maltreatment and Delinquency: The Question of Intervening Processes." *Journal of Research in Crime and Delinquency.*

Junger, Marianne and Ineke Haen Marshall "The Interethnic Generalizability of Social Control Theory: An Empirical Test." *Journal of Research in Crime and Delinquency.*

Alston, Reginald J., Debra Harley and Karen Lenhoff "Hirschi's Social Control Theory: A Sociological Perspective on Drug Abuse Among Persons With Disabilities." *The Journal of Rehabilitation.*

Test Bank

Essay Questions

1. Describe the relationship between socialization and crime. What are the prominent elements of socialization that contribute or not to a criminal career?
2. Compare and contrast the Social Learning Theories. Are the Learning Theories valid? Why or why not?
3. Describe Social Control Theory. What is the relationship between crime and self-concept? Define the elements of the social bond and their relationship to deviance.
4. Define Differential Association. Describe the basic principles of differential association. Does Differential Association have any impact on current social policy?
5. What is Labeling Theory? What are the consequences of labeling an individual? Differentiate between primary and secondary deviance.

Fill In The Blank

1. According to Akers, **Differential Reinforcement** is the principal that both deviant and conventional behavior is learned.

2. According to neutralization theory, **Techniques of Neutralization** are the ability of delinquent youth to neutralize moral constraints so they may drift into criminal acts.

3. **Subterranean Behaviors** are the morally tinged influences, which have become entrenched in the culture but are publicly, condemned.

4. **Reflective role-taking** is when one believes that others view them as antisocial or troublemakers, and they take on attitudes and roles that reflect this assumption.

5. People who create the rules are **Moral Entrepreneurs.**

6. **Primary Deviance** involves norm violations or crimes that have very little influence on the actor and can be quickly forgotten.

7. **Secondary Deviance** occurs when a deviant event comes to the attention of significant others or social control agents who apply a negative label.

8. **Neutralize** is the principle that becoming a criminal is a learning process in which potential delinquents and criminals master techniques that enable them to counterbalance or neutralize conventional value and drift back and forth between illegitimate and conventional behavior.

9. A youth's self-evaluation based on his or her perceptions of how others evaluate him or her is **Reflected Appraisal**.

10. Communication via symbols is **Symbolic Interaction**.

11. **Social Process Theories** hold that criminality is a function of individual socialization.

12. When behavior is punished, this is referred to as **Negative Reinforcement**.

13. Some individuals have **self-control**, which is manifested through a strong moral sense, which renders them incapable of hurting others and violating social norms.

14. **Containment Theory** argues that a strong self-image insulates a youth from the pressures and pulls of criminogenic influences in the environment.

15. **Attachment** refers to a person's sensitivity to and interest in others.

Multiple Choice

1. Small groups of friends who share activities and confidences are called:
    a. Cliques
    b. Crowds
    c. Gangs
    d. Friends
    (Answer = a)

2. An enduring label that taints a person's identity and changes him or her in the eyes of others is known as:
    a. Socialization
    b. Drift
    c. Cliques
    d. Crowds
    (Answer = d)

3. The process of human development and enculturation is known as:
    a. Stigma
    b. Socialization
    c. Drift
    d. Primary deviance
    (Answer = b)

4. Loosely organized groups of children who share interests and activities are known as:
   a. cliques
   b. gangs
   c. friends
   d. crowds
   (Answer = d)

5. People's behavior, including criminal activity, is controlled by people's attachment and commitment to conventional institutions, individuals, and processes is known as:
   a. commitment to conformity
   b. Negative affective states
   c. Positive affective states
   a. Primary deviance
   (Answer = a)

6. According to Sutherland, the principle that criminal acts are related to a person's exposure to an excess amount of antisocial attitudes and values is:
   a. Labeling theory
   b. Differential reinforcement
   c. Social learning theory
   d. Differential association
   (Answer = d)

7. The view that involves norm violations or crimes that have very little influence on the actor and can be quickly forgotten is known as:
   a. Anomie
   b. Primary deviance
   c. Secondary deviance
   d. Social control theory
   (Answer = b)

8. This occurs when a deviant event comes to the attention of significant others or social control agents who apply a negative label and is known as:
   a. Secondary deviance
   b. Primary deviance
   c. Anomie
   d. Social control theory
   (Answer = a)

9. The movement from one extreme of behavior to another, resulting in behavior that is sometimes conventional, free, or deviant and at other times constrained and sober is:
    a. Stigma
    b. Conduct disorder
    c. Drift
    d. Relative deprivation
    (Answer = c)

10. People who create rules are:
    a. Poor
    b. Moral entrepreneurs
    c. Deviant
    d. Academics
    (Answer = b)

11. The view according to Ackers is that both deviant and conventional behavior is learned is called:
    a. Differential Association
    b. Labeling theory
    c. Social reaction theory
    d. Differential Reinforcement
    (Answer = d)

12. A youth's self-evaluation based on his or her perceptions of how others evaluate him or her is known as:
    a. Reflected appraisal
    b. Primary deviance
    c. Secondary deviance
    d. Stigma
    (Answer = a)

13. When one believes that others view them as antisocial or troublemakers, they take on attitudes and roles that reflect this assumption:
    a. Reflected appraisal
    b. Reflective role-taking
    c. Stigma
    d. Primary deviance
    (Answer = b)

14.The principle that becoming a criminal is a learning process in which potential delinquents and criminals master techniques that enable them to counterbalance or neutralize conventional value and drift back and forth between illegitimate and conventional behavior is known as:
   a. Drift
   b. Labeling theory
   c. Reflected appraisal
   d. Neutralize
   (Answer = d)

15.The theory, which maintains that everyone has the potential to become a criminal, but that their bond to society controls most people, is known as:
   a. Social learning theory
   b. Differential association
   c. Differential reinforcement
   d. Social control theory
   (Answer = d)

16. People become criminals when significant members of society label them as such and they accept those labels, as a personal identity is known as:
   a. Social strata
   b. Social learning theory
   c. Social control theory
   d. Social reaction theory
   (Answer = d)

17.People learn the techniques and attitudes of crime from close and intimate relationships with criminal peers is known as:
   a. Social reaction theory
   b. Social learning theory
   c. Social control theory
   d. Labeling theory
   (Answer = b)

18. The morally tinged influences, which have become entrenched in the culture but are publicly, condemned is known as:
   a. Techniques of neutralization
   b. Symbolic interaction
   c. Subterranean behaviors
   d. Labeling theory
   (Answer = c)

19. Communication via symbols is known as:
   a. Symbolic interaction
   b. Labeling theory
   c. Subterranean behaviors
   d. Techniques of neutralization
   (Answer = a)

20. The ability of delinquent youth to neutralize moral constraints so they may drift into criminal acts is known as:
   a. Symbolic interaction
   b. Techniques of neutralization
   c. Subterranean behaviors
   d. Labeling theory
   (Answer = b)

21. The National Crime Victimization Survey estimates how many crimes occur each year?
   a. 1 million
   b. 2 million
   c. 12 million
   d. 26 million
   (Answer = d)

22. Today, more than _____ million Americans live in poverty.
   a. 1
   b. 2
   c. 10
   d. 30
   (Answer = d)

23. Children growing up in homes where a parent suffers from mental impairment are at risk for:
   a. Success
   b. Delinquency
   c. Scholarships
   d. Successful careers
   (Answer = b)

24. One national survey found that about ____ percent of student's aged 12 through 19 report violent or property victimization at school each year.
   a. 10%
   b. 5%
   c. 15%
   d. 40%
   (Answer = c)

25. How many fights occur on school grounds each year?
    a. 90
    b. 900
    c. 9000
    d. 190,000
    (Answer = d)

26. Criminal behavior is learned through human interaction is:
    a. Control theory
    b. Labeling theory
    c. Social control theory
    d. Social learning theory
    (Answer = d)

27. Some people are labeled "criminal" by police and court authorities; labeled people are known as troublemakers, criminals and are shunned by conventional society. This is:
    a. Social learning theory
    b. Control theory
    c. Labeling theory
    d. Social control theory
    (Answer = c)

28. Human behavior is controlled through close associations with institutions and individuals is known as:
    a. Control theory
    b. Social learning theory
    c. Labeling theory
    d. Social control theory
    (Answer = a)

29. When friends or parents demonstrate their disapproval of crime:
    a. Association occurs
    b. Disassociation occurs
    c. Definitions favorable toward criminality
    d. Definitions unfavorable toward criminality
    (Answer = d)

30. Differential associations may vary in:
    a. Frequency
    b. Duration
    c. Priority
    d. All of the above
    (Answer = d)

31. The age of children when they first encounter definitions of criminality is:
    a. Frequency
    b. Duration
    c. Priority
    d. Intensity
    (Answer = c)

32. The importance and prestige attributed to individual or groups from whom the definitions are learned is:
    a. Priority
    b. Duration
    c. Intensity
    d. Frequency
    (Answer = c)

33. When behavior is punished, this is referred to as:
    a. Direct conditioning
    b. Reconditioning
    c. Labeling
    d. Negative reinforcement
    (Answer = d)

34. When young offenders claim their unlawful acts were simply not their fault, it is known as:
    a. Denial of responsibility
    b. Denial of injury
    c. Denial of victim
    d. Condemnation of the condemners
    (Answer = a)

35. By denying the wrongfulness of an act, criminals are able to neutralize illegal behavior and this is known as:
    a. Denial of responsibility
    b. Denial of victim
    c. Condemnation of the condemners
    d. Denial of injury
    (Answer = d)

36. Criminals sometimes neutralize wrongdoing by maintaining that the victim of crime "had it coming." This is known as:
    a. Denial of responsibility
    b. Denial of injury
    c. Denial of victim
    d. Condemnation of the condemners
    (Answer = c)

37. When an offender views the world as a corrupt place with a dog-eat-dog code, it is called:
    a. Denial of responsibility
    b. Denial of injury
    c. Condemnation of the condemners
    d. Denial of victim
    (Answer = c)

38. Novice criminals often argue that they are caught in the dilemma of being loyal to their own peer group while at the same time attempting to abide by the rules of ht larger society and this is known as:
    a. Denial of responsibility
    b. Appeal to higher loyalties
    c. Denial of injury
    d. Denial of victim
    (Answer = b)

39. A strong moral sense which renders individuals incapable of hurting others and violating social norms is:
    a. Self-control
    b. Out of control
    c. Drift
    d. Reflected appraisal
    (Answer = a)

40. Theory which argues that a strong self-image insulates a youth from the pressures and pulls of criminogenic influences in the environment is known as:
    a. Self-containment theory
    b. Containment theory
    c. Labeling theory
    d. Socialization
    (Answer = b)

True/False

T   1.   Children growing up in homes where a parent suffers from a mental impairment are also at risk for delinquency.

F   2.   There is no link between child abuse, neglect, sexual abuse and crime.

F   3.   Schools have no contribution to criminality when they label problem youths, and set them apart from conventional society.

T   4.   Research indicates that many school dropouts, especially those, who have been expelled, face a significant chance of entering a criminal career.

T   5. A popular government supported program designed to reduce the number of students who drop out of school is the Communities in Schools network.

F   6. Social learning theories assume people are born "bad" and learn to be "good".

F   7. One of the most prominent social learning theories is Karl Marx's differential association theory.

T   8. When behavior is punished, this is referred to as negative reinforcement.

T   9. Subterranean values are the morally tinged influences, which have become entrenched in the culture but are publicly condemned.

F   10. Cliques refer to the movement from one extreme of behavior to another.

T   11. Offenders frequently respect and admire honest, law-abiding persons.

T   12. When young offenders sometimes claim their unlawful acts were simply not their fault, it is known as denial of responsibility.

F   13. When an offender views the world as a corrupt place with a dog-eat-dog code, it is known a denial of injury.

T   14. Some individuals have self-control, which is manifested through a strong moral sense, which renders them incapable of hurting others and violating social norms.

T   15. Hirschi argues that the social bond a person maintains with society is divided into four main elements: attachment, commitment, involvement and belief.

Chapter Nine

Conflict Theory

Summary

Chapter Nine begins with a discussion of Marxist thought. The development of Conflict Theory is presented and then Marxist Criminology. There are many elements of Marxism and each of the theories is examined. Chapter Nine concludes with the implications of Social Conflict Theory on our Social Policy.

Learning Objectives

After reading this chapter the student should be able to:
- Develop an understanding of Marxist thought.
- Explore Marx on Crime.
- Define Conflict Theory.
- Describe the contribution of Wilhem Bonger.
- Distinguish between the contributions of Ralf Dahrendorf and George Vold.
- Discuss Conflict Criminology.
- List the research on Conflict Theory.
- Provide an analysis of Conflict Theory.
- Define Marxist Criminology.
- Describe the development of a Radical Criminology.
- Understand the fundamentals of Marxist Criminology.
- Define Left Realism.
- Examine Radical Feminist Theory.
- Describe Power-Control Theory.
- Explore Social Conflict Theory and the impact on social policy.

Chapter Overview

Chapter Outline

I. Introduction

    A. Conflict theorists goal:

        1. To explain crime within economic and social contexts

2. To express the connection between the nature of social class, crime and social control.
   B. Theorist concerned with:
      1. the role government plays in creating a crimogenic environment
      2. the relationship between personal or group power and the shaping of criminal law
      3. the prevalence of bias in the justice system operations
      4. The relationship between a capitalist free-enterprise economy and crime rates.
   C. Theorists view crime as the outcome of the class struggle.
   D. Consider acts of racism, sexism, imperialism, unsafe working conditions, inadequate child care, substandard housing, pollution of the environment, and war making as a tool of foreign policy as "true crimes".
   E. Conflict theory - has several independent branches. First, the inter-group conflict and rivalry that exists in every society causes crime. Second the crime-producing traits of capitalist society. Others are devoted to feminist, new realist, peacemaking and post-modern thought.

II. **Marxist Thought**
   A. Karl Marx - lived in time of unrestrained capitalist expansion
   B. Industrial Revolution - Large factories
   C. Moved to Paris
   D. Met Friedrich Engels (1820-1895) - friend and economic patron
   E. 1847 - Marx and Engels joined the Communist League

III. **Productive Forces and Productive Relations**
   A. 1848 - Marx published his famous communist manifesto
      1. Focused on the economic conditions perpetuated by the capitalist system.
      2. Development had turned workers into a dehumanized mass that merely existed at the mercy of the capitalist employers.
   B. Identified the economic structures in society that control all human relations.
      1. Production has two components:
         a. Productive forces - technology, energy sources and material resources
         b. Productive relations - the relationships that exist among the people producing goods and services.
      2. Most important relations in industrial culture between:
         a. Capitalist bourgeoisie - the owners of production
         b. Proletariat - people who do the actual work
         c. Lumpen proletariat - the bottom of society - the fringe members who produce nothing and live off the work of others.

IV. **Surplus Value**
   A. Marx held that laboring class produces goods that exceed wages in value - the theory of surplus value.
   B. Excess value goes to capitalists as profit.
   C. Capitalists find ways to produce cheaply
      1. Pay workers lowest possible wages
      2. Replace workers with labor-saving machinery

V. **Marx on Crime**
   A. The product of law enforcement policies akin to a labeling process theory.
   B. A connection between criminality and the inequities found in the capitalist system.

VI. **Developing a Conflict Theory on Crime**
   A. Marx and Engels influenced the development of social conflict thinking.
   B. Conflict theory first applied to Bonger, Dahrendorf and Vold.

VII. **The Contribution of Willem Bonger**
   A. Born 1876 in Holland and committed suicide in 1940 rather than submit to Nazi rule.
   B. Believed crime is of social origin and crime lies within the boundaries of normal human behavior.
   C. No act is naturally immoral or criminal.
   D. Response to crime is applying penalties considered more severe than spontaneous moral condemnation.
   E. Society is divided into have and have not groups.
   F. Every society that is divided into the ruling class and an inferior class, the penal law serves the will of the ruling class.
   G. The legal system discriminate against the poor by defending the actions of the wealthy.
   H. Upper-class individuals will commit crime if
      1. They have a good opportunity to make a financial gain
      2. Their lack of moral sense enables them to violate social rules.
      3. When wealth is distributed unequally, those who are poor will be crime-prone.
      4. Concluded that crime will disappear if society progresses from competitive capitalism to monopoly capitalism - relatively few enterprises control the means of production.

VIII. **The Contribution of Ralf Dahrendorf**
   A. Argues that modern society is organized into imperatively coordinated associations.
      1. Those who posses authority and those who lack authority.
      2. Domination of one society does not mean dominating another, society is a plurality of competing interest groups.
   B. Wrote *Class and Class Conflict in Industrial Society*
      1. Attempted to show how society changed since Marx works
      2. Argued that Marx did not foresee the changes occurring in the labor classes.
      3. Workers divided into:
         a. unskilled
         b. skilled
         c. semiskilled
   C. Proposed a unified conflict theory of human behavior:
      1. Social change is everywhere, all of the time.
      2. Social conflict is everywhere, all of the time.

3. Every element in society contributes to its disintegration and change.

4. Others base every society on the coercion of some of its members.

IX.   The Contribution of George Vold

   A. Argued that crime can be explained by social conflict.

   B. Laws created by politically-oriented groups who seek the government's assistance to help them defend their rights and protect their interests.

   C. Criminal acts are a consequence of direct contact between forces struggling to control society.

X.   Conflict Theory - became prominent during the 1960's.

   A. Criminologists began to view the justice system as a mechanism to control the lower class and maintain the status quo.

   B. Publications contributed to the development of conflict theory:

   1. Lemert's *Social Pathology*

   2. Becker's *Outsiders*

XI.   Developing a Conflict Theory

   A. William Chambliss and Robert Seidman wrote: *Law, Order and Power* - documented how the justice system protects the rich and powerful.

   1. Described the control of the political and economic system affects how criminal justice is administered.

   2. Showed how the definitions of crime favor those who control the justice system.

   3. Analyzed the role of conflict in contemporary society.

   B. Their work demonstrated the major objective of conflict theory: how justice in U.S. is skewed.

   1. Those who deserve to be punished the most (wealthy white-collar criminals) are actually punished the least, those crimes are relatively minor and committed out of economic necessity receive the stricter sanctions.

   C. Power Relations

   1. According to conflict view, those who define crime are in power.

   2. Power - the ability of persons and groups to determine and control the behavior of others and to shape public opinion to meet their personal needs.

   3. Unequal distribution of power causes conflict.

   D. The Social Reality of Crime - theory embraced by Richard Quinnery

   1. Criminal definitions (law) represent those who hold power

   2. Criminal definitions are based on:

   a. changing social conditions

   b. emerging interests

   c. increasing demands that political, economic, and religious interests be protected

   d. changing conceptions of public interest

   e. concepts of crime are controlled by the powerful

   f. The criminal justice system works to secure the needs of the powerful.

   E. Norm Resistance - produced by interaction between authorities and subject.

XII.   Research on Conflict Theory

A. Comparing crime rates of members of powerless groups with those of member of the elite classes.

B. Examining the criminal justice systems operations.

C. Studies that show that the criminal justice system is quick to take action when the victim of crime is wealthy, white and male, but it is disinterested when the victim is poor, black, and female.

XIII. **Analysis of Conflict Theory**

A. Conflict Theory has had an important niche in the criminological literature.

XIV. **Marxist Criminology**

A. View crime as a function of the capitalist mode of production.

B. Capitalist society - those in political power control the legal definition of crime and how the system enforces the law.

C. The rich use the fear of crime as a tool to maintain their control over society.

XV. **The Development of a Radical Criminology**

A. 1968 - British sociologists formed the National Deviancy Conference

B. 1973 - Radical theory published in *The New Criminology* by Ian Taylor, Paul Walton and Jock Young.

C. Scholars in America started following

D. Primarily at University of California at Berkeley - the criminology program

E. 1980's - The Left Realism School - started by scholars of the Middlesex Polytechnic and the University of Edinburgh in Great Britain.

XVI. **Fundamentals of Marxist Criminology**

A. Ignore formal theory construction

B. The nature of society controls the direction of its criminality.

C. Economic Structure and Surplus Value

  1. Ownership and control is the principal basis of power in U.S. society.

  2. As surplus value increases, more people are displaced from productive relationships and the size of the "marginal" population increases.

  3. Marginalization - a larger portion of the population is forced to live in areas, known as structural locations or conducive to crime.

XVII. **Instrumental Marxism** - view the criminal justice system as a method of controlling the poor, have-not members of society; the state is the tool of the capitalists.

A. Concepts of Instrumental Marxism - According to theorists, legal relations in the U.S. secure an economic infrastructure that centers on a capitalist mode of production.

B. Integrative-Constitutive Theory - Gregg Barak and Stuart Henry

  1. The act of making people criminals is a crime.

  2. Aspects of Crime

    a. Crimes of Reduction - when the offended party experiences a loss of some quality relative to their present standing.

    b. Crimes of Repression - when members of a group are prevented from achieving their fullest potential because of racism, sexism or some other status bias.

C. The Essence of Instrumental Marxism

1. The state, law and ruling class are a single entity.
2. The economic, social and political interests of the ruling class shape law.
3. Law is constructed and used by the ruling class to its advantage.

XVIII. Structural Marxism
   A. Law is used to maintain the long-term interests of the capitalist system
   B. Law is used to control members of any class who pose a threat to its existence.
   C. Law is designed to keep the capitalist system working efficiently.

XIX. Research on Marxist Criminology
   A. Correctionalism - research conducted, which unmasks the weak and powerless members of society so they can be better, dealt with by the legal system.
   B. Macrolevel issues - how the accumulation of wealth affects crime rates
   C. Microlevel issues - the effect of criminal interactions on the lives of individuals living in a capitalist society.
   D. Crime, the Individual and the State
      1. Crime and its control are a function of capitalism
      2. The justice system is biased among the working class and favors upper-class interests.
   E. Historical Analysis
      1. To show changes in criminal law correspond to the development of capitalist economy.
      2. Research between nineteenth century convict work and capitalism.

XX. Critique of Marxist Criminology
   A. Great deal of criticism
   B. Some charge that Marxists unfairly neglect the efforts of the capitalist system to regulate itself.

XXI. Emerging Forms of Conflict Theory
   A. Left Realism - connected to British scholars John Lea and Jock Young
      1. Street criminal prey on the poor and disenfranchised, thus making them doubly abused, first by the capitalist system and then by members of their own class.
      2. Preemptive deterrence - an approach of community efforts trying to eliminate or reduce crime before it becomes necessary to employ police.
      3. Marginalized youth - youth that feel they are not a part of society and have nothing to lose by committing crime.
   B. Radical Feminist Theory - a number of feminist writers have attempted to explain the cause of crime, gender differences in the crime rate and the exploitation of female victims.
   C. Marxist Feminist - view gender inequality as stemming from the unequal power of men and women in a capitalist society.
      1. Patriarchy, or male supremacy, continues to be support by capitalists.
      2. Patriarchy and Crime - link criminal behavior patterns to the gender conflict created by the economic and social struggles common in post-industrial societies.
         a. Double Marginality - capitalists control the labor of workers, while men control women both economically and biologically.

b. Females in a capitalist society commit fewer crimes than males; they are isolated in families and have fewer opportunities than men.

c. Elite deviance - white-collar and economic crimes.

d. Doing gender - dominating women to prove their manliness

e. Crime is a vehicle for men to do gender.

3. Radical Feminism - view the cause of female crime as originating with the onset of male supremacy (patriarchy), the subsequent subordination of women, male aggression, and the efforts of men to control females sexually.

4. How the Justice System Penalizes Women.

   a. Juvenile System views the majority of female delinquents as sexually precocious girls who have to be brought under control.

   b. Females more likely to be arrested for sexual misconduct than their male counterpart.

   c. Girls more likely to undergo physical exam then boys.

   d. Girls more likely to be sent to a detention facility before trial.

   e. Longer detention for girls than boys.

XXII. Power-Control Theory - John Hagan and associates

A. 1989 *Structural Criminology*

B. Crime and Delinquency are a function of:

   1. class position (power)

   2. family functions (control)

   3. Parents reproduce the power relationships they hold in the workplace.

C. Testing Power-Control Theory - received a great deal of attention

   1. Not all research is supportive.

XXIII. Post-Modern Theory

A. Post-modernists have embraced semiotics and/or deconstructionist analysis as a method of understanding all human relations including human behavior.

B. Semiotics - using language as signs or symbols beyond their literal meaning.

C. Post-modernists believe that language is value-laden and can promote inequities that are present in the rest of the social structure.

XXIV. Peacemaking Criminology

A. The purpose of criminology is to promote a peaceful and just society.

B. Peacemakers view the efforts of the state to punish and control as crime encouraging rather than crime discouraging.

C. Advocate rather than prison, policies such as mediation and conflict resolution.

XXV. Social Conflict Theory and Social Policy

A. Conflict causes crime.

B. Restorative Justice - peacemaking movement which has adopted non-violent methods and applied them

XXVI. Reintegrative Shaming

A. John Braithwaite's book *Crime, Shame and Reintegration*

B. Shame - power tool of informal social control

1. Stigmatization - an ongoing process of degradation in which the offender is branded as an evil person and cast out of society.
2. Reintegrative Shaming - disapproval is extended to the offenders' evil deeds, while at the same time they are cast as respected people who can be reaccepted by society.

XXVII. **Concepts of Restoration**
   A. Restoration - turning the justice system into a "healing" process rather than being a distributor of retribution and revenge.
   B. Restorative vs. Traditional Justice
      1. Legalistic View of Justice - society is defined as an aggregation of people who share common values over which the State has jurisdiction.
      2. Restorative Justice View - that "society" is made up of many competing interests and values making it difficult to derive a universal code that applies to all people.
      3. Restorative Justice is guided by:
         a. Community ownership of conflict (including crime);
         b. Material and symbolic reparation for victims and community; and,
         c. Social reintegration of the offender.

XXVIII. **Restoration Programs** - involve diverting the formal court process.
   A. Sentencing Circles - crime victims and their families are brought together with offenders and their families in an effort to formulate a sanction that addresses the needs of each party.
   B. Negotiation
   C. Mediation
   D. Consensus-building
   E. Peacemaking
   F. To reduce the conflict and harm and restore rather than punish.

XXIX. The Challenge of Restorative Justice
   A. The difficult task of balancing the needs of offenders with those of their victims.
   B. May risk ignoring the offender's need and increasing the likelihood of re-offending.
   C. Programs, which focus on the offender, may turn off victims.

XXX. Summary

Key Terms

Conflict Theory - The view that the inter-group conflicts and rivalry that exists in every society causes crime.

Willem Bonger - (1876-1940) Bonger believed that crime is of social and not biological origin and that, with the exception of a few special cases, crime lies within the boundaries of normal human behavior.

Correctionalism - Research conducted by mainstream liberal/positivist criminologists is designed to unmask the weak and powerless members of society so they can be better dealt with by the legal system.

Ralf Dahrendorf - Argued that modern society is organized into imperatively coordinated associations. These associations comprise two groups: those who possess authority and use it for social domination and those who lack authority and are dominated.

Left Realism - A branch of conflict theory that holds that crime is a "real" social problem experienced by the lower classes and radical scholars must address those lower-class concerns about crime.

George Vold - Argued that crime could also be explained by social conflict. Politically oriented groups who seek the government's assistance to help them defend their rights and protect their interests create laws.

Marxist Feminists - Radical Feminist Theorists that view gender inequality as stemming from the unequal power of men and women in a capitalist society. They view gender inequality as a function of female exploitation by fathers and husbands.

Social Reality of Crime - According to Richard Quinney, criminal definitions (law) represent the interests of those who hold power in society.

Radical Feminist - Area of Criminology where a number of feminist writers have attempted to explain the cause of crime, gender differences in the crime rate, and the exploitation of female victims from a radical feminist perspective.

Patriarchy - Male supremacy.

Surplus Value - Marx held that the laboring class produces goods that exceed wages in value (the theory of surplus value).

Paternalistic - Leaders are seen as father figures and others are treated as children.

Left Realism School - Started in the early 1980's by scholars affiliated with the Middlesex Polytechnic and the University of Edinburgh in Great Britain.

Instrumentalists - Group of Marxists who view the criminal law and criminal justice system solely as an instrument for controlling the poor, have-not members of society; the state is the "tool" of the capitalists.

Marginalization - People who are thrust outside of the economic mainstream.

Structural Location - Areas conducive to crime.

Integrative-Constitutive Theory - Barak and Henry's view that crime and its control cannot be separated from the structural and cultural contexts in which it is produced.

Peacemaking Criminology - One of the newer movements of radical theory. For members of the peacemaking movement, the main purpose of criminology is to promote a peaceful and just society.

Demystify - To unmask the true purpose of law and justice.

Discussion Exercise

Divide the class into three groups. Have each group review one of the Conflict theorists: Bonger, Dahrendorf, or Vold. Compare and contrast the theorists, the culture in which they lived, the economic times, and the relevance of their theory in today's pop culture.

InfoTrac Assignment

GETTING STARTED: Search term words for subject guide: Marx, Ralf Dahrendorf, Radical Criminology, Left Realism, Radical Feminist Theory, Power-Control Theory.

CRITICAL THINKING PROJECT: Using the search term "Radical Criminology," find articles that discuss this important Conflict Theory. Examine this theory and compare it to other theories of crime.

Here are three articles:

Currie, Elliott "Radical Criminology or Just Criminology- Then, and Now." *Social Justice*.

Shank, Gregory "Looking Back: Radical Criminology and Social Movements." *Social Justice*.

Cardarelli, Albert P. and Stephen C. Hicks "Radicalism in Law and Criminology: A Retrospective View of Critical Legal Studies and Radical Criminology." *Journal of Criminal Law and Criminology*.

Test Bank

Essay Questions

1. Describe Karl Marx's theory on crime. What influence has Marx had on current social policy?
2. Compare and contrast the theory contributions of Willem Bonger, Ralf Dahrendorf, and George Vold.
3. Define Conflict Theory. What research has been conducted to validate conflict theory? Provide the current analysis of conflict theory.
4. What is Radical Criminology? Which criminologists influenced this theory?
5. What is Left Realism theory? What are the roots of left realism and how did it evolve? What are the current social implications of left realism theory?

Fill In The Blank

1. Areas conducive to crime are known as **Structural Locations**.

2. According to Richard Quinney, **The Social Reality of Crime** is that criminal definitions (law) represent the interests of those who hold power in society.

3. **Radical Feminist** is the area of Criminology where a number of feminist writers have attempted to explain the cause of crime, gender differences in the crime rate, and the exploitation of female victims.

4. **Integrative-Constitutive Theory** is Barak and Henry's view that crime and its control cannot be separated from the structural and cultural contexts in which it is produced.

5. **Paternalistic** occurs when leaders are seen as father figures and others are treated as children.

6. **Left Realism School** began in the 1980's by scholars affiliated with the Middlesex Polytechnic and the University of Edinburgh in Great Britain.

7. **Marginalization** are people who are thrust outside of the economic mainstream.

8. The purpose of **Peacemaking Criminology** is to promote a peaceful and just society.

9. **Ralf Dahrendorf** argued that modern society is organized into imperatively coordinated associations: those who possess authority and those who lack authority.

10. In 1848, Marx issues his famous **Communist Manifesto**.

11. **Productive Forces** include such things as technology, energy sources and material resources.

12. The relationships, which exist among the people producing the goods and services, is **Productive Relations**.

13. The owners of the means of production are the **capitalist bourgeoisie**.

14. **The proletariat** are the people who do the actual labor.

15. Hegel argued that for every idea, or thesis, there exists an opposing argument, or **Antithesis**.

Multiple Choice

1. The view that the inter-group conflicts and rivalry that exists in every society causes crime is known as:
   a. Conflict Theory
   b. Radical Feminist Theory
   c. Surplus Value
   d. Peacemaking Criminology
   (Answer = a)

2. Which theorist believed that crime is of social and not biological origin and that, with the exception of a few special cases, crime lies within the boundaries of normal human behavior?
   a. Karl Marx
   b. George Vold
   c. Ralf Dahrendorf
   d. Willem Bonger
   (Answer = d)

3. The view that Marx held that the laboring class produces goods that exceed wages in values is known as:
   a. Left realism
   b. Surplus value
   c. Stigma
   d. Drift
   (Answer = b)

4. Areas, which are conducive to crime, are known as:
   a. Gated communities
   b. Beverly Hills
   c. Structural locations
   d. All of the above
   (Answer = c)

5. Research conducted by mainstream liberal/positivist criminologists is designed to unmask the weak and powerless members of society so they can be better dealt with by the legal system is known as:
   a. Correctionalism
   b. Patriarchy
   c. Marginalization
   d. Structural location
   (Answer = a)

6. To unmask the true purpose of law and justice is to:
   a. Socialize
   b. Educate
   c. Label
   d. Demystify
   (Answer = d)

7. Which theorist argued that crime could also be explained by social conflict?
   a. Willem Bonger
   b. George Vold
   c. Ralf Dahrendorf
   d. Karl Marx
   (Answer = b)

8. A group of Marxists who view the criminal law and criminal justice system solely as an instrument for controlling the poor, have-not members of society is known as:
   a. Instrumentalists
   b. Peacemakers
   c. Left realists
   d. Surplus values
   (Answer = a)

9. The theory according to Richard Quinney that criminal definitions represent the interests of those who hold power in society is:
   a. Marxist feminism
   b. Radical feminism
   c. Social reality of crime
   d. Integrative-Constitutive theory
   (Answer = c)

162

10. Which theorist argued that modern society is organized into imperatively coordinated associations: those who possess authority and those who lack authority?
    a. Willem Bonger
    b. Ralf Dahrendorf
    c. George Vold
    d. Karl Marx
    (Answer = b)

11. The area of criminology where a number of feminist writers have attempted to explain the cause of crime, gender differences in the crime rate and the exploitation of female victims is called:
    a. Differential Association
    b. Labeling theory
    c. Social reaction theory
    d. Radical Feminist
    (Answer = d)

12. For members of this movement, the main purpose of criminology is to promote a peaceful and just society and it is known as:
    a. Peacemaking Criminology
    b. Marxist Feminists
    c. Left Realism School
    d. Integrative-Constitutive Theory
    (Answer = a)

14. Male supremacy is also known as:
    a. paternalistic
    b. patriarchy
    c. left realism
    d. marginalization
    (Answer = b)

14. When leaders are seen as father figures and others are treated as children this is known as:
    a. patriarchy
    b. radical feminist
    c. surplus value
    d. paternalistic
    (Answer = d)

15. Barak and Henry's view that crime and its control cannot be separated from the structural and cultural contexts in which it is produced is known as:
    a. Social learning theory
    b. Differential association
    c. Differential reinforcement
    d. Integrative-Constitutive Theory
    (Answer = d)

16. The branch of conflict theory which holds that crime is a "real" social problem experienced by the lower classes and radical scholars must address those lower-class concerns about crime is known as:
    a. Marginalization
    b. Social learning theory
    c. Social control theory
    d. Left Realism
    (Answer = d)

17. Those theorists who view gender inequality as a function of female exploitation by fathers and husbands are known as:
    a. Left Realists
    b. Marxist Feminists
    c. Peacemakers
    d. Instrumentalists
    (Answer = b)

18. This occurs when people are thrust outside of the economic mainstream.
    a. Techniques of neutralization
    b. Symbolic interaction
    c. Marginalization
    d. Subterranean behaviors
    (Answer = c)

19. This school of thought was begun in the 1980's by scholars affiliated with the Middlesex Polytechnic and the University of Edinburgh in Great Britain and is known as:
    a. Left Realism School
    b. School of Hard Knocks
    c. Social Reality School
    d. Peacemaker School
    (Answer = a)

164

20. Conflict theorists are concerned with which of the following?
    a. The role government plays in creating a crimiogenic environment
    b. The relationship between personal or group power and the shaping of criminal law
    c. The prevalence of bias in the justice system operations
    d. All of the above
    (Answer = d)

21. In 1848 Karl Marx issued his famous:
    a. Communist manifesto
    b. Declaration of independence
    c. Constitution
    d. Declaration of war
    (Answer = a)

22. Productive forces include such things as:
    a. Technology
    b. Energy sources
    c. Material resources
    d. All of the above
    (Answer = d)

23. The relationships which exist among the people producing goods and services is known as:
    a. Productive forces
    b. Productive relations
    c. Capitalist bourgeoisie
    d. The proletariat
    (Answer = b)

24. The owners of the means of production are called:
    a. Productive forces
    b. Productive relations
    c. Capitalist bourgeoisie
    d. The proletariat
    (Answer = c)

25. The people who do the actual work are called:
    a. Productive forces
    b. Productive relations
    c. Capitalist bourgeoisie
    d. The proletariat
    (Answer = d)

26. The bottom of society are those who produce nothing and live, parasitically, of the work of other are called:
    a. Productive forces
    b. Capitalist bourgeoisie
    c. The proletariat
    d. Lumpen proletariat
    (Answer = d)

27. In Marxist, theory, what term refers to position in relation to others?
    a. Stigma
    b. Productive forces
    c. Class
    d. Labels
    (Answer = c)

28. Hegel argued that for every idea, or thesis, there exists an opposing argument or:
    a. Antithesis
    b. Subthesis
    c. Hypothesis
    d. Dialectic method
    (Answer = a)

29. When relatively few enterprises control the means of production it is called:
    a. Competitive capitalism
    b. Real capitalism
    c. Wealth distribution
    d. Monopoly capitalism
    (Answer = d)

30. Dahrendorf proposed a unified conflict theory of human behavior, which says which of the following?
    a. Every society is at every point subject to processes of change.
    b. Every society displays at every point dissent and conflict.
    c. Every element in a society renders a contribution to its disintegration and change.
    d. All of the above
    (Answer = d)

31. The ability of persons and groups to determine and control the behavior of others and to shape public opinion to meet their personal interests is:
    a. Class
    b. Status
    c. Power
    d. Stigma
    (Answer = c)

32. Quinney wrote that criminal definitions are based on which of the following factors?
    a. Changing social conditions
    b. Emerging interests
    c. All of the above
    d. None of the above
    (Answer = c)

33. Those in society who dominate are referred to as:
    a. Subjects
    b. Criminals
    c. Defendants
    d. Authorities
    (Answer = d)

34. Those who are controlled and have little ability to control the law are known as:
    a. Subjects
    b. Authorities
    c. Judges
    d. Attorneys
    (Answer = a)

35. Interaction between authorities and subjects eventually produces open conflict between the two groups and is known as:
    a. Norms
    b. Norm confidence
    c. Norm denial
    d. Norm resistance
    (Answer = d)

36. The law represents the values of the majority, legal codes are designed to create a just society and by breaking the law, criminals are predators who violate the rights of others is known as:
    a. Conflict view of crime
    b. Power-control theory
    c. Consensus view of crime
    d. Left realism
    (Answer = c)

37. Crimes that occur when members of a group are prevented from achieving their fullest potential because of racism, sexism or some other status bias are called:
    a. Crimes of reduction
    b. Crimes of seduction
    c. Crimes of repression
    d. Crimes of depression
    (Answer = c)

38. Crimes that occur when the offended party experiences a loss of some quality relative to their present standing are known as:
   a. Crimes of repression
   b. Crimes of reduction
   c. Crimes of seduction
   d. Crimes of depression
   (Answer = b)

39. Which group disagrees with the view that the relationship between law and capitalism is unidimensional, always working for the rich and against the poor?
   a. Structural Marxists
   b. Capitalists
   c. Realists
   d. Economists
   (Answer = a)

40. Marxists devote considerable attention to the study of relationships between which of the following?
   a. Crime
   b. Victims
   c. The state
   d. All of the above
   (Answer = d)

True/False

T   1. The writings of Karl Marx and Friedrich Engels greatly influenced the development of social conflict thinking.

F   2. Willem Bonger believed that crime is of a biological origin not a social origin.

F   3. Upper-class individuals will commit crime if (a) they sense a poor opportunity to make a financial gain; and (b) their abundance of moral sense enables them to violate social rules.

T   4. Conflict theory came into criminological prominence during the 1960s.

T   5. According to the conflict view, those define crime in power

F   6. Structural locations are those locations that have no crime

F   7. Instrumentalists view the criminal law and criminal justice system solely as an instrument for controlling the elite, have members of society.

T 8. According to the instrumental view, capitalist justice serves the powerful and rich and enables them to impose their morality and standards of behavior on the entire society.

T 9. Integrative-Constitutive Theory is a recent effort to show that crime and its control cannot be separated from the structural and cultural contexts in which it is produced.

F 10. Crimes of repression occur when the offended party experiences a loss of some quality relative to their present standing.

T 11. Patriarchy first emerged in pre-capitalist agricultural societies in which a male head presided over his family, controlling work, and the marriages of its members.

T 12. Radical feminists focus on the social forces that shape women's lives and experiences to explain female criminality.

F 13. Analyses of national surveys support the radical perspective by showing that about 10% of adolescent girls are sexually harassed in school.

T 14. Girls are more likely to be sent to a detention facility before trial, and the length of their detention averaged three times that of the boys.

T 15. Post-modernists rely on semiotics to conduct their research efforts.

Chapter Ten

Developmental Theories: Latent Trait and Life Course

Summary

Chapter Ten examines the Developmental Theories. The Developmental Theories can be divided into either Latent Trait Theories or Life Course Theories. An examination of the Latent Trait Theories is presented with explanations of Human Nature Theory, General Theory of Crime, Differential Coercion Theory and Control Balance Theory. Next, the Developmental Theories are defined with discussions of The Glueck Research, Life Course Concepts, Theories of the Criminal Life Course, The Social Development Model, Farrington's Theory of Delinquent Development, Interactional Theory and Age-Graded Theory. The chapter concludes with a comparison of Latent Trait and Life Course theories: their commonalities and their distinctions.

Learning Objectives

After reading this chapter the student should be able to:
- Define Latent Trait Theories.
- Review Human Nature Theory.
- Understand the various components of Differential Coercion Theory.
- Develop an understanding of Control Balance Theory.
- Realize the distinction between the various Life Course Theories.
- To understand the Glueck Research.
- Explore the Life Course Concepts.
- Be able to define the Theories of the Criminal Life Course.
- Understand the Social Development Model.
- Develop an understanding of Farrington's Theory of Delinquent Development.
- Evaluate Interactional Theory.
- Review Sampson and Laub: Age-Graded Theory.

Chapter Overview

Introduction
Latent Trait Theories
       Human Nature Theory
       General Theory of Crime
       Differential Coercion Theory
       Control Balance Theory
Life Course Theories
       The Glueck Research
       Life Course Concepts
       Theories of the Criminal Life Course
       The Social Development Model (SDM)
       Farrington's Theory of Delinquent Development
       Interactional Theory
       Sampson and Laub: Age-Graded Theory
Commonalities and Distinctions
Summary

Chapter Outline

I.   **Introduction** - Developmental theories fall into two groups: latent trait and life course theories.

II.   **Latent Trait Theories** - explain the flow of crime over the life cycle.

       A.   Latent traits - either present at birth or established early in life and remain stable over time. Suspected latent traits include:

           1. Defective intelligence

           2. Impulsive personality

           3. Genetic abnormalities

           4. The physical-chemical functioning of the brain

           5. Environmental influences on brain function

               a. Drugs

               b. Chemicals

               c. Injuries

       B.   Crime and Human Nature

1. James Q. Wilson and Richard Herrnstein (1985) wrote *Crime and Human Nature*.
2. Personal traits, genetics, intelligence and body build outweigh social variables as predictors of criminal activity.

C. General Theory of Crime - Michael Gottfredson and Travis Hirschi wrote *A General Theory of Crime* - they modified Hirschi's social control theory with biosocial, psychological, routine activities and rational choice theories.

1. The Act and the Offender
   a. The criminal offender and the criminal act are separate concepts.
2. What Makes People Crime-Prone?
   a. The tendency to commit crime to a person's level of self-control.
   b. People with limited self-control tend to be impulsive.
   c. Those with low self-control enjoy risky, exciting, or thrilling behaviors with immediate gratification - more likely to enjoy criminal acts.
   d. Root of poor self-control to inadequate child-rearing practices.
   e. Low self-control develops early in life and remains stable into adulthood.
3. Self-Control and Crime
   a. Principles of self-control theory explain all varieties of criminal behavior.
4. Supporting Evidence for the GTC
   a. Research identified indicators of impulsiveness and self-control to determine if the correlated with criminal activity.
   b. A number of studies have indicated successfully this correlation.
5. Analyzing the General Theory of Crime - several questions remain unanswered:
   a. Tautological - may involve circular reasoning.
   b. Personality Disorder - saying one lacks self-control implies a personality defect making them impulsive or rash.
   c. Ecological/individual Differences - GTC fails to address individual and ecological patterns in the crime rate.
   d. Racial and Gender Differences - little evidence that males are more impulsive than girls; Gottfredson and Hirschi explain racial differences as a failure of African-Americans in child-rearing.
   e. Moral Beliefs - General theory ignores the moral concept of right and wrong.
   f. People Change - General Theory assumes that criminal propensity does not change; opportunities change.
   g. Modest Relationship- Self-control is a modest fact and there are other forces which predict the onset of criminal behavior.
   h. Cross-cultural Differences - Evidence shows the criminals in other countries do not lack self-control and GTC may be culturally limited.

     i. Misreads Human Nature - makes flawed assumptions about people; assumes that people are selfish, self-serving and hedonistic and must be controlled.

D.   Differential Coercion Theory

1. Mark Colvin wrote *Crime and Coercion* - suggested that self-control is produced by experiences a person has with destructive forces called coercion.

2. Two types of coercion:
   a. Inter-personal coercion - direct, involving the use or threat of force and intimidation from parents, peers and significant others.
   b. Impersonal coercion - involves pressures beyond individual control, such as economic and social pressure caused by unemployment, poverty, or competition among businesses or other groups.

3. A person's ability to maintain self-control is a function of the amount, type and consistency of coercion they experience as they go through life.

4. Coercion and Criminal Careers - Colvin found that chronic offenders grew up with parents using erratic control and in an inconsistent fashion.

E.   Control-Balance Theory - by Charles Tittle

1. Control has 2 elements:
   a. The amount of control one can exercise over others.
   b. The amount of control one is subject to by others.

2. Conformity results when these 2 elements are in balance; control imbalances produce deviant and criminal behaviors.

3. Control deficit - occurs when one's desires or impulses are limited by others ability to regulate or punish their behavior.

4. Control surplus - occurs when the amount of control one exercises over others is in excess of the ability others have to control or modify the person's behavior.

5. People sensing a deficit of control turn to 3 types of behavior to restore balance
   a. Predation - direct forms of physical violence such as robbery, sexual assault or other forms of physical violence.
   b. Defiance - designed to challenge and control mechanisms but stop short of physical harm: vandalism, curfew violations, and unconventional sex.
   c. Submission - passive obedience to the demands of others such as submitting to physical or sexual abuse without response.

6. Those with an excess of control may engage in:
   a. Exploitation - using others to commit crime, such as contract killers or drug runners.
   b. Plunder - using power without regard for others, such as committing a hate crime or polluting the environment.
   c. Decadence - involves spur of the moment, irrational acts such as child molesting.

III. **Life Course Theories**
   A. Even as toddlers, people begin relationships and behaviors that determine their adult life course.
   B. People must learn to conform to social rules and function effectively in society.
   C. Transitions are expected to occur in order: finish school, marriage, etc.
   D. Disruptions in life's major transitions can be destructive and may cause criminality.
   E. Positive life experience may help some criminals desist from crime for a while; a negative life experience may cause them to resume their activities.
   F. As people mature, the factors that influence their behavior change.
   G. Multidimensional Theories - criminality has multiple roots, including maladaptive personality traits, educational failure and family relations.
   H. The Glueck Research - Sheldon and Eleanor Glueck - Harvard University - 1930's - popularized research on the life cycle of delinquent careers.
      1. Conducted longitudinal research studies to determine the factors that predicted persistent offending.
      2. Found children who are antisocial early in life are most likely to continue their offending careers into adulthood.
      3. Identified a number of personal and social factors related to persistent offending - the most important family relations.
      4. Measured biological and psychological traits such as body type, intelligence and personality.
      5. Found children with low intelligence, with a background of mental disease and had a powerful physique were the most likely to become persistent offenders.
   I. Life Course Concepts - the factors that produce crime and delinquency at one point in the life cycle may not be relevant at another; as people mature, the social, physical and environmental influences on their behavior are transformed.
      1. Problem Behavior Syndrome - a group of antisocial behaviors that cluster together and typically involve:
         a. Family dysfunction
         b. Sexual and physical abuse
         c. Substance abuse
         d. Smoking
         e. Precocious sexuality
         f. Early pregnancy
         g. Educational underachievement
         h. Suicide attempts
         i. Sensation seeking
         j. Unemployment
   J. Pathways to Crime - Rolf Loeber and associates identified paths to crime:

1. Authority Conflict Pathway - begins at an early age with stubborn behavior which leads to defiance and then to authority avoidance.
2. Covert Pathway - begins with minor, underhanded behavior (lying, shoplifting) that leads to property damage then to more serious criminality.
3. Overt Pathways - escalates to aggressive acts beginning with aggression leading to physical and fighting and then to violence.

K. Age of Onset - early onset of deviance strongly predicts later and more serious criminality.
   1. The continuity of crime - children repeatedly in trouble will continue to be antisocial throughout their life course.
   2. "Adolescent Limiteds" and "Life-Course Persisters"
      a. Life-course persisters - those who begin offending at an early age and continue to offend well into adulthood.
      b. Adolescent limiteds - begin to mimic the antisocial behavior of more troubled teens, only to reduce the frequency of their offending as they mature to around age 18.
   3. Life Course Theories
      a. Early onset predicts more lasting crime.

L. The Social Development Model (SDM)
   1. A number of community-level risk factors make some people more susceptible to developing antisocial behaviors.
   2. As children mature, elements of socialization control their developmental process.
      a. Perceived opportunities for involvement in activities and interactions with others.
      b. The degree of involvement and interaction with parents.
      c. The children's ability to participate in these interactions.
      d. The reinforcement they perceive for their participation.
   3. To control the risk of antisocial behavior, a child must maintain pro-social bonds.
   4. Children's antisocial behavior also depends on the quality of their attachments to parents and other influential relations.
   5. SDM holds that commitment and attachment to conventional institutions; activities and beliefs insulate youth from crime influences.

M. Farrington's Theory of Delinquent Development - longitudinal study since 1982 - uses self-report data, interviews and psychological testing.
   1. Found traits present in persistent offenders can be observed as early as age 8.
   2. Future criminals receive poor parental supervision.
   3. Deviant behavior tends to be versatile rather than specialized.
   4. By age 30, former delinquents are likely to be separated or divorced and an absent parent.
   5. Nonoffenders and Desisters

a. Nonoffenders - those, who exhibit factors that, put them at risk of offending, but remain a nonoffender.

b. Desisters - those who begin a criminal career and then later desist.

6. What Caused Offenders to Desist?

    a. Holding a good job

    b. Physical relocation

    c. Marriage

7. Theoretical Modeling

    a. Childhood factors predict teenage antisocial behavior and adult dysfunction.

    b. Personal and social factors are associated with criminal propensity.

    c. Adolescents who have crimogenic tendencies are motivated to offend by their desire for material goods, excitement, and status with peers.

    d. Life events influence behavior.

    e. The chance of offending in any particular situation depends on the perceived costs and benefits of crime and noncrime alternatives.

    f. Factors that encourage criminality at one time during the life course may inhibit it in another.

    g. Adult criminal behavior is predicted by external and internal behaviors.

N. Interactional Theory - Terrence Thornberry

1. Seriously delinquent youths form belief systems that are consistent with their deviant lifestyle.

2. Delinquents form a criminal peer group of individuals with the same interests as their own.

3. Testing Interactional Theory

    a. Current testing and ample evidence supportive of its premise: crime and social relations are Interactional.

    b. Research indicates association with delinquents does increase delinquent involvement.

    c. Delinquency related to weakened attachments to family and education.

    d. Suggests criminality is part of a dynamic social process and not just an outcome.

O. Sampson and Laub: Age-Graded Theory

1. Robert Sampson and John Laub (1993) *Crime in the Making*

2. The stability of delinquent behavior can be affected by events that occur later in life.

3. Turning Points and Social Capital

    a. Life events that enable an adult offender to desist from crime.

    b. Marriage

    c. Career

4. Social Capital - positive relations with individuals and institutions that are life sustaining.

5. Accumulating Social Capital
   a. Building social capital and strong social bonds reduces the likelihood of long-term deviance.

6. Testing Age-Graded Theory
   a. Empirical research shows people change over the life course and factors which predict delinquency in adolescence may have less of an impact on adult crime.
   b. Evidence supports once begun, criminal careers can be reversed if life conditions improve.
   c. Research supports accumulating social capital reduces crime rates.

7. Persistence and Desistance

IV. Commonalities and Distinctions

A. A criminal career has a beginning and an ending.

B. Factors affecting criminal careers could include:
1. Structural factors
   a. Income
   b. Status
2. Socialization factors
   a. Family
   b. Peer Relations
3. Biological factors
   a. Size
   b. Strength
4. Psychological factors
   a. Intelligence
   b. Personality
5. Opportunity factors
   a. Free time
   b. Inadequate police protection
   c. A supply of easily stolen merchandise

C. Latent trait theories assume that it is not people but criminal opportunities that change.

V. Summary

Key Terms

Developmental Criminology - A branch of criminology that examines change in a criminal career over the life course. Developmental factors include biological, social, and psychological change. Among the topics of developmental criminology are desistance, resistance, escalation, and specialization.

Latent Trait - A stable feature, characteristic, property, or condition, present at birth or soon after, that makes some people crime-prone over the life course.

Human Nature Theory - A view that both biological and psychological traits influence the crime-noncrime choice.

General Theory of Crime (GTC) - Gottfredson and Hirschi consider the criminal offender and the criminal act as separate concepts. Self-control is seen as a stabilizing force. Social bonds and self-control are acquired through early experiences with effective parenting. Those without self-control are more prone to crime.

Life Course Theory - A view that even as toddlers, people begin relationships and behaviors that will determine their adult life course.

Problem Behavior Syndrome (PBS) - Some theorists believe that criminality may be a part of a group of antisocial behaviors that cluster together and typically involve family dysfunction, sexual and physical abuse, substance abuse, smoking, precocious sexuality and early pregnancy, educational underachievement, suicide attempts, sensation seeking and unemployment.

Authority Conflict Pathway - One of the Pathways to Crime. Authority Conflict Pathway begins at an early age with stubborn behavior. This leads to defiance and to authority avoidance.

Covert Pathway - One of the Pathways to Crime. Covert Pathway begins with minor, underhanded behavior that leads to property damage. This behavior eventually escalates to more serious forms of criminality, ranging from joy riding to breaking and entering.

Overt Pathway - One of the Pathways to Crime. Overt Pathway escalates to aggressive acts beginning with aggression, leading to physical fighting and then to violence.

Adolescent-Limited - Most offenders antisocial behavior peaks during adolescence and then diminishes.

Life-Course Persister - A small group of offenders who begin their career at an early age and then continue to offend well into adulthood.

Social Development Model (SDM) - A view that a number of community-level risk factors make some people susceptible to develop antisocial behaviors.

Interactional Theory - A view that seriously delinquent youths form belief systems that are consistent with their deviant lifestyle.

Turning Points - Life events which enable adult offenders to desist from crime. Examples include marriage and career.

Social Capital - Positive relations with individuals and institutions that are life-sustaining.

Discussion Exercise

Conduct an anonymous survey of student's deviant behavior as adolescents. Have class analyze results and discuss delinquent behavior in terms of the developmental theories.

InfoTrac Assignment

GETTING STARTED: Search term words for subject guide: Developmental Theories, Latent Trait Theories, Glueck Research, Social Development Model, Sampson and Laub.

CRITICAL THINKING PROJECT: Using the search term "Developmental Theory," find articles that discuss this important theory. Examine this theory and compare it to other theories of crime.

Here are three articles:

Blum, Nathan J., George E. Williams, Patrick C. Friman and Edward R. Christophersen "Disciplining Young Children: The Role of Verbal Instructions and Reasoning." *Pediatrics*.

Gruen, Arno "Reductionist Biological Thinking and the Denial of Experience and Pain In Developmental Theories." *The Journal of Humanistic Psychology*.

Farrall, Stephen "Developmental Theories of Crime and Delinquency." *British Journal of Criminology*.

Test Bank

Essay Questions

1. Compare and contrast the Developmental Theories: Latent Trait and Life Course. What are the commonalities and distinctions?

2. Describe Latent Trait Theories. Where did they get their origin? What is the foundation for Latent Trait Theories? Are they valid theories?

3. Define the General Theory of Crime. Which theorist is this theory attributed to and what is the foundation?

4. What are the areas of General Theory of Crime, which remain unanswered? Do these unanswered areas truly matter in our study of crime causation?

5. Define Differential Coercion Theory. What is its origin and which theorist is credited with this theory? Distinguish between the various types of coercion.

Fill In The Blank

1. As part of the **General Theory of Crime** Gottfredson and Hirschi consider the criminal offender and the criminal act as separate concepts.

2. A view that both biological and psychological traits influence the crime-noncrime choice is the **Human Nature Theory**.

3. **Life-Course Persister** is the small group of offenders who begin their career at an early age and then continue to offend well into adulthood.

4. **Latent Trait** is a stable feature, characteristic, property, or condition; present at birth or soon after that makes some people crime-prone over the life course.

5. **Interactional Theory** is a view that seriously delinquent youths form belief systems that are consistent with their deviant lifestyles.

6. When a theory involves circular reasoning, it is **Tautological**.

7. **Inter-personal coercion** is direct, involving the use or threat of force and intimidation from parents, peers and significant others.

8. **Impersonal coercion** involves pressures beyond individual control, such as economic and social pressure caused by unemployment, poverty, or competition among businesses or other groups.

9. **Coercive ideation** is where the world is conceived as full of coercive forces that can only be overcome through the application of equal or even greater coercive responses.

10. **Control deficit** occurs when a persons desires or impulses are limited by other people's ability to regulate or punish their behavior.

11. **Control surplus** occurs when the amount of control one can exercise over others is in excess of the ability others have to control or modify the person's behavior.

12. **Predation** involves direct forms of physical violence such as robbery, sexual assault or other forms of physical violence.

13. **Defiance** is designed to challenge control mechanisms but stop short of physical harm: vandalism; curfew violations; unconventional sex.

14. **Submission** involves passive obedience to the demands of others such as submitting to physical or sexual abuse without response.

15. **Decadence** involves spur of the moment, irrational acts such as child molesting.

Multiple Choice

1. Most offenders antisocial behavior peaks during adolescence and then diminishes and this is known as:
   a. Adolescent-limited
   b. Life-course persister
   c. Overt pathway
   d. Social capital
   (Answer = a)

2. Life events which enable adult offenders to desist from crime are known as:
   a. Anniversaries
   b. Birthdays
   c. Special occasions
   d. Turning points
   (Answer = d)

3. The view that a number of community-level risk factors make some people susceptible to develop antisocial behaviors is known as:
   a. Left realism
   b. Social development model
   c. Social capital
   d. Developmental criminology
   (Answer = b)

4. Positive relations with individuals and institutions that are life sustaining are known as:
   a. Adolescent-limited
   b. Social development model
   c. Social capital
   d. Turning points
   (Answer = c)

5. The pathway to crime that begins at an early age usually with stubborn behavior is known as:
   a. Authority conflict pathway
   b. Covert pathway
   c. Overt pathway
   d. Social capital
   (Answer = a)

6. The pathway to crime that begins with minor, underhanded behavior that leads to property damage is known as:
   a. Social capital
   b. Authority conflict pathway
   c. Overt pathway
   d. Covert pathway
   (Answer = d)

7. The branch of criminology that examines change in a criminal career over the life course is known as:
   a. Social development model
   b. Developmental criminology
   c. General theory of crime
   d. Social control theory
   (Answer = b)

8. Some theorists believe that criminality may be a part of a group of antisocial behaviors that cluster together and typically involve family dysfunction, sexual and physical abuse, substance abuse, smoking, precocious sexuality and early pregnancy, educational underachievement, suicide attempts, sensation seeking and unemployment and this is known as:
   a. Problem behavior syndrome
   b. General theory of crime
   c. Social development model
   d. Human nature theory
   (Answer = a)

9. A pathway of crime in that aggressive acts begin with aggression, leading to physical fighting and then to violence is:
   a. Social capital
   b. Authority conflict pathway
   c. Overt pathway
   d. Covert pathway
   (Answer = c)

10. The view that even as toddlers, people begin relationships and behaviors that will determine their adult life course is known as:
    a. Social development model
    b. Life course theory
    c. Interactional theory
    d. Human nature theory
    (Answer = b)

11. The theory where Gottfredson and Hirschi consider the criminal offender and the criminal act as separate concepts is called:
    a. Differential Association
    b. Labeling theory
    c. Social reaction theory
    d. General theory of crime
    (Answer = d)

12. The view that both biological and psychological traits influence the crime-noncrime behavior is known as:
    a. Human nature theory
    b. Peacemaking Criminology
    c. Marxist Feminists
    d. Left Realism School
    (Answer = a)

13. A small group of offenders who begin their career at an early age and then continue to offend well into adulthood are known as:
    a. Adolescent-limited
    b. Life-course persister
    c. Social capital
    d. None of the above
    (Answer = b)

14. A stable feature, characteristic, property, or condition, present at birth or soon after that makes some people crime-prone over the life course is known as:
    a. Life-course persister
    b. Overt pathway
    c. Social capital
    d. Latent trait
    (Answer = d)

15. A view that seriously delinquent youths form belief systems that are consistent with their deviant lifestyle is known as:
   a. Human nature theory
   b. Social learning theory
   c. Differential association
   d. Interactional theory
   (Answer = d)

16. According to The General Theory of Crime: an impulsive personality would consist of which of the following:
   a. Physical
   b. Insensitive
   c. Risk-taking
   d. All of the above
   (Answer = d)

17. When a theory involves circular reasoning it is known as:
   a. Ecological
   b. Tautological
   c. Biological
   d. Psychological
   (Answer = b)

18. Which of the following are types of coercion?
   a. inter-personal
   b. impersonal
   c. all of the above
   d. none of the above
   (Answer = c)

19. Coercion that is direct, involving the use or threat of force and intimidation from parents, peers and significant is known as:
   a. Inter-personal
   b. Impersonal
   c. Latent
   d. Personal
   (Answer = a)

20. Coercion that involves pressures beyond individual control, such as economic and social pressure caused by unemployment, poverty, or competition among businesses or other groups is known as:
    a. Personal
    b. Latent
    c. Inter-personal
    d. Impersonal
    (Answer = d)

21. This occurs when a persons desires or impulses are limited by other people's ability to regulate or punish their behavior is known as:
    a. Control deficit
    b. Control surplus
    c. Exploitation
    d. Defiance
    (Answer = a)

22. This occurs when the amount of control one can exercise over others is in excess of the ability others have to control or modify the person's behavior is known as:
    a. Defiance
    b. Exploitation
    c. Control deficit
    d. Control surplus
    (Answer = d)

23. Direct forms of physical violence such as robbery, sexual assault or other forms of physical violence is known as:
    a. Submission
    b. Predation
    c. Defiance
    d. All of the above
    (Answer = b)

24. _____ is designed to challenge control mechanisms but stop short of physical harm: vandalism; curfew violations; unconventional sex.
    a. Predation
    b. Submission
    c. Defiance
    d. All of the above
    (Answer = c)

25. Passive obedience to the demands of others such as submitting to physical or sexual abuse without response is called:
    a. Predation
    b. Defiance
    c. Exploitation
    d. Submission
    (Answer = d)

26. Those who have an excess of control and involve using others to commit crime are known as:
    a. Predation
    b. Defiance
    c. Submission
    d. Exploitation
    (Answer = d)

27. Spur of the moment, irrational acts are known as:
    a. Exploitation
    b. Predation
    c. Defiance
    d. Decadence
    (Answer = c)

28. Which theory says that even as toddlers, people begin relationships and behaviors that will determine their adult life course?
    a. Life course theory
    b. Social control theory
    c. Differential association
    d. Labeling theory
    (Answer = a)

29. Life course theorist conclude which of the following factors influence criminality?
    a. Social
    b. Personal
    c. Economic
    d. All of the above
    (Answer = d)

30. When one has problem behaviors in the social realm, they may exhibit which of the following?
    a. Family dysfunction
    b. Unemployment
    c. Educational underachievement
    d. All of the above
    (Answer = d)

31. When one has problem behaviors in the personal realm, they may exhibit which of the following?
    a. Family dysfunction
    b. Unemployment
    c. Substance abuse
    d. All of the above
    (Answer = c)

32. When one has problem behaviors in the environmental realm, they may exhibit which of the following?
    a. Family dysfunction
    b. Substance abuse
    c. Racism
    d. All of the above
    (Answer = c)

33. Which of the following are pathways to crime?
    a. Authority conflict pathway
    b. Covert pathway
    c. Overt pathway
    d. All of the above
    (Answer = d)

34. Those who begin their offending career at a very early age and then continue to offend well into adulthood are known as:
    a. Life-course persisters
    b. Adolescent limiteds
    c. Subjects
    d. Authorities
    (Answer = a)

35. Which group of delinquents begin to mimic the antisocial behavior of more troubled teens, only to reduce the frequency of their offending as they mature to around age 18?
    a. Life-course persisters
    b. Subjects
    c. Authorities
    d. Adolescent limiteds
    (Answer = d)

36. What percent of violent female offenders begin their criminal careers at a very young age?
    a. 20%
    b. 30%
    c. 60%
    d. 90%
    (Answer = c)

37. According to which theory, a number of community-level risk factors make some people susceptible to developing antisocial behaviors is known as:
    a. General theory of crime
    b. Differential association
    c. Social development model
    d. Labeling theory
    (Answer = c)

38. Children are socialized and develop bonds to their families through which of the following interactions and processes?
    a. Perceived opportunities for involvement in activities and interactions with others
    b. The degree of involvement and interaction with parents
    c. The children's ability to participate in these interactions
    d. All of the above
    (Answer = d)

39. Which theorist is associated with Interactional theory?
    a. Terence Thornberry
    b. Karl Marx
    c. Travis Hirschi
    d. Edwin Sutherland
    (Answer = a)

40. Which theory holds that seriously delinquent youth form belief systems that are consistent with their deviant lifestyle?
    a. Differential association
    b. Labeling theory
    c. Social conflict theory
    d. Interactional theory
    (Answer = d)

True/False

T   1.   Gottfredson and Hirschi suggest that low self-control is a function of an impulsive personality.

F   2.   Inter-personal coercion involves pressures beyond individual control, such as economic and social pressure cause by unemployment, poverty, or competition among businesses or other groups.

F   3.   Impersonal coercion is direct, involving the use or threat of force and intimidation from parents, peers and significant others.

T   4.   Control Balance Theory expands upon the concept of personal control as a predisposing element for criminality.

T   5.   Control deficit occurs when a person desires or impulses are limited by other people's ability to regulate or punish their behavior.

F   6.   Disruptions in life's major transitions can be constructive and ultimately can promote success.

F   7.   Life course theories also recognize that as people mature, the factors that influence their behavior never change.

T   8.   Life course theories are inherently multidimensional.

T   9.   The Gluecks identified a number of personal and social factors related to persistent offending, the most important of which was family relations.

F   10.   The Gluecks research was highly praised for nearly 30 years as the study of crime and delinquency shifted almost exclusively to social factors.

T   11.   As they reach their mid-teens, adolescent-limited delinquents begin to mimic the antisocial behavior of more troubled teens, only to reduce the frequency of their offending as they mature to around age 18.

T   12.   Early-onset delinquents also appear to be more violent than their older peers, who are likely to be involved in nonviolent crimes such as theft.

F   13.   About 100% of violent female offenders began their criminal careers at a very young age.

T   14.   As children mature within their environment, elements of socialization control their developmental process.

T   15. To control the risk of antisocial behavior, a child must maintain pro-social bonds.

Chapter Eleven

Violent Crime

Summary

Chapter Eleven discusses the various types of violent crime in our society. The chapter begins with an examination of the roots of violence and various factors that predispose individuals to violence. The common-law crimes of rape, murder, assault and battery are explained and explanations for cause are offered. The chapter concludes with a discussion on terrorism and the various forms and causes.

Learning Objectives

After reading this chapter the student should be able to:
- Understand the roots of violence.
- Define the personal traits of violence.
- Understand the role of ineffective families and violence.
- Distinguish between Murder and Homicide.
- Explain the functions of the Criminal Law.
- Describe the history of rape.
- Understand the types and causes of rape.
- Understand the differences between assault and battery.

Chapter Overview

Introduction
The Root of Violence
      Personal Traits
      Ineffective Families

Evolutionary
Factors/Human Instinct
Exposure to Violence
Cultural Values
National Values
Substance Abuse
Firearm Availability
Forcible Rape
History of Rape
Incidence of Rape
Types of Rape
The Causes of Rape
Rape and the Law
Murder and Homicide
Degrees of Murder
The Nature and Extent of Murder
Murderous Relations
Types of Murders
Assault and Battery
Nature and Patterns of Assault
Assault in the Home
Robbery
Emerging Forms of Interpersonal Violence
Hate Crimes
Workplace Violence
Terrorism
Forms of Terrorism
Extent of Terrorism
Causes of Terrorism
Responses to Terrorism
Summary

Chapter Outline

I.   **Introduction**
II.   **The Roots of Violence**
       A. Personal Traits - Psychologist Dorothy Otnow Lewis and her associates found
          murderous youths suffer:
          1. Major neurological impairment
             a. Abnormal EEGs
             b. Multiple psychomotor impairment
             c. Severe seizures

2. Low intelligence
3. Psychotic close relatives
4. Psychotic symptoms
    a. Paranoia
    b. Illogical thinking
    c. Hallucinations
B. Ineffective Families - the following are linked to persistent violent offending.
    1. Absent or deviant parents
    2. Inconsistent discipline
    3. Lack of supervision
    4. Physical punishment without support, warmth and care
    5. Abused Children
        a. Research indicates that abused children engage in delinquent behaviors more than unabused children.
        b. Lonnie Athens, criminologist, links violence to child abuse and classifies aggressive people into the following:
            1. Nonviolent
            2. Violent - those who attack others physically with the intention of harming them.
            3. Incipiently violent - those who are willing and ready to attack but limit themselves to violent ultimatums and/or intimidating physical gestures.
        c. Athens, found 4 distinct types of violent acts:
            1. Physically defensive - perpetrator sees his violent act as one of self-defense.
            2. Frustrative - offender acts out of anger due to frustration when they cannot get their way.
            3. Malefic - victim is considered to be extremely evil or malicious.
            4. Frustrative-malefic - a combined type.
        d. Antisocial careers are created in a series of stages that begin with brutal episodes:
            1. Brutalization process - young victim begins the process of developing a belligerent, angry demeanor. Brutalization can result from subjugation, personal horrification, and violent coaching by peers.
            2. Brutalized youth may become belligerent and angry. They respond with violent performances of angry, hostile behavior.
            3. Virulency stage - emerging criminals develop a violent identity that makes them feared; they enjoy intimidating others.
            4. Violentization process - one must complete the full cycle - belligerence, violence performances and virulencey to become socialized into violence.
C. Evolutionary Factors/Human Instinct
    1. Freud believed that human aggression and violence are produced by instinctual drives.

        a. Eros - life instinct - drives people to self-fulfillment and enjoyment

        b. Thanatos - death instinct - produces self-destruction

           1. externally - violence or sadism

           2. internally - suicide, alcoholism, or other self-destructive habits.

    2. Evolutionary theories suggest that violent behavior is mostly committed by males.

D. Exposure To Violence - those constantly exposed to violence are more likely to adopt violent methods.

    1. Crusted Over - condition children living in violence adopt; they do not let others inside, nor do they express their feelings. They exploit others and allow themselves to be exploited.

E. Substance Abuse - influences violence by the following:

    1. Psychopharmacological relationship - High does of PCI and amphetamines may produce violent, aggressive behavior. Alcohol abuse associated with all forms of violence.

    2. Economic Compulsive behavior - drug users resort to violence to support their habit.

F. Firearm Availability - if weapons are available, violence escalates.

G. Cultural Values

    1. Subculture of violence - areas where violence seems to cluster together. Violence influences lifestyles, socialization, and interpersonal relationships. Usually found in areas with concentrated poverty and social disorganization.

    2. Social Movements - members of radical political and social movements contributes to violence.

    3. Ganging - members likely to own guns, drug trafficking, and turf protection.

    4. Regional Values - South has higher rates of violence and homicide.

H. National Values - Some nations have higher rates of violence: United States, Sri Lanka, Angola, Uganda and the Philippines.

III.   **Forcible Rape** - the carnal knowledge of a female forcibly and against her will.

A. History of Rape - Babylonian Law - punishable by death

    1. Rape and the Military - throughout history, rape has been associated with armies and warfare.

B. Incidence of Rape

    1. UCR data - 90,000 rapes or attempted rapes reported to police in 2000.

    2. NCVS data - 260,000 rapes and attempted rapes took place.

C. Types of Rape/Rapists

    1. Anger Rape - sexuality becomes a way of expressing and discharging pent-up anger and rage.

    2. Power Rape - does not want to harm the victim, but wants to possess her sexually.

    3. Sadistic Rape - involves sexuality and aggression. Victim may be tormented, bound or tortured.

    4. Gangs vs. Individual Rape -

      a.   Gang rapes usually more severe. Victim more likely to call police and to consider suicide.

   5. Serial Rape - rapists who commit more than one rape in their lifetime.

   6. Acquaintance Rape - involves someone known to the victim, including family members and friends.

      a.   Date Rape - sexual attack during a courting relationship.

      b.   Martial Rape - forcible sex between people who are legally married.

      c.   Statutory Rape - the victim is underage.

D. The Causes of Rape

   1. Evolutionary/Biological Factors - rape may be instinctual, developed over the ages as a means of perpetuating the species.

   2. Male Socialization - a function of modern male socialization.

      a.   Virility mystique - belief that males must separate their sexual feelings from needs for love, respect and affection.

   3. Hypermasculinity - men who have a callous sexual attitude and believe that violence is manly.

   4. Psychological Abnormality - view that rapists suffer from a personality disorder or mental illness.

   5. Social Learning - perspective that men learn to commit rapes as they learn other behavior.

   6. Sexual Motivation

      a.   Power and control

      b.   Sexual Gratification

E. Rape and the Law - created the most conflict in the law

   1. Proving Rape - extremely challenging for prosecutors

   2. Suspiciousness - U.S. sexism causes a cultural suspiciousness of women - often seen as provocateurs in sexual encounters with men.

   3. Consent - must prove that the attack was forced and the victim did not give voluntary content to the attacker.

   4. Reform - efforts include:

      a.   Changing the language of statutes

      b.   Dropping the condition of victim resistance

      c.   Changing the requirement of use of force to include threat of force or injury.

      d.   Shield laws - protect women form being questioned about sexual history unless it directly bears on the case.

   5. The Limits of Reform - prosecutors may still influence their decision on the circumstances of the crime.

IV. **Murder and Homicide** - the unlawful killing of a human being with malice aforethought." - the most serious crime and can be punished by death.

A. Degrees of Murder

   1. First-degree murder - person kills after premeditation and deliberation.

      a.   Premeditation - killing considered beforehand and it was motivated by more than a desire to engage in violence.

     b. Deliberation - killing planned after careful thought rather than impulse.

  2. Second-degree murder - killer must have malice aforethought but not premeditation or deliberation.

  3. Manslaughter - homicide without malice.

     a. Voluntary manslaughter - killing committed in heat of passion or during a sudden quarrel that provoked violence.

     b. Involuntary manslaughter - killing that occurs when one is negligent and without regard for the harm they may cause others.

  4. "Born and Alive" - whether a murder victim can be a fetus that has not been delivered - feticide.

B. The Nature and Extent of Murder

  1. Currently on the decline in the U.S.

  2. Tends to be an urban crime.

  3. Victims and offenders tend to be males.

  4. About 1/3 of murder victims are under 25.

  5. About 1/2 of murder offenders are under 25.

  6. Half of murder victims are African-American and half are Caucasian.

  7. Murder, tends to be, intra-racial.

  8. Infanticide - murders which involve very young children.

  9. Eldercide - murders which involve senior citizens.

C. Murderous Relations - murders occur more frequently among people with relationships rather than strangers.

  1. Spousal Relations

  2. Personal Relations

  3. Student Relations

D. Serial Murder

  1. Serial Murderers and Their Motivations

     a. Long histories of violence

     b. Maintain superficial relationships with others

     c. Have trouble relating to the opposite sex

     d. Feel guilty about their interest in sex

     e. Sociopaths, who from early childhood demonstrate bizarre behavior and this behavior extends to the pleasure they reap from killing, their ability to ignore or enjoy their victims' suffering, and their propensity for basking in the media limelight when apprehended for their crimes.

  2. Female Serial Killers

     a. Estimated 10-15% of serial killers are women.

     b. More likely to poison or smother their victims.

     c. More likely to lure victims to their death.

  3. Controlling Serial Killers

     a. FBI developed a profiling system to identity potential suspects.

     b. Justice Department's Violent Criminal Apprehension Program - computerized information service, gathers information and matches offense characteristics on violent crimes around the country.

V.   Assault and Battery

A. Battery - offensive touching, such as slapping, hitting or punching a victim.
B. Assault - requires no actual touching, but involves either attempted battery or intentionally frightening the victim by word or deed.
C. Nature and Patterns of Assault
    1. Common in our society
    2. Road rage - motorists who assault each other.
D. The Nature and Extent of Assaults
    1. FBI recorded less than 910,000 assaults in year 2000.
    2. Assaults on the decline.
    3. Offenders are more often:
        a. Young
        b. Male
        c. White
    4. Emergency Room Data
        a. 1.4 million people treated for violence-related injuries
        b. 40% of injuries were serious
        c. 60% did not involve a weapon
E. Assault in the Home - intrafamily violence is an enduring problem in U.S.
    1. Child Abuse
        a. Actual physical beatings administered to a child by hands, feet, weapons, belts, sticks, burning and so on.
        b. Neglect - Not providing a child with the care and shelter to which he or she is entitled.
    2. Sexual Abuse - exploitation of children through rape, incest, and molestation by parents or other adults.
    3. Causes of Child Abuse
        a. Family violence perpetuated from one generation to the next.
        b. Abusive parent behavior can often be traced to negative childhood experiences.
        c. Blended families have been linked to abuse.
        d. Parents may become abusive if isolated from friends, neighbors or relatives.
    4. Spousal Abuse - occurred throughout recorded history.
    5. The Nature and Extent of Spousal Abuse
        a. 60-70% of evening calls to police involve domestic disputes.
        b. 1 in 5 high school girls suffered sexual or physical abuse from a boyfriend.
        c. Batters tend to fall into 2 categories:
            1. Pit Bulls - emotions are quick to erupt, are driven by deep insecurity and dependence on the wives and partners they abuse; tend to become stalkers, unable to let go of relationships once they have ended.

2. Cobras - coolly and methodically inflict pain and humiliation on their mates. See violence as an unavoidable part of life.
F. Robbery - the taking or attempting to take anything of value for the care, custody or control of a person or persons by force or threat of force or violence and/or by putting the victim in fear.
G. Emerging Forms of Interpersonal Violence
   1. Hate Crimes - Violent acts directed toward a particular person or members of a group because the target s share a discernible racial, ethnic, religious or gender characteristic.
      a. The Roots of Hate - generally spontaneous incidents motivated by the victims' walking, driving, shopping or socializing in an area where the attackers do not feel they belong.
         1. McDevit and Levin identify 3 types of hate crimes:
            a. Thrill-seeking hate crimes
            b. Reactive hate crimes
            c. Mission hate crimes
   2. Nature and Extent of Hate Crime
      a. During 2000, reported 8,063 bias-motivated crimes
      b. Resulted in 19 murders
      c. 60% involve a violent act
      d. 60% are motivated by race
   3. Punishing Hate Crimes - some argue that punishment should be more severe than the same crime without the bias.
   4. Workplace Violence - typical offender is middle-aged white male who faces termination in a worsening economy.
      a. The Extent of Workplace Violence
         1. More than 2 million U.S. residents become victims of violent workplace crime.
      b. Can Workplace Violence Be Controlled?
         1. Use of restorative justice tactics is helpful.
         2. Aggressive job retraining.
         3. Continued medical coverage after layoffs.
   5. Stalking - a course of conduct directed at a specific person that involves repeated physical or visual proximity, nonconsensual communication, or verbal, written, or implied threats sufficient to cause fear in a reasonable person.
      a. Affects 1.4 million victims annually.
      b. Most victims know their stalker.
      c. Women are most likely to be stalked by an intimate partner.
VI. **Terrorism**
   A. What is Terrorism?
      1. Involves the illegal use of force against innocent people to achieve a political objective.

2. U.S. State Department says terrorism - premeditated, politically motivated violence perpetrated against noncombatant targets by sub-national groups or clandestine agents usually intended to influence an audience.
3. International terrorism - terrorism involving citizens or the territory of more than one country.
4. Terrorist Group - any group practicing, or that has significant subgroups that practice, international terrorism.

B. Terrorists and Guerillas - interchangeable terms
1. Terrorists:
   a. Urban focus.
   b. Operate in small bands or cadres - 3 to 5 members
   c. Target the property or person of their enemy
2. Guerillas:
   a. Located in rural areas
   b. Attack the military, police and government officials
   c. Organizations grow large

C. A Brief History of Terror - throughout history
1. Assassination of Julius Caesar - March 15, 44 B.C.
2. Middle Ages
3. French Revolution
4. World War II

D. Contemporary Forms of Terrorism
1. Revolutionary Terrorists - use violence to frighten those in power and to replace the existing government with a regime that holds acceptable political or religious views.
2. Political Terrorists - directed at those who oppose the terrorists' political ideology.
3. Nationalist Terrorism - promotes the interests of a minority ethnic or religious group that feels it has been persecuted under majority rule and wants independence.
4. Cause-Based Terrorism - Against individuals and/or governments to whom they object.
5. Environmental Terrorism - acts to prevent the use of land or animals for human consumption.
6. State-Sponsored Terrorism - occurs when a repressive governmental regime forces its citizens into obedience, oppresses minorities, and stifles political dissent.
7. Nuclear Terrorism - the threat or act with nuclear weapons.
8. Criminal Terrorism - sometimes terrorist groups become involved in common law crimes such as drug dealing and kidnapping to fund their activities.

E. What Motivates Terrorism?
1. Emotionally disturbed individuals who act out their psychosis within the confines of violent groups.
2. Hold extreme ideological beliefs that prompt their behavior.

3. May be motivated by feelings of alienation and failure to comprehend post-technological society.

 F. Responses to Terrorism - U.S. policy:

  1. Make no concessions and strike no deals.

  2. Bring terrorist to justice for their crimes.

  3. Isolate and apply pressure on states that sponsor terrorism to force them to change their behavior and

  4. Bolster the counter-terrorism capabilities of those countries that work with U.S. and require assistance.

VII. Summary

Key Terms

Instrumental Violence - Violence designed to improve the financial or social position of the criminal.

Expressive Violence - Violence that is designed not for profit or gain but to vent rage, anger, or frustration.

Electroencephalogram (EEG) - The most important measure of neurophysiological functioning. An EEG records the electrical impulses given off by the brain.

Brutalization Process - According to Athens, the first stage in a violent career during which parents victimize children, causing them to develop a belligerent, angry demeanor.

Eros - The most basic human drive present at birth; the instinct to preserve and create life.

Thanatos - According to Freud, the instinctual drive toward aggression and violence.

Subculture of Violence - In this subculture, a potent theme of violence influences lifestyles, the socialization process, and interpersonal relationships.

Systemic Link - Violent behavior that results from the conflict inherent in the drug trade.

Rape - (from the Latin rapere, to take by force) is defined in common law as "the carnal knowledge of a female forcibly and against her will."

Acquaintance Rape - Rape by someone known to the victim, possibility including family members and friends.

Date Rape - Rape involving people in some form of courting relationship.

Martial Rape - Rape of a woman by her husband.

Martial Exemption - The practice in some states of prohibiting the prosecution of husbands for the rape of their wives.

Statutory Rape - Sexual relations between an underage minor female and an adult male. Sex does not have to be forced or coerced; the law says that young girls are incapable of giving informed consent.

Virility Mystique - The belief that males must separate their sexual feelings from needs for love, respect, and affection.

Hypermasculine - Men who typically have a callous sexual attitude and believe that violence is manly.

Consent - In a rape case, the absence of consent is essential to prove that the rape did occur.

Shield Laws - Laws that protect women from being questioned about their sexual history unless it directly bears on the case.

Felony Murder - Killing a human being with malice aforethought.

Thrill Killing - The most common form of serial murderer. Thrill killers strive for either sexual sadism or dominance.

Serial Murder - The killing of a large number of people over time by an offender who seeks to escape detection.

Mass Murder - The killing of a large number of people in a single incident by an offender who typically does not seek concealment or escape.

Battery - Requires offensive touching, such as slapping, hitting, or punching a victim.

Assault - Requires no actual touching, but involves either attempted battery or intentionally frightening the victim by word or deed.

Child Abuse - Any physical, emotional, or sexual trauma to a child for which no reasonable explanation, such as an accident, can be found. Child abuse can also be a function of neglecting to give proper care and attention to a young child.

Neglect - Not providing a child with the care and shelter to which he or she is entitled.

Sexual Abuse - The exploitation of children through rape, incest and molestation by parents or other adults.

Robbery - The taking or attempting to take anything of value from the care, custody or control of a person or persons by force or threat of force or violence and/or by putting the victim in fear.

Hate Crimes - Bias Crimes, which are violent acts, directed toward a particular person or members of a group merely because the targets share a discernible racial, ethnic, religious or gender characteristic.

Bias Crimes - See Hate Crime.

Workplace Violence - Irate employees or former employees attacking coworkers or sabotaging machinery and production lines. Workplace violence is now considered the third leading cause of occupational injury or death.

Conventional Criminals - Those who violate the law who believe their actions will ultimately benefit society.

Terrorism - An act that must carry with it the intent to disrupt and change the government and must not be merely a common-law crime committed for greed or egotism.

Guerrilla - Located in rural areas and attack the military, the police and government officials.

Discussion Exercise

Assign groups to various terrorism events that have occurred in the last 10 years in the United States and abroad. Key events may include the September 11, 2001 attack on the United States, the Oklahoma City Bombing, events in the Middle East and the Unabomber.

InfoTrac Assignment

GETTING STARTED: Search term words for subject guide: Violence, Forcible Rape, Murder, Homicide, Assault, Battery, Hate Crimes, Terrorism.

CRITICAL THINKING PROJECT: Using the search term "Murder," find relevant articles.

Here are three articles:

Gesalman, Anne Belli and Lynette Clemetson "A Crazy System: As the Yates Family Assesses Andrea's Life Sentence, A Nation Ponders Its Method of Coping With Madness." *Newsweek.*

"Catching the Killer; U.S. Seeks Justice for Death of U.S. Journalist." *Current Events.*

Breslau, Karen "A Deadly Weapon: A Dog is No Different Than a Gun. Or So the Jury Ruled in Convicting California's Most Notorious Pet Owners." *Newsweek.*

Test Bank

Essay Questions

1. Define Terrorism. What are the various forms of terrorism? What is the United States plan against terrorism? Is this sufficient?

2. Describe the events of 9/11 in the United States. What type of terrorist acts were committed? Who was responsible and what was the purpose of the attack? What type of terrorist were involved in the 9/11 attack against the United States?
3. Compare and contrast Assault and Battery. Where do these crimes occur most frequently and what are the some of the precipitators?
4. What are Hate Crimes? Give three examples of recent hate crimes. How should we punish hate crime offenders? What can be done to prevent hate crimes?
5. Define Workplace Violence. Which occupations are most likely to encounter workplace violence? What are some methods that may be used to cut-down or eliminate violence in the workplace?

Fill In The Blank

1. Rape involving people in some form of courting relationship is known as **Date Rape**.

2. Serial killers who strive for either sexual sadism or dominance or known as **Thrill Killers**.

3. According to Freud, **Thanatos** is the instinctual drive toward aggression and violence.

4. **Electroencephalogram** is the most important measure of neurophysiological functioning.

5. **Eros** is the most basic human drive present at birth; the instinct to preserve and create life.

6. An act that must carry with it the intent to disrupt and change the government and must not be merely a common-law crime committed for greed or egotism is known as **Terrorism**.

7. **Systemic Link** is violent behavior that results from the conflict inherent in the drug trade.

8. **Expressive Violence** is violence that is designed not for profit or gain but to vent rage, anger or frustration.

9. **Felony Murder** is killing a human being with malice aforethought.

10. **Subculture of violence** occurs where a potent theme of violence influences lifestyles, the socialization process and interpersonal relationships.

11. **Statutory Rape** occurs when there are sexual relations between an underage minor female and an adult male.

12. **Shield Laws** are laws that protect women from being questioned about their sexual history unless it directly bears upon the case.

13. **Sexual Abuse** is the exploitation of children through rape, incest and molestation by parents or other adults.

14. **Serial Murder** involves the killing of a large number of people over time by an offender who seeks to escape detection.

15. **Guerillas** are individuals located in rural areas that attack the military, the police and government officials.

Multiple Choice

1. Rape by someone known to the victim, possibility including family members and friends is known as:
   a. Acquaintance Rape
   b. Date Rape
   c. Stranger Rape
   d. Gang Rape
   (Answer = a)

2. Requires no actual touching, but involves either attempted battery or intentionally frightening the victim by word or deed is known as:
   a. Battery
   b. Rape
   c. Murder
   d. Assault
   (Answer = d)

3. Those who violate the law who believe their actions will ultimately benefit society are known as:
   a. Terrorists
   b. Conventional criminals
   c. Serial killers
   d. Rapists
   (Answer = b)

4. In a rape case, the absence of _____ is essential to prove that the rape did occur.
   a. Assault
   b. Penetration
   c. Consent
   d. All of the above
   (Answer = c)

5. Any physical, emotional, or sexual trauma to a child for which no reasonable explanation, such as an accident, can be found is known as:
   a. Child abuse
   b. Elder abuse
   c. Hate crimes
   d. Cruelty to animals
   (Answer = a)

6. According to Athens, the first stage in a violent career during which parents victimize children, causing them to develop a belligerent, angry demeanor is known as:
   a. Honeymoon stage
   b. Verbal abuse
   c. Child abuse
   d. Brutalization process
   (Answer = d)

7. Another name for hate crime is:
   a. Terrorism
   b. Bias crime
   c. Serial killing
   d. Gang rape
   (Answer = b)

8. The crime which requires offensive touching, such as slapping, hitting, or punching a victim is known as:
   a. Battery
   b. Assault
   c. Rape
   d. Murder
   (Answer = a)

9. The belief that males must separate their sexual feelings from needs for love, respect and affection is:
   a. Hypermasculine
   b. Martial exemption
   c. Virility mystique
   d. Subculture of violence
   (Answer = c)

10. When irate employees or former employees attack coworkers or sabotage machinery and production lines it is known as:
   a. Terrorism
   b. Workplace violence
   c. Stalking
   d. Instrumental violence
   (Answer = b)

11. Rape involving people in some form of courting relationship is called:
   a. Stranger rape
   b. Gang rape
   c. Serial killer rape
   d. Date rape
   (Answer = d)

12. The most common form of serial murder where killer strive for either sexual sadism or dominance is known as:
   a. Thrill killing
   b. Random killing
   c. Accidental killing
   d. Felony murder
   (Answer = a)

13. According to Freud, the instinctual drive toward aggression and violence is known as:
   a. Terrorism
   b. Thanatos
   c. Thrill killing
   d. Hate crimes
   (Answer = b)

14. An act that must carry with it the intent to disrupt and change the government and must not be merely a common-law crime committed for greed or egotism is known as:
   a. Statutory rape
   b. Felony murder
   c. Assault
   d. Terrorism
   (Answer = d)

15. The most important measure of neurophysiological functioning is known as:
   a. An IQ test
   b. TB test
   c. Metal Detectors
   d. Electroencephalogram
   (Answer = d)

16. The most basic human drive present at birth; the instinct to preserve and create life is known as:
    a. Ego
    b. Id
    c. Superego
    d. Eros
    (Answer = d)

17. Violence that is designed not for profit or gain but to vent rage, anger or frustration is known as:
    a. Terrorism
    b. Expressive violence
    c. Stalking
    d. Gang banging
    (Answer = b)

18. Killing a human being with malice aforethought is known as:
    a. assault
    b. battery
    c. felony murder
    d. misdemeanor murder
    (Answer = c)

19. Individuals are located in rural areas and attack the military, the police and government officials and are known as:
    a. Guerillas
    b. Cobras
    c. Pit-bulls
    d. Snakes
    (Answer = a)

20. Violent acts directed toward a particular person or members of a group merely because the targets share a discernible racial, ethnic, religious or gender characteristic are known as:
    a. Instrumental violence
    b. Felony murder
    c. Subculture of violence
    d. Hate crimes
    (Answer = d)

21. Men who typically have a callous sexual attitude and believe that violence is manly are known as:
   a. Hypermasculine
   b. Feminist
   c. Virility mystique
   d. All of the above
   (Answer = a)

22. Violent behavior that results from the conflict inherent in the drug trade is known as:
   a. Subculture of violence
   b. Shield laws
   c. Sexual abuse
   d. Systemic link
   (Answer = d)

23. A potent theme of violence influences lifestyles, the socialization process and interpersonal relationships is in which subculture?
   a. Thanatos
   b. Subculture of violence
   c. Terrorists
   d. Serial killers
   (Answer = b)

24. Sexual relations between an underage minor female and an adult male is known as:
   a. Consent
   b. Marital rape
   c. Statutory rape
   d. Gang rape
   (Answer = c)

25. Laws that protect women from being questioned about their sexual history unless it directly bears on the case are called:
   a. Statutory laws
   b. Marital laws
   c. Real estate laws
   d. Shield laws
   (Answer = d)

26. The exploitation of children through rape, incest and molestation by parents or other adults is known as:
   a. Terrorism
   b. Thrill killing
   c. Robbery
   d. Sexual abuse
   (Answer = d)

27. The killing of a large number of people over time by an offender who seeks to escape detection is known as:
    a. Mass murder
    b. Hate crimes
    c. Serial murder
    d. Martial rape
    (Answer = c)

28. The taking or attempting to take anything of value form the care, custody or control of a person or persons by force or threat of force or violence and/or by putting the victim in fear is known as:
    a. Robbery
    b. Rape
    c. Murder
    d. Felony murder
    (Answer = a)

29. The carnal knowledge of a female forcibly and against her will is known as:
    a. Robbery
    b. Murder
    c. Felony murder
    d. Rape
    (Answer = d)

30. The killing of a large number of people in a single incident by an offender who typically doe not seek concealment or escapes is which of the following?
    a. Rape
    b. Serial murder
    c. Gang banging
    d. Mass murder
    (Answer = d)

31. The rape of a woman by her husband is known as:
    a. Gang rape
    b. Serial rape
    c. Marital rape
    d. Sexual abuse
    (Answer = c)

32. The practice in some states of prohibiting the prosecution of husbands for the rape of their wives is known as:
    a. Shield laws
    b. Marital rape
    c. Marital exemption
    d. Sexual abuse
    (Answer = c)

33. Violence designed to improve the financial or social position of the criminal is known as:
    a. Subculture of violence
    b. Expressive violence
    c. Hate crimes
    d. Instrumental violence
    (Answer = d)

34. Athens finds that people can be classified into which of the following based on their aggressive tendencies?
    a. Nonviolent
    b. Brutalization
    c. Frustrative-malefic
    d. Malefic
    (Answer = a)

35. Which of the following are types of violent acts?
    a. Physically defensive
    b. Frustrative
    c. Malefic
    d. All of the above
    (Answer = d)

36. Which of the following are stages that lead to antisocial behavior?
    a. Brutalization process
    b. Virulency stage
    c. All of the above
    d. None of the above
    (Answer = c)

37. According to the most recent UCR data, about _____ rapes or attempted rapes were reported to U.S. police in 2000.
    a. 9,000,000
    b. 900,000
    c. 90,000
    d. 9
    (Answer = c)

38. When an attacker does not want to harm his victim as much as he wants to possess her sexually, it is known as:
    a. Anger rape
    b. Gang rape
    c. Serial rape
    d. Power rape
    (Answer = d)

39. Which rapist is bound up in ritual - tormenting their victim, binding her or torturing her?
    a. Sadistic rapist
    b. Anger rapist
    c. Gang rapist
    d. Power rapist
    (Answer = a)

40. Men who engage in multiple rapes are known as:
    a. Gang rapist
    b. Power rapist
    c. Anger rapist
    d. Serial rapist
    (Answer = d)

True/False

T   1.   Evolutionary theories in criminology suggest that violent behavior is predominantly committed by males because over the course of human existence, sexually aggressive males have been the ones most likely to produce children.

F   2.   People who are constantly exposed to violence at home, at school, or in the environment will never adopt violent methods themselves.

F   3.   Substance abuse has no link to violence in our society.

T   4.   The Uniform Crime Report indicate that two thirds of all murders and about 40 percent of all robberies involve firearms.

T   5.   Membership in radical political and social movements contribute to violence.

F   6.   The virility mystique is that men typically have a callous sexual attitude and believe that violence is manly.

F   7.   Hypermasculine men typically believe that males must separate their sexual feelings from needs for love, respect, and affection.

T   8. A number of states and the federal government have replaced rape laws with the more sexually neutral crimes of sexual assault.

T   9. Most states and the federal government have developed shield laws, which protect women from being questioned about their sexual history unless it directly bears on the case.

F   10. Murder is defined as the lawful killing of a human being with malice aforethought.

T   11. Murders in which involve senior citizens are the victims are referred to as eldercide

T   12. The younger the child the greater the risk for infanticide.

F   13. Most murders occur among strangers.

T   14. An estimated 10 to 15 percent of serial killers are women.

T   15. Thrill killers strive for either sexual sadism or dominance.

Chapter Twelve

Property Crimes

Summary

Chapter Twelve describes the various property crimes in our society. The chapter begins with a brief history of theft and an explanation of modern thieves. The various types of larceny/theft are defined with special emphasis on the crime of burglary. Chapter Twelve concludes with a description of arson and the various types of arsonists.

Learning Objectives

After reading this chapter the student should be able to:
- Be able to explain the history of theft.
- Distinguish between occasional criminals and professional criminals.
- Understand the varieties of larceny.
- Explain auto theft and methods of combating auto theft.
- Describe false pretense or fraud.
- Understand embezzlement.
- Define burglary.
- Understand the nature and extent of burglary.
- Explore the rationale for one seeking a career in burglary.
- Define arson.

Chapter Overview

Introduction
A Brief History of Theft
Modern Thieves
      Occasional Criminals
      Professional Criminals
Larceny/Theft

Chapter Outline

I. Introduction

II. A Brief History of Theft

A. Economic crimes - acts in violation of the criminal law designed to bring financial reward to the offender.

B. Theft has been recorded throughout history.

1. 11th Century -Crusades - inspired peasants and noblemen to prey upon passing pilgrims.

2. 13th Century - Peasants poached the king's game and robbed strangers.

3. 14th Century - Livestock thieves - stealing cattle and sheep.

4. 15th and 16th Century - Hundred Years War - foreign mercenaries looted and pillaged the countryside.

5. 18th Century - 3 groups of property criminals were active:

   a. Skilled Thieves - worked in larger cities. Pickpockets, forgers and counterfeiters. Gathered in flash houses-public meeting places. Gang headquarters.

   b. Smugglers - Transported goods without bothering to pay tax or duty.

   c. Poachers - lived in the country and lived on game that belonged to the landlord.

III. Modern Thieves

A. Occasional Criminals

1. Commit most of the annual property and theft-related crimes and do not see themselves as criminals.

2. Situational inducement - short-term influences on a person's behavior that increase risk-taking.

B. Professional Criminals - skilled, theft-oriented, career criminal

1. Sutherland's Professional Criminal - thieves who use no force or physical violence in their crimes and live solely by their wits and skill.
2. Professional Criminals: The Fence - a buyer and seller of stolen merchandise.
   a. Upfront Cash - all deals are cash transactions.
   b. Knowledge of dealing: learning the ropes - knowledge of the trade.
   c. Connections with suppliers of stolen goods - able to engage in long-term relationships with suppliers of high-value stolen goods.
   d. Connections with buyers - must have continuous access to buyers of stolen merchandise.
   e. Complicity with law enforcers - must work out a relationship with law enforcement officials to stay in business.
3. The Nonprofessional Fence - significant portion of all fencing is done by amateur or occasional criminals.
   a. Associational fences - amateur bartering stolen goods for services.
   b. Neighborhood hustlers - buy and sell stolen property as one way to make a living.
   c. Amateur receivers - strangers approached publicly by one offering a deal on commodities.

IV. **Larceny/Theft** - early common-law crime created by English judges - act where one took for his/her own uses the property of another.
   A. Larceny Today
      1. Petit (petty) Larceny
         a. Small amounts of money or property
         b. Punished as a misdemeanor.
      2. Grand Larceny
         a. Involves merchandise of greater value
         b. Considered a felony
         c. Punished in State prison
   B. Varieties of Larceny
      1. Shoplifting - common form of theft - taking of goods from retail stores.
         a. Boosters or Heels - professional shoplifters who steal intending to resell stolen merchandise to pawnshops or fences.
         b. Snitches - majority of shoplifters - amateur pilfers - systematic shoplifters who steal for their own use.
         c. Controlling Shoplifting
            1. Less than 10% of shoplifting incidents are detected by store employees.
            2. Customers are unwilling to report crimes.
         d. Prevention Strategies
            1. Target Removal Strategies - using display dummy goods while locking up the "real" merchandise.
            2. Target Hardening Strategies - locking goods into place or having them monitored by electronic systems.

3. Electronic Article Surveillance Systems - tags with small electronic sensors that trip sound and light alarms if not removed.
4. Source Tagging - process of manufacturers embedding the tag in packaging or in the product itself.
5. Situational measures - place the most valuable goods in the least vulnerable places, use warning signs and closed-circuit cameras.
2. Bad Checks - knowingly and intentionally drawing money on a nonexistent or underfunded bank account.
   a. Naïve check forgers - amateurs who do not believe their actions will hurt anyone; usually have a financial crisis that demands an immediate resolution.
   b. Closure - naïve check writers who have a financial crisis such as pressing bills or lost money at the track.
   c. Systemic Forgers - make a substantial living by passing bad checks.
3. Credit Card Theft - major problem in the U.S.
C. Auto Theft - common larceny offense.
   1. Categories of Auto Theft
      a. Joyriding - do not steal for profit, but to experience the benefits associated with owning an automobile. Often teenagers.
      b. Short-term transportation - similar to joyriding. Theft of a car to go from one place to another.
      c. Long-term transportation - intend to keep cars for personal use.
      d. Profit - for monetary gain. Some are professionals who resell expensive cars; others are amateurs who may strip the vehicle of parts.
      e. Commission of another crime - some steal cars to use in other crimes.
   2. Which cars are taken most?: According to National Insurance Crime Bureau:
      a. Toyota Camry
      b. Honda Accord
      c. Followed by: Oldsmobile Cutlass, Honda Civic, Jeep Cherokee, Chevy Pickup, Toyota Corolla, Chevrolet Caprice, Ford Taurus and Ford F150 Pickup
   3. Carjacking - Type of auto theft where gunmen approach car and force the owner to give up the keys.
D. Combating Auto Theft
   1. Increase the risk of apprehension
   2. Information hot-lines
   3. Lojack System - hidden tracking device installed in cars
   4. Publicity campaigns
E. False Pretense or Fraud - misrepresenting a fact that a victim willingly gives up property to the offender, who keeps it.
   1. Confidence Games - Run by swindlers who aspire to separate the victim from his or her money.
      a. Mark - that target of a con man or woman
      b. Pigeon drop - most common con game.

F. Embezzlement - when one who is trusted with property fraudulently keeps it for their own use or the use of others.

V. **Burglary** - forcible entry into a home or place of work for theft.
   A. The Nature and Extent of Burglary - UCR reports 2 million burglaries in 2000; NVCS reported 3.4 million residential burglaries in 2000.
      1. Residential Burglary
      2. Commercial Burglary
   B. Careers in Burglary
      1. Good burglar - professional burglars who have distinguished themselves:
         a. technical competence
         b. maintenance of personal integrity
         c. specialization in burglary
         d. financial success
         e. ability to avoid prison sentences
      2. The Burglary "Career Ladder."
         a. Young novices - learn the trade from older more experienced burglars.
         b. Novices - continue to get tutoring as long as they develop their own markets (fences) for stolen goods.
         c. Journeyman stage - forays in search of lucrative targets and careful planning.
      3. Repeat Burglary - research indicates that many burglars will return to the "scene of the crime" in order to repeat their offenses.

VI. **Arson** - willful and malicious burning of a home, public building, vehicle, or commercial building.
   A. Motives for Arson
      1. Adult arsonists - severe emotional turmoil.
      2. Juvenile arsonists - associated with conduct problems, disobedience, aggressiveness, anger, hostility and resentment over parental rejection.
      3. Professional arsonist - engage in arson for profit. People looking to collect insurance money, but afraid to set the fire, may hire a professional arsonist.
      4. Arson fraud - a business owner burning his or her own property, or hiring someone to do it, to escape financial problems.

VII. **Summary**

Key Terms

✓**Fence** - A buyer and seller of stolen merchandise.

Closure - Cashing forged checks perhaps for a financial crisis.

✓**Street Crimes** - Common theft-related offenses. These crimes include the major forms of common theft: larceny, embezzlement, and theft by false pretenses.

✓**Systematic Forgers** - Professionals who make a substantial living by passing bad checks.

Burglary - Forcible entry into a person's home or place of work for the purpose of theft.

Joyriding - Car theft usually motivated by a teenager's desire to acquire the power, prestige, sexual potency, and recognition associated with an automobile.

Flash Houses - Public meeting places often taverns that served as headquarters for gangs in the 18th century.

Carjacking - A type of auto theft involving gunmen approaching a car and forcing the owner to give up the keys.

Occasional Criminals - Amateur criminals whose decision to steal is spontaneous and whose acts are unskilled, unplanned and haphazard.

False Pretenses - Also known as fraud, involves misrepresenting a fact in a way that causes a victim to willingly give his/her property to the wrongdoer, who then keeps it.

Professional Criminals - Criminals who make a significant portion of their income from crime. They pursue their craft with vigor, attempting to learn from older, experienced criminals the techniques that will earn them the most money with the least risk.

Fraud - See False Pretenses.

Economic Crimes - Acts in violation of the criminal law designed to bring financial reward to an offender.

Confidence Games - Run by swindlers who aspire to separate a victim from his/her hard-earned money.

Situational Inducement - Occasional property crimes occur when there is an opportunity to commit crime.

Pigeon Drop - The most common con game. A method of swindling money out of an innocent victim.

Constructive Possession - When an individual voluntarily and temporarily gives up custody of their property but still believes that their property is legally theirs.

Good Burglar - A burglar who has technical competence, maintains personal integrity, specializes in burglary, has financial success and the ability to avoid prison sentences.

Boosters - See Heels.

Arson - The intentional or negligent burning of a home, structure, or vehicle for criminal purposes such as profit, revenge, fraud, or crime concealment.

Heels - Also known as boosters. Professional shoplifters who steal with the intention of reselling stolen merchandise to pawnshops or fences.

Arson Fraud - A business owner burning his/her property, or hiring someone to do it, to escape financial problems.

Snitches - Usually respectable persons who do not conceive of themselves as thieves, but are systematic shoplifters who steal merchandise for their own use.

Naïve Check Forgers - The majority of check forgers who do not believe their actions will hurt anyone. They cash bad checks usually because of a financial crisis.

Discussion Exercise

Have class research current statistics for petty property crimes and white-collar property crimes. Discuss the results. What are the similarities? What are the differences?

InfoTrac Assignment

GETTING STARTED: Search term words for subject guide: Theft, Thieves, Professional Criminals, Larceny, Auto Theft, False Pretenses, Fraud, Embezzlement, Burglary, Arson.

CRITICAL THINKING PROJECT: Using the search term "Arson," find relevant articles.

Here are three articles:

Colman, Adrian "Arson." *Youth Studies Australia.*

"Off To Jail." *Maclean's.*

"They Can Kiss That Arsonist Job Goodbye." *American City & County.*

Test Bank

Essay Questions

1. Provide a brief history of Theft. Define Theft. What is the common-law definition of theft?
2. Who would be considered modern thieves? Compare and contrast occasional criminals with professional criminals.
3. What is larceny/theft? Describe the varieties of larceny?

4. Define auto theft? What are the various categories of auto theft? What types of individuals are most likely to commit which types of auto theft?

5. Describe some of the methods that have been implemented to discourage auto theft? Are these methods working? Which automobiles are most likely to be stolen in our society?

Fill In The Blank

1. Common theft-related offenses are referred to as **Street Crimes**.

2. **Snitches** are usually respectable persons who do not conceive of themselves as thieves, but are systematic shoplifters who steal merchandise for their own use.

3. **False Pretense** involves misrepresenting a fact in a way that causes a victim to willingly give his or her property to the wrongdoer, who then keeps it.

4. **Situational Inducement** is the concept that describes occasional property crimes occurs when there is an opportunity to commit crime.

5. **Professional Criminals** are criminals who make a significant portion of their income from crime.

6. A method of swindling money out of an innocent victim is known as **Pigeon Drop**.

7. **Occasional Criminals** are amateur criminals whose decision to steal is spontaneous and whose acts are unskilled, unplanned and haphazard.

8. **Naïve Check Forgers** are the majority of check forgers who do not believe their actions will hurt anyone.

9. **Joyriding** is a type of car theft usually motivated by a teenager's desire to acquire the power, prestige, sexual potency, and recognition associated with an automobile.

10. **Heels** are professional shoplifters who steal with the intention of reselling stolen merchandise to pawnshops or fences.

11. **Good Burglar** is a burglar who has technical competence, maintains personal integrity, specializes in burglary, and has financial success and the ability to avoid prison sentences.

12. **Fraud** is another name for false pretense.

13. **Flash Houses** are public meeting places that served as headquarters for gangs in the 18th century.

14. A **Fence** is a buyer and seller of stolen merchandise.

15. **Arson Fraud** involves a business owner burning his or her property, or hiring someone to do it, to escape financial problems.

Multiple Choice

1. The intentional or negligent burning of a home, structure, or vehicle for criminal purposes such as profit, revenge, fraud, or crime concealment is known as:
   a. Arson
   b. Burglary
   c. Robbery
   d. Murder
   (Answer = a)

2. When an individual voluntarily and temporarily gives up custody of their property but still believes that the property is legally theirs is known as:
   a. Closure
   b. Confidence games
   c. Boosters
   d. Constructive possession
   (Answer = d)

3. Cons run by swindlers who aspire to separate a victim from his or her hard-earned money is known as:
   a. Constructive possession
   b. Confidence games
   c. Carjacking
   d. Closure
   (Answer = b)

4. Cashing forged checks for a financial crisis is known as:
   a. Boosters
   b. Heels
   c. Closure
   d. Constructive possession
   (Answer = c)

5. A type of auto theft involving gunmen approaching a car and forcing the owner to give up the keys is known as:
   a. Carjacking
   b. Situation inducement
   c. Joyriding
   d. False pretenses
   (Answer = a)

6. Forcible entry into a person's home or place of work for the purpose of theft is known as:
   a. Arson
   b. Murder
   c. Homicide
   d. Burglary
   (Answer = d)

7.Another name for boosters is:
   a. Arson
   b. Heels
   c. Snitches
   d. Fence
   (Answer = b)

8.A business owner burning his or her property, or hiring someone to do it, to escape financial problems is known as:
   a. Arson fraud
   b. Closure
   c. Burglary
   d. Carjacking
   (Answer = a)

9. Professionals who make a substantial living by passing bad checks are:
   a. Snitches
   b. Occasional criminals
   c. Systematic forgers
   d. Naïve check forgers
   (Answer = c)

10. Common theft-related offense which usually include larceny, embezzlement, and theft by false pretense are known as:
   a. Snitches
   b. Street crimes
   c. Terrorism
   d. Burglary
   (Answer = b)

11. Usually respectable persons who do not conceive of themselves as thieves, but are systematic shoplifters who steal merchandise for their own use are called:
   a. Systematic forgers
   b. Professional criminals
   c. Burglars
   d. Snitches
   (Answer = d)

12. Occasional property crimes, which occur when there is an opportunity to commit crime, are known as:
   a. Situational Inducement
   b. Systematic Forgers
   c. False Pretenses
   d. Burglar
   (Answer = a)

13. Criminals who make a significant portion of their income from crime are known as:
   a. Occasional criminals
   b. Professional criminals
   c. Naïve check forgers
   d. Snitches
   (Answer = b)

14. A method of swindling money out of an innocent victim is known as:
   a. situation inducement
   b. systematic forgers
   c. false pretenses
   d. pigeon drop
   (Answer = d)

15. Amateur criminals whose decision to steal is spontaneous and whose acts are unskilled, unplanned and haphazard are known as:
   a. professional criminals
   b. systematic forgers
   c. snitches
   d. occasional criminals
   (Answer = d)

16. The majority of check forgers who do not believe their actions will hurt anyone and usually cash bad checks because of a financial crisis are known as:
   a. professional criminals
   b. systematic forgers
   c. good burglars
   d. naïve check forgers
   (Answer = d)

17. Car theft usually motivated by a teenager's desire to acquire the power, prestige, sexual potency, and recognition associated with an automobile is known as:
   a. carjacking
   b. joyriding
   c. closure
   d. situational inducement
   (Answer = b)

18. Professional shoplifters who steal with the intention of reselling stolen merchandise to pawnshops or fences are known as:
    a. naïve check forgers
    b. good burglars
    c. heels
    d. snitches
    (Answer = c)

19. A burglar, who has technical competence, maintains personal integrity, specializes in burglary, has financial success and the ability to avoid prison sentences is known as:
    a. good burglar
    b. occasional criminal
    c. snitch
    d. shoplifter
    (Answer = a)

20. Another name for fraud is:
    a. Fence
    b. Flash houses
    c. Fake
    d. False pretense
    (Answer = d)

21. Public meeting places often taverns that served, as headquarters for gangs in the 18th century were known as:
    a. Flash houses
    b. Pigeon drops
    c. Boosters
    d. Heels
    (Answer = a)

22. A buyer and seller of stolen merchandise is known as:
    a. snitches
    b. professional criminals
    c. occasional criminals
    d. fence
    (Answer = d)

23. Also known as fraud, involves misrepresenting a fact in a way that causes a victim to willingly give his or her property to the wrongdoer, who then keeps it is known as:
    a. street crimes
    b. false pretense
    c. naïve check forgers
    d. joyriding
    (Answer = b)

24. Acts in violation of the criminal law designed to bring financial reward to an offender are known as:
    a. Street crimes
    b. Situational inducement
    c. Economic crimes
    d. Snitches
    (Answer = c)

25. By the 18th century which of the following property criminals were active?
    a. skilled thieves
    b. smugglers
    c. poachers
    d. all of the above
    (Answer = d)

26. Thieves who typically worked in the larger cities and were often pickpockets, forgers and counterfeiters were is known as:
    a. smugglers
    b. poachers
    c. burglars
    d. skilled thieves
    (Answer = d)

27. Thieves who moved freely in sparsely populated areas and transported goods, such as spirits, gems, gold and spices without bothering to pay tax or duty were known as:
    a. Skilled thieves
    b. Poachers
    c. Smugglers
    d. Burglars
    (Answer = c)

28. Thieves who typically lived in the county and supplemented their diet and income with game that belonged to a landlord were known as:
    a. Poachers
    b. Skilled thieves
    c. Smugglers
    d. Burglars
    (Answer = a)

29. Who wrote the classic book, *The Professional Thief*?
    a. Freud
    b. Marx
    c. Darwin
    d. Sutherland
    (Answer = d)

30. According to the Typology of Professional Thieves, which of the following do professional thieves engage in?
    a. Pickpocket
    b. Shoplifter
    c. Jewel thief
    d. All of the above
    (Answer = d)

31. A successful fence must meet which of the following conditions?
    a. Upfront cash
    b. Knowledge of dealing
    c. Connections with buyers
    d. All of the above
    (Answer = d)

32. Amateur fences who barter stolen goods for services are known as:
    a. Neighborhood hustlers
    b. Professional fences
    c. Associational fences
    d. Amateur receivers
    (Answer = c)

33. Those who buy and sell property as one of the many ways they make a living are known as:
    a. Associational fences
    b. Amateur receivers
    c. Professional fences
    d. Neighborhood hustlers
    (Answer = d)

34. Complete strangers approached in a public place by one offering a great deal on valuable commodities would be called:
    a. Amateur receivers
    b. Associational fences
    c. Professional fences
    d. Neighborhood hustlers
    (Answer = a)

35. Larceny is divided into which of the following?
    a. Petit larceny
    b. Grand larceny
    c. All of the above
    d. None of the above
    (Answer = c)

36. The FBI reports about how many larcenies each year?
    a. 1 million
    b. 10 million
    c. 7 million
    d. 1 billion
    (Answer = c)

37. In England about what percent of the population has been convicted of shoplifting by the age of 40?
    a. 100
    b. 50
    c. 5
    d. 1
    (Answer = c)

38. Which of the following are prevention strategies to reduce or eliminate shoplifting?
    a. electronic article surveillance systems
    b. source tagging
    c. target removal strategies
    d. all of the above
    (Answer = d)

39. Using dummy or disabled goods on display while having the "real" merchandise kept under lock and key is known as:
    a. Target removal strategies
    b. Target hardening strategies
    c. Electronic surveillance systems
    d. Source tagging
    (Answer = a)

40. Locking goods into place or having them monitored by electronic systems is known as:
    a. Target removal strategies
    b. Electronic surveillance systems
    c. Source tagging
    d. Target hardening strategies
    (Answer = d)

True/False

T   1. Economic crimes can be defined as acts in violation of the criminal defined to bring financial reward to an offender.

F   2. National surveys indicate that between 55 and 75 percent of the U.S. population are victims of theft offenses each year.

227

F   3. Theft is a phenomenon unique to modern times; the theft of personal property has not been known throughout recorded history.

T   4. By the eighteenth century, three separate groups of property criminals were active: skilled thieves, smugglers and poachers.

T   5. Occasional property crime occurs when there is an opportunity or situational inducement to commit crime.

F   6. Burglary was one of the earliest common-law crimes created by English judges to define acts in which one person took for his or her own use the property of another.

F   7. Larceny is usually separated by state statute into big larceny and small larceny.

T   8. Shoplifting is a common form of theft involving the taking of goods from retail stores.

T   9. Retail security measures all to the already high cost of crime, all of which is passed on to the consumer.

F   10. One major problem with combating shoplifting is that many customers who observe pilferage gladly report it to security agents.

T   11. Motor vehicle theft is another common larceny offense.

T   12. Thieves who steal cars for long-term transportation intend to keep the cars for their personal use.

F   13. A large portion of auto thieves steal cars to use in other crimes, such as robberies and thefts.

T   14. About 50,000 carjackings occur each year.

T   15. Both the victims and offenders in carjackings tend to be young black men.

Chapter Thirteen

White-Collar and Organized Crime

Summary

Chapter Thirteen provides a discussion of White-Collar and Organized Crime. The history of White-Collar Crime and its current components are included. Various causes and methods of control of White-Collar Crime are emphasized. The chapter concludes with a discussion of Organized Crime. The various characteristics and activities of Organized Crime are included. Methods of control and the future of Organized Crime conclude the chapter.

Learning Objectives

After reading this chapter the student should be able to:
- Be able to define the concept of white-collar crime.
- Understand the white-collar crime problem.
- Explain the International white-collar crime problem.
- Describe stings and swindles.
- Understand chiseling.
- Distinguish between embezzlement and employee fraud.
- Define client fraud.
- Understand corporate crime.
- Explore the cause of white-collar crime.
- Describe techniques for controlling white-collar crime.
- Define organized crime.
- Understand the characteristics of organized crime.
- Discuss the activities of organized crime.
- Examine the future of organized crime.

Chapter Overview

Introduction
White-Collar Crime
      Redefining White-Collar Crime
      The White-Collar Crime Problem
      International White-Collar Crime
Components of White-Collar Crime
      Stings and Swindles
      Chiseling
      Individual Exploitation of Institutional Position
      Influence Peddling and Bribery
      Embezzlement and Employee Fraud
      Client Fraud
      Corporate Crime
      High-Tech Crime
The Cause of White-Collar Crime
      Greedy or Needy?
White-Collar Law Enforcement Systems
      Controlling White-Collar Crime
Organized Crime
      Characteristics of Organized Crime
      Activities of Organized Crime
      The Concept of Organized Crime
      Organized Crime Groups
      Controlling Organized Crime
      The Future of Organized Crime
Summary

Chapter Outline

I.   **Introduction**
II.   **White-Collar Crime** - 1930's - Edwin Sutherland - described the criminal activities of the rich and powerful. White-collar crime - crime committed by a respectable, high social status person in the course of his occupation.
     A. Redefining White-Collar Crime

1. Much broader than Sutherland's original definition
2. Includes middle-income Americans and corporate titans who use their marketplace for criminal activity.
3. Tax evasion
4. Credit card fraud
5. Bankruptcy fraud
6. Pilfering
7. Soliciting bribes or kickbacks
8. Embezzlement
9. Land swindles
10. Securities theft
11. Medical fraud
12. Antitrust violations
13. Price-fixing
14. False Advertising

    B. The White-Collar Crime Problem
        1. Difficult to estimate because white-collar crime is usually overlooked by victimologists.

III. Components of White-Collar Crime

    A. Stings and Swindles - stealing through deception by individuals who use their institutional or business position to bilk people out of their money.
        1. Religious Swindles - an example a swindle.
    B. Chiseling - regularly cheating an organization, its consumers or both.
        1. Professional Chiseling - professionals who use their positions to cheat their clients
            a. Pharmacist - charges for name brand and substitutes with generic.
        2. Securities Fraud - brokers using their position to cheat individual clients
            a. Churning - by repeated, excessive and unnecessary buying and selling of stock
            b. Front running - brokers place personal orders ahead of a large customer's order to profit from the market effects of the trade
            c. Bucketing - skimming customer-trading profits by falsifying trade information.
            d. Insider trading - Using one's position of trust to profit from inside business information.
    C. Individual Exploitation of Institutional Position - occurs when victim has a right to service and offender threatens to withhold service unless a payment or bribe is forthcoming.
        1. Exploitation in Government and Industry
    D. Influence Peddling and Bribery
        1. Taking of kickbacks - from contractors in return for awarding them contracts
        2. Exploitation - forcing victims to pay for services to which they have a clear right.
        3. Influence Peddling in Government

a. HUD - 1980's - officials tried to defraud the government of $4 billion to $8 billion.

b. Knapp Commission - found corrupt police officers in New York City.

4. Influence Peddling in Business

a. Gulf Oil paid $4 million to South Korean ruling party.

b. Burroughs Corporation paid $1.5 million to foreign officials.

E. Embezzlement and Employee Fraud - individuals' use their positions to embezzle company funds or appropriate company property for themselves.

1. Blue-Collar Fraud

a. Pilferage - employee theft

2. Management Fraud

a. Converting company assets for personal benefit

b. Fraudulently receiving increases in compensation (such as raises and bonuses)

c. Fraudulently increasing personal holdings of company stock

d. Retaining one's present position within the company by manipulating accounts

e. Concealing unacceptable performance from stockholders.

F. Client Fraud - theft by an economic client from an organization that advances credit to its clients or reimburses them for services rendered.

1. Health Care Fraud

2. Bank Fraud

3. Tax Evasion

a. Passive neglect - not paying taxes, not reporting income, or not paying taxes when due.

b. Affirmative tax evasion - keeping double books, making false entries, destroying books or records, concealing assets, or covering up sources of income.

G. Corporate Crime - socially injurious acts committed by people who control companies to further their business interests.

1. Illegal Restraint of Trade and Price-Fixing - regulated by the Sherman Antitrust Act

a. Restraint of Trade - involves a contract or conspiracy designed to stifle competition, create a monopoly, artificially maintain prices, or otherwise interfere with free market competition.

b. Division of markets - firms divide a region into territories and each firm agrees not to compete in the others' territories.

c. Tying arrangement - corporation requires customers of one of its services to use other services it offers.

d. Group boycotts - company boycotts retail stores that do not comply with its rules or desires.

e. Price-fixing - conspiracy to set and control the price of a necessary commodity-is considered an absolute violation of the act.

2. Deceptive Pricing - when contractors provide the government or other corporations with incomplete or misleading information on how much it actually cost to fulfill the contracts they were bidding on or use mischarges once the contracts are signed.

3. False Claims and Advertising - illegal to knowingly and purposely advertise a product as possessing qualities that the manufacturer realizes that it does not have.

4. Environmental Crimes

H. High-Tech Crime - involve the theft of information, resources or funds.

1. Internet Crimes
   a. Internet Securities Fraud
      1. Market manipulation - individual tries to control the price of stock by interfering with the natural forces of supply and demand.
         a. Pump and dump - erroneous and deceptive information is posted online to get unsuspecting investors to become interested in a stock, while those spreading the information sell previously purchased stock at an inflated price.
         b. Cyber-smear - reverse pump and dump; negative information is spread online about a stock driving down its price and allowing people to buy it at an artificially low price before rebuttals by the company's officers re-inflate the price.
      2. Fraudulent offerings of securities - cyber criminals create websites to fraudulently sell securities.
      3. Illegal touting - individuals make securities recommendations and fail to disclose they are being paid to disseminate their favorable opinions.
   b. Identity Theft - person uses the Internet to steal someone's identity and/or impersonate them in order to open a new credit card account or conduct some other financial transaction.

2. Computer Crimes - new trend in employee theft and embezzlement.
   a. Theft of services - computer used for unauthorized purposes or an unauthorized user penetrates the computer system.
   b. Use of data in a computer system for personal gain.
   c. Unauthorized use of computers employed for various types of financial processing to obtain assets.
   d. Theft of property by computer for personal use or conversion to profit.
   e. Making the computer itself the subject of a crime - planting a virus.
   f. The Trojan Horse - one computer is used to reprogram another for illicit purposes.
   g. The Salami Slice - Employee sets up dummy account in the company's computerized records. A small amount is subtracted from customers' accounts and added to the account of the thief.
   h. Super-zagging - Tinkering with the company computer program to issue checks to ones personal account.

i.   The Logic Bomb - Program looking for an error in company computer. When error occurs, the thief exploits the situation and steals money, secrets, commits sabotage or the like.

j.   Impersonation - unauthorized person uses the identity of an authorized person to access the computer system.

k.   Data leakage - person illegally obtains data from a computer system by leaking it out in small amounts.

IV.   The Cause of White-Collar Crime

A. Some individuals rationalize their behavior.

B. Some see no harm; since they see that it does not hurt anyone.

C. Some do not see their actions as crimes.

D. Some feel justified.

E. Greedy or Needy?

1. Corporate Culture Theory - some business enterprises cause crime by placing excessive demands on employees while at the same time maintaining a business climate tolerant of employee deviance.

2. The Self-Control View - Hirschi and Gottfredson maintain the motives that produce white-collar crimes are the same as those that produce any other criminal behaviors: the desire for relatively quick, relatively certain benefit, with minimal effort.

V.   White-Collar Law Enforcement Systems - detection is primarily in the hands of administrative departments and agencies like the FBI.

A. Controlling White-Collar Crime - rarely prosecuted and when convicted, receives relatively light sentences.

1. Compliance Strategies - aim for law conformity without the necessity of detecting, processing, or penalizing individual violators.

a. Set up administrative agencies to oversee business activity.

2. Deterrence Strategies - involve detecting criminal violations, determining who is responsible, and penalizing the offenders to deter future violations.

3. Is the Tide Turning? - Growing evidence that white-collar crime deterrence strategies have become normative.

VI.   Organized Crime - the ongoing criminal enterprise groups whose ultimate purpose is personal economic gain through illegitimate means.

A. Characteristics of Organized Crime

1. A conspiratorial activity, involving the coordination of numerous persons in the planning and execution of illegal acts or in the pursuit of a legitimate objective by unlawful means.

2. Has economic gain as its primary goal.

3. Not limited to providing illicit services.

4. Employs predatory tactics, such as intimidation, violence and corruption.

5. Groups are very quick and effective in controlling their members, associates and victims.

6. Not synonymous with the Mafia. The Mafia is a common stereotype of organized crime.

7. Does not include terrorists dedicated to political change.

234

B. Activities of Organized Crime
1. Providing illicit materials
2. Using force to enter into and maximize profits in legitimate businesses.
3. Narcotic distribution
4. Loansharking
5. Prostitution
6. Gambling
7. Theft Rings
8. Pornography
9. Other illegal enterprises.
C. The Concept of Organized Crime
1. Alien Conspiracy Theory - organized crime is a direct offshoot of a criminal society - the Mafia - that first originated in Italy and Sicily and now controls racketeering in major U.S. cities.
a. The Mafia is centrally coordinated by a national committee that settles disputes, dictates policy and assigns territory.
b. La Cosa Nostra.
D. Emerging Organized Crime Groups
1. Eastern European Crime Groups
E. Controlling Organized Crime
1. Interstate and Foreign Travel or Transportation in Aid of Racketeering Enterprises Act (Travel Act) - aimed directly at organized crime.
2. Organized Crime Control Act - 1970 - called Racketeer Influenced and Corrupt Organization Act (RICO).
a. Created new categories of offenses in racketeering activity.
F. The Future of Organized Crime
1. Indications that organized crime is on the decline.
2. Some large gangs are becoming similar to traditional organized crime.
3. Due to the demand for certain illegal goods and services, organized crime will never be totally eliminated.

VII. Summary

Key Terms

Entrepreneurship - One willing to take risks for profit in the marketplace.

White-Collar Crime - According to Sutherland, a crime committed by a person of respectability and high status in the course of his occupation. A more contemporary definition would be crime activities for economic gain.

Organized Crime - A conspiratorial activity, involving the coordination of numerous persons in the planning and execution of illegal acts or in the pursuit of a legitimate objective by unlawful means.

Enterprise - An organized crime group that profits from the sale of illegal goods and services, such as narcotics, pornography and prostitution.

Churning - A white-collar crime in which a stockbroker makes repeated trades to fraudulently increase his/her commissions.

Insider Trading - Securities chiseling can also involve one's position of trust to profit from inside business information. The information can then be used to buy and sell securities, giving the trader an unfair advantage over the general public, which lacks this information.

Arbitrage - The practice of buying large blocks of stock in companies that are believed to be the target of corporate buyouts or takeovers.

Pilferage - Theft by employees through stealth or deception.

Corporate Crime - A component of white-collar crime which involves situations in which powerful institutions or their representatives willfully violate the laws that restrain these institutions from doing social harm or require them to do social good.

Organizational Crime - Crime that involves large corporations and their efforts to control the marketplace and earn huge profits through unlawful bidding, unfair advertising, monopolistic practices, or other illegal means.

Sherman Antitrust Act - The legal basis which restraints trade violations and subjects criminal or civil sanctions on any person who shall make any contract or engage in any combination or conspiracy in restraint of interstate commerce.

Division of Markets - Firms divide a region into territories and each firm agrees not to compete in the others' territories.

Tying Arrangement - In which a corporation requires customers of one of its services to use other services it offers. For example, it would be an illegal restrain of trade if a railroad required that companies doing business with it or supplying it with materials ship all goods they produce on trains owned by the rail line.

Group Boycott - In which an organization or company boycotts retail stores that do not comply with its rules or desires.

Price-Fixing - a conspiracy to set and control the price of a necessary commodity-is considered an absolute violation of the act.

Compliance - A white-collar enforcement strategy that encourages law-abiding behavior through both the threat of economic sanctions and the promise of rewards for conformity.

Alien Conspiracy Theory - Organized crime is made up of a national syndicate of 25 or so Italian-dominated crime families that call themselves La Cosa Nostra.

Racketeer Influenced and Corrupt Organization Act (RICO) - In 1970 Congress passed the Organized Crime Act. Title IX of the act, has been called the Racketeer Influenced and Corrupt Organization Act.

Forfeiture - The seizure of personal property by the state as a civil or criminal penalty.

Discussion Exercise

Have the class review various groups of Organized Crime. Discuss the different groups, their area of operation, and their specific crime area.

InfoTrac Assignment

GETTING STARTED: Search term words for subject guide: White-Collar Crime, Swindles, Embezzlement, Fraud, High-Tech Crime, Organized Crime.

CRITICAL THINKING PROJECT: Using the search term "Organized Crime," find relevant articles.

Here are three articles:

Cooper, John "Cleaning Up Dirty Money." *CMA Management*.

Young, Vicki M. "Counterfeit Probe: U.S. Attorney Charges New York Mobsters." *WWD*.

"Cosa Nostra, Continued." *The Economist (US)*.

Test Bank

Essay Questions

1. Define White-Collar crime. Compare and contrast Sutherland's original definition of white-collar crime with today's more updated definition.
2. Describe the various components of White-Collar crime. What are the various types of crimes that individuals commit under the heading of White-Collar Crime?
3. What is the cause of White-Collar Crime? Do individuals commit White-Collar Crime for need or for greed and why?

4. What are some of the measures being used to control White-Collar Crime in the United States? Describe the philosophy of investigation and punishment of White-Collar Crime.

5. Compare and contrast the views of White-Collar Crime and low-income, street crime. Are the sentencing strategies equal?

Fill In The Blank

1. Crime that involves large corporations and their efforts to control the marketplace and earn huge profits through unlawful bidding, unfair advertising, monopolistic practices, or other illegal means is referred to as **Organizational Crime**.

2. **Insider Trading** is information that is used to buy and sell securities, giving the trader an unfair advantage over the general public.

3. **Churning** is a white-collar crime in which a stockbroker makes repeated trades to fraudulently increase his or her commissions.

4. **Compliance** is a white-collar enforcement strategy that encourages law-abiding behavior through both the threat of economic sanctions and the promise of rewards for conformity.

5. **Corporate Crime** is a component of white-collar crime which involves situations in which powerful institutions or their representatives willfully violate the laws that restrain these institutions from doing social harm or require them to do social good.

6. Firms which divide a region into territories and each firm agrees not to compete in the others' territories is known as **Division of Markets**.

7. An **Enterprise** is an organized crime group that profits from the sale of illegal goods and services, such as narcotics, pornography and prostitution.

8. One willing to take risks for profit in the marketplace is called an **Entrepreneurship.**

9. **Forfeiture** is the seizure of personal property by the state as a civil or criminal penalty.

10. **Group Boycott** is where an organization or company boycotts retail stores that do not comply with its rules or desires.

11. **Front Running** is when brokers place personal orders ahead of a large customer's order to profit from the market effects of the trade.

12. **Bucketing** is skimming customer-trading profits by falsifying trade information.

13. **Exploitation** involves forcing victims to pay for services to which they have a clear right.

14. When government employees **Take Kickbacks,** they are taking money from contractors in return for awarding them contracts.

15. **Check Kiting** is a scheme whereby a client with accounts in two or more banks takes advantage of the time required for checks to clear in order to obtain unauthorized use of bank funds.

Multiple Choice

1. The view Organized Crime is made up of a national syndicate of 25 or so Italian - dominated crime families that call themselves La Cosa Nostra is known as:
   a. Alien conspiracy theory
   b. Division of markets
   c. Sherman antitrust act
   d. Tying arrangement
   (Answer = a)

2. The practice of buying large blocks of stock in companies that are believed to be the target of corporate buyouts or takeovers is known as:
   a. Churning
   b. Compliance
   c. Enterprise
   d. Arbitrage
   (Answer = d)

3. A white-collar crime in which a stockbroker makes repeated trades to fraudulently increase his or her commissions is known as:
   a. Compliance
   b. Churning
   c. Forfeiture
   d. Pilferage
   (Answer = b)

4. A white-collar enforcement strategy that encourages law-abiding behavior through both the threat of economic sanctions and the promise of rewards for conformity is known as:
   a. Churning
   b. Enterprise
   c. Compliance
   d. Pilferage
   (Answer = c)

5. A component of white-collar crime, which involves situations in which powerful institutions or their representatives willfully violate the laws that restrain these institutions from doing social harm or require them to do social good, is known as:
   a. Corporate Crime
   b. Insider trading
   c. Enterprise
   d. Tying arrangement
   (Answer = a)

6. Firms that divide a region into territories and each firm agrees not to compete in the others' territories is known as:
   a. Compliance
   b. Churning
   c. Forfeiture
   d. Division of markets
   (Answer = d)

7.An organized crime group that profits from the sale of illegal goods and services, such as narcotics, pornography and prostitution is known as:
   a. Entrepreneurship
   b. Enterprise
   c. Compliance
   d. Tying arrangement
   (Answer = b)

8.One willing to take risks for profit in the marketplace is known as:
   a. Entrepreneurship
   b. Enterprise
   c. Compliance
   d. Tying arrangement
   (Answer = a)

9. The seizure of personal property by the state as a civil or criminal penalty is known as:
   a. pilferage
   b. price-fixing
   c. forfeiture
   d. arbitrage
   (Answer = c)

10. When an organization or company boycotts retail stores that do not comply with its rules or desires it is known as:
   a. forfeiture
   b. group boycott
   c. enterprise
   d. Entrepreneurship
   (Answer = b)

11. Information used to buy and sell securities, giving the trader an unfair advantage over the general public is called:
   a. group boycott
   b. division of markets
   c. enterprise
   d. insider trading
   (Answer = d)

12. Crime that involves large corporations and their efforts to control the marketplace and earn huge profits through unlawful bidding, unfair advertising, monopolistic practices, or other illegal means is known as:
   a. Organizational Crime
   b. Tying arrangement
   c. Insider trading
   d. Enterprise
   (Answer = a)

13. When a corporation requires customers of one of its services to use other services it offers it is known as:
   a. Price-fixing
   b. Tying arrangement
   c. Enterprise
   d. Compliance
   (Answer = b)

14. The legal basis which restraints trade violations and subjects criminal or civil sanctions on any person who shall make any contract or engage in any combination or conspiracy in restraint of interstate commerce is known as:
   a. RICO
   b. Division of markets
   c. Arbitrage
   d. Sherman Antitrust Act
   (Answer = d)

15. In 1970 Congress passed the Organized Crime Act also known as:
    a. Division of markets
    b. Arbitrage
    c. Sherman Antitrust Act
    d. RICO
    (Answer = d)

16. A conspiracy to set and control the price of a necessary commodity is known as:
    a. Arbitrage
    b. Churning
    c. Compliance
    d. Price-fixing
    (Answer = d)

17. Theft by employees through stealth or deception is known as:
    a. Price-fixing
    b. Pilferage
    c. Insider trading
    d. Forfeiture
    (Answer = b)

18. A conspiratorial activity, involving the coordination of numerous persons in the planning and execution of illegal acts or in the pursuit of a legitimate objective by unlawful means is known as:
    a. Enterprise
    b. Division of markets
    c. Organized crime
    d. Corporate crime
    (Answer = c)

19. According to Sutherland, a crime committed by a person of respectability and high status in the course of his occupation is known as:
    a. White-Collar Crime
    b. Division of labor
    c. Organized crime
    d. Enterprise
    (Answer = a)

20. Regularly cheating an organization, its consumers or both is known as:
    a. Churning
    b. Compliance
    c. Corporate crime
    d. Chiseling
    (Answer = d)

21. Broker fraud in, which brokers place personal orders ahead of a large customer's order to profit from the market effects of the trade, is known as:
   a. Front running
   b. Bucketing
   c. Churning
   d. All of the above
   (Answer = a)

22. Skimming customer trading profits by falsifying trade information is known as:
   a. Front running
   b. Churning
   c. Chiseling
   d. Bucketing
   (Answer = d)

23. When government employees take money from contractors in return for awarding them contracts, it is known as:
   a. Exploitation
   b. Taking of kickbacks
   c. Front running
   d. Churning
   (Answer = b)

24. Forcing victims to pay for services to which they have a clear right is known as:
   a. Churning
   b. Front running
   c. Exploitation
   d. Taking of kickbacks
   (Answer = c)

25. Which act make it a criminal offense to bribe foreign officials or to make other questionable overseas payments?
   a. Sherman Antitrust Act
   b. 1977 White-Collar Crime Act
   c. RICO Act
   d. Foreign Corrupt Practices Act
   (Answer = d)

26. What percentage of employees report being involved in pilferage?
   a. 10%
   b. 20%
   c. 25%
   d. 35%
   (Answer = d)

27. Which of the following are types of management fraud?
    a. Converting company assets for personal benefit
    b. Fraudulently receiving increases in compensation
    c. All of the above
    d. None of the above
    (Answer = c)

28. Bank fraud can encompass which of the following?
    a. Check kiting
    b. Check forging
    c. Sale of stolen checks
    d. All of the above
    (Answer = d)

29. A scheme whereby a client with accounts in two or more banks takes advantage of the time required for checks to clear in order to obtain unauthorized use of bank funds is known as:
    a. Check forging
    b. Sale of stolen checks
    c. Auto title fraud
    d. Check kiting
    (Answer = d)

30. Simply not paying taxes, not reporting income, or not paying taxes when due is known as:
    a. Affirmative tax evasion
    b. Check forging
    c. Check kiting
    d. Passive neglect
    (Answer = d)

31. Keeping double books, making false entries, destroying books or records, concealing assets, or covering up sources of income is known as:
    a. Passive neglect
    b. Check kiting
    c. Check forging
    d. Affirmative tax evasion
    (Answer = d)

32. Some of the acts associated with corporate crime are:
    a. Price-fixing
    b. Illegal restraint of trade
    c. All of the above
    d. None of the above
    (Answer = c)

33. A contract or conspiracy designed to stifle competition, create a monopoly, artificially maintain prices, or otherwise interfere with free market competition is known as:
    a. Division of markets
    b. Tying arrangement
    c. Group boycotts
    d. Restraint of trade
    (Answer = d)

34. When an individual tries to control the price of stock by interfering with the natural forces of supply and demand, it is called:
    a. Market manipulation
    b. Fraudulent offerings of securities
    c. Illegal touting
    d. Enterprises
    (Answer = a)

35. Which of the following are types of market manipulation?
    a. Pump and dump
    b. Cyber-smear
    c. All of the above
    d. None of the above
    (Answer = c)

36. Erroneous and deceptive information is posted online to get unsuspecting investors to become interested in a stock, while those spreading the information sell previously purchased stock at an inflated price is called:
    a. Cyber-smear
    b. Fraudulent offerings of securities
    c. Pump and dump
    d. Illegal touting
    (Answer = c)

37. A reverse pump and dump: negative information is spread online about a stock driving down its price and allowing people to buy it at an artificially low price before rebuttals by the company's officers re-inflate the price is known as:
    a. Illegal touting
    b. Pump and dump
    c. Cyber-smear
    d. Fraudulent offerings of securities
    (Answer = c)

38. When individuals make securities recommendations and fail to disclose that they are being paid to disseminate their favorable opinions, this is known as:
    a. Fraudulent offerings of securities
    b. Cyber-smear
    c. Pump and dump
    d. Illegal touting
    (Answer = d)

39. When a person uses the Internet to steal someone's identity and/or impersonate them in order to open a new credit card account or conduct some other financial transaction, it is known as:
    a. Identity theft
    b. Cyber-smear
    c. Pump and dump
    d. Illegal touting
    (Answer = a)

40. The fraud attributable to the misrepresentation of a product advertised for sale through an Internet auction site or the non-delivery of merchandise or goods purchased through an Internet auction site is known as:
    a. Non-delivery of goods/services
    b. Pyramid schemes
    c. Credit card theft
    d. Online auction/retail
    (Answer = d)

True/False

T   1. Securities chiseling can involve using one's position of trust to profit from inside business information referred to as insider trading.

F   2. Exploitation involves taking money from contractors in return for awarding them contracts they could have won on merit.

F   3. Taking of kickbacks involves forcing victims to pay for services to which they have a clear right.

T   4. Blue-collar employees may be involved in systematic theft of company property, commonly called pilferage.

T   5. Bank fraud can encompass such diverse schemes as check kiting, check forgery, false statements on loan applications, sale of stolen checks, bank credit card fraud, unauthorized use of ATMs, auto title fraud, and illegal transactions with offshore banks.

F   6. A division of markets involves a contract or conspiracy designed to stifle competition, create a monopoly, artificially maintain prices, or otherwise interfere with free market competition.

F   7. A tying arrangement is where an organization or company boycotts retail stores that do not comply with its rules or desires.

T   8. Price-fixing is a conspiracy to set and control the price of a necessary commodity.

T   9. Deceptive pricing occurs when contractors provide the government or other corporations with incomplete or misleading information on how much it will actually cost to fulfill the contracts they are bidding on or use mischarges once they are signed.

F   10. Market manipulation occurs when Cyber criminals create websites specifically designed to fraudulently sell securities.

T   11. Business opportunity/"Work at Home" is the offering of a phony job opportunity, often with associated charges such as "processing or application" fees.

T   12. Financial Institution Fraud is the misrepresentation of the truth or concealment of a material fact by a person to induce a business, organization, or other entity that manages money, credit, or capital to perform a fraudulent activity.

F   13. Ponzi/Pyramid Schemes are the unauthorized use of a credit/debt card or credit/debt card number to fraudulently obtain money or property.

T   14. Non-Delivery of Goods/Services are the non-delivery of goods or services which were purchased or contracted remotely through the Internet.

T   15. When a computer is used to reprogram another for illicit purposes, it is known as the Trojan Horse.

Chapter Fourteen

Public Order Crimes

Summary

Chapter Fourteen discusses the various Public Order Crimes. A definition of homosexuality is provided with various attitudes and the current laws in our society. A variety of deviant sexual activities are discussed with a section on prostitution. Pornography is included and the impact that it is having on our society. Finally, Chapter Fourteen discusses the use of drugs in our culture. A variety of drugs are examined with explanations of the various Federal drug laws.

Learning Objectives

After reading this chapter the student should be able to:
- Distinguish between law and morality.
- Define morality.
- Understand the various attitudes towards homosexuality.
- Develop an understanding of homosexuality and the law.
- Define paraphilias.
- Recognize the different types of prostitution.
- Debate the issue of legalizing prostitution.
- Recognize the dangers of pornography.
- Understand the issues of pornography and the law.
- Explore the various types of substance.
- Describe the most commonly used drugs.
- Understand the extent of substance abuse.
- Develop an understanding of AIDS and the correlation with drug use.
- Recognize the causes of substance abuse.
- Review the drug control strategies.

Chapter Overview

Introduction
Law and Morality
    Debating Morality
Homosexuality
    Attitudes Toward Homosexuality
    Homosexuality and the Law
Paraphilias
Prostitution
    Incidence of Prostitution
    Types of Prostitution
    Becoming a Prostitute
    Legalize Prostitution?
Pornography
    The Dangers of Pornography
    Does Pornography Cause Violence?
    Pornography and the Law
    Controlling Sex for Profit
Substance Abuse
    When Did Drug Use Begin?
    Alcohol and Its Prohibition
    Commonly Abused Drugs
    The Extent of Substance Abuse
    AIDS and Drug Use
    The Causes of Substance Abuse
    Types of Drug Users
    Drugs and Crime
    Drugs and the Law
    Drug Control Strategies
Summary

Chapter Outline
I.   **Introduction**
II.   **Law and Morality**

A. Debating Morality
   1. Social Harm
      a. Immoral acts can be distinguished from crimes on the basis of the social they cause.
      b. Acts believed to be extremely harmful to the public are outlaws; those, which only harm the actor, are tolerated.
   2. Moral Crusaders
      a. Moral entrepreneurs - rule creators operating with an absolute certainty that their way is right and that any means are justified to get their way.
      b. Take on issues such as prayer in school, the right to legal abortions, and the distribution of sexually explicit books and magazines.
      c. Risk engaging in immoral conduct trying to protect society from those considered immoral.

III. **Homosexuality -** erotic interest in one's own sex.
   A. Gay Bashing - violent acts directed at people because of their sexual orientation.
   B. Homosexuality - an adult motivated by a definite preferential erotic attraction to members of the same sex and who usually (but not necessarily) engage in overt sexual relations with them.
   C. Homosexual behavior has existed in most societies.
   D. Attitudes Toward Homosexuality
      1. Throughout history, homosexuals have been the subjects of discrimination, sanction, and violence.
      2. Bible forbids homosexuality.
      3. Homosexuals killed by Hebrews, Christians and many nations.
      4. Homophobia - extremely negative overreaction to homosexuals.
   E. Homosexuality and the Law
      1. No longer a crime in the U.S.
      2. Military - don't ask; don't tell policy.
      3. Many states have changed their laws.
      4. Is the Tide Turning?
         a. Increased social tolerance.
         b. Many support gays in the military
         c. Equal housing, employment, inheritance rights and social security benefits for same sex couples.

IV. **Paraphilias**
   A. Bizarre or abnormal sexual practices involving recurrent urges focused on:
      1. Nonhuman objects
      2. Humiliation or the experience of receiving or giving pain
      3. Children or others that cannot give consent.
      4. Outlawed sexual behavior includes:
         a. Asphyxiophilia - using a noose, ligature, plastic bag, mask, volatile chemicals, or chest compression, attempting partial asphyxia and oxygen deprivation to the brain to enhance sexual gratification.

b. Frotteurism - rubbing against or touching a nonconsenting person in a crowd, elevator, or other public place.

c. Voyeurism - obtaining sexual pleasure from spying on a stranger while they disrobe or engage in sexual behavior with another.

d. Exhibitionism - deriving sexual pleasures from exposing the genitals to surprise or shock a stranger.

e. Sadomasochism - deriving pleasure from receiving pain or inflicting pain on another.

f. Pedophilia - attaining sexual pleasure through sexual activity with prepubescent children.

V. **Prostitution** - the granting of nonmarital sexual access, established by mutual agreement of the prostitutes, their clients, and their employers, for remuneration.

A. Incidence of Prostitution

1. UCR indicates that about 90,000 prostitution arrests are made annually.

B. Types of Prostitutes

1. Streetwalkers - prostitutes working the streets in plain sight; also known as hustlers or hookers.

2. Bar Girls - Called B-girls spend time in bars, drinking and waiting to be picked up by customers.

3. Brothel Prostitutes - Bordellos, cathouses, sporting houses and houses of ill repute - large establishments usually run by a madam that house several prostitutes.

4. Call Girls - Aristocrats of prostitution. Some net over $100,000 annually.

5. Escort Services/Call Houses

a. Escort Services are usually fronts for prostitution rings.

b. Call Houses - Madams receive calls and arrange for prostitution service.

6. Circuit Travelers - Groups of 2 or 3 traveling to lumber, labor and agricultural camps.

7. Skeezers - Women who barter drugs for sex.

8. Massage Parlors/Photo Studios

C. Becoming A Prostitute

1. Prostitutes often come from troubled homes.

2. Most prostitutes grew up with absent fathers.

3. Conflict with school authorities, poor grades

4. Drug Abuse

5. Psychological Disturbance

6. Sexual Abuse and Prostitution

a. Initiated into sex by family members at age 10 to 12.

b. Many flee an abusive home.

c. Vulnerable on the street.

d. Get hooked into the sex trade.

7. International Sex Trade

a. Some kidnapped and forced into prostitution.

b. Sex tourism - men from wealthy countries frequent semi-regulated sex areas in need countries, like Thailand, to procure young girls forced or sold into prostitution.
8. Controlling Prostitution
    a. The Federal Mann Act (1925) prohibited bringing women into the country or transporting them across state lines for the purpose of prostitution. Often called the "white slave act".
    b. Prostitution, today, is a misdemeanor.
    c. Illegal in all states but Nevada.
D. Legalize Prostitution

VI. Pornography
A. Child Pornography - estimated that each year over a million children are believed to be used in pornography or prostitution.
B. Does Pornography Cause Violence?
1. Some studies indicate that viewing sexually explicit material actually has little effect on sexual violence.
2. Violent Pornography
    a. Studies that men exposed to violent pornography are more likely to act aggressively and hold aggressive attitudes toward women.
C. Pornography and the Law
1. All states and the federal government prohibit the sale and production of pornographic material.
2. Punishing Obscenity creates moral and legal dilemmas.
    a. Art or Pornography.
    b. The 1st Amendment and a variety of cases protect art.
D. Controlling Pornography - little evidence that it can be controlled or eliminated by legal means alone.
1. Technological Change
    a. Home Video Tapes
    b. Internet

VII. Substance Abuse
A. When Did Drug Use Begin? - Has been around for thousands of years.
B. Alcohol and Its Prohibition
1. 18th Amendment - 1919 - prohibited the sale of alcoholic beverages.
2. 21st Amendment - 1933 - repealed prohibition.
C. The Extent of Substance Abuse
1. Monitoring the Future (MTF)
    a. Annual self-report survey of drug abuse of high school students conducted by the Institute of Social Research (ISR) at the University of Michigan.
    b. 45,000 high school students - 8th, 10th, and 12th grades.
    c. Drug use declined from 1980 until 1990.
    d. Increased until 1996.
    e. Marijuana is currently on the decrease.
    f. Drug ecstasy has been increasing in popularity.

2. The National Household Survey of Drug Abuse
   a. Conducted by the Department of Health and Human Services National Institute on Drug Abuse
   b. Interviews approximately 70,000 people at home annually.
   c. Shows that alcohol and drug abuse have stabilized or declined.
3. Are the Surveys Accurate?
   a. Respondents may overreport, underreport, forget or be unaware.
   b. Significant population missing - those who are homeless, in prison, in drug rehab clinics, in AIDS clinics and those who refuse to participate.
   c. Surveys administered each year so problems should be consistent.
D. AIDS and Drug Use
1. Drug use linked to the threat of AIDS.
2. About $1/4^{th}$ of adult AIDS cases have occurred among IV drug users.
E. What Causes Substance Abuse?
1. Subcultural View - lower-class problem
   a. Racial prejudice
   b. Devalued identities
   c. Low self-esteem
   d. Poor socioeconomic status
   e. High level of mistrust, negativism and deviance found in poor areas.
2. Psychodynamic View - suggest that drugs help youth control or express unconscious needs and impulses.
   a. Drinking alcohol may reflect on oral fixation.
   b. Weak ego.
   c. Low frustration tolerance.
   d. Anxiety.
   e. Fantasies of omnipotence.
3. Genetic Factors
   a. People whose parents are substance abusers may have a greater chance of developing a problem than children of nonusers.
4. Social Learning
   a. Drug abuse may result from observing parental drug use.
5. Problem Behavior Syndrome (PBS) - for some substance abuse is one of many social problems.
   a. Rational Choice - some use drugs and alcohol to enjoy the effects.
F. Is There a Drug Gateway?
1. Most people fall into drug abuse slowly, beginning with alcohol and following with marijuana and then more serious drugs.
G. Types of Drug Users
1. Adolescents Who Distribute Small Amounts of Drugs
2. Adolescents Who Frequently Sell Drugs
3. Teenage Drug Dealers Who Commit Other Delinquent Acts
4. Adolescents Who Cycle in and out of the Justice System
5. Drug-Involved Youths Who Continue to Commit Crimes as Adults
6. Outwardly Respectable Adults Who are Top-Level Dealers

a. Smugglers - import drugs into the United States.

    1. Generally men, middle-aged with strong organizational skills, established connections, capital to invest and a willingness to take large business risks.

7. Adult Predatory Drug Users Who are Frequently Arrested

    a. Getting arrested, doing time, using multiple drugs, and committing predatory crimes are a way of life.

    b. Become street junkies.

8. Adult Predatory Drug Users Who are Rarely Arrested

    a. Commit hundreds of crime each year and are rarely arrested.

    b. Sometimes referred to as stabilized junkies.

9. Less Predatory Drug-Involved Adult Offenders

    a. Petty criminals who avoid violent crime.

10. Women Who Are Drug-Involved Offenders

    a. Often involved in prostitution and low-level drug dealing.

H. Drugs and Crime - research shows association between drug use and crime.

    1. User Surveys - show that people who take drugs have extensive involvement in crime.

    2. Surveys of Known Criminals - testing known criminals to determine the extent of their substance abuse.

    3. The Drug-Crime Connection

        a. Police may apprehend muddle-headed substance abusers than clear-thinking abstainers.

        b. Most criminals are substance abusers.

        c. Drug use weakens the social bond that leads to antisocial behavior.

I. Drugs and the Law

    1. Pure Food and Drug Act - 1906 - required manufacturers to list the amounts of habit-forming drugs in products on the labels, but did not restrict their use.

    2. Harrison Narcotics act - 1914 - restricted importation, manufacture, sale, and dispensing of narcotics.

    3. Harrison Narcotics Act - 1922 - revised to allow importation of opium and coca leaves for qualified medical practitioners.

    4. Marijuana Tax Act - 1937 - required registration and tax payment by all that imported, sold, or manufactured marijuana.

    5. Boggs Act of 1951 - provided mandatory sentences for violating federal drug laws.

    6. Durham-Humphrey Act of 1951 - made it illegal to dispense barbiturates and amphetamines without a prescription.

    7. Narcotic Control Act of 1956 - increased penalties for drug offenders.

    8. Drug Abuse Control Act - 1965 - set up stringent guidelines for the legal use and sale of mood-modifying drugs.

    9. Comprehensive Drug Abuse Prevention and Control Act - 1970 - set up unified categories of illegal drugs and associated penalties with their sale, manufacture, or possession.

10. 1984 Controlled Substances Act - set new, stringent penalties for drug dealers.
11. The Anti-Drug Abuse Act of 1986 - set new standards for minimum and maximum sentences for drug offenders.
12. Anti-Drug Abuse Act of 1988 - created national drug policy under a "drug czar", set treatment an prevention priorities and imposed the death penalty for drug-related killings.

J. Drug Control Strategies
1. Source Control - deter drug sale and importation through the apprehension of dealers and enforcing laws with heavy penalties.
2. Interdiction Strategies - Using Border Patrol and military personnel to intercept drug suppliers as they enter the country.
3. Law Enforcement Strategies - Local, state and federal law enforcement agencies fighting actively against drugs.
4. Punishment Strategies - Courts can severely punish known drug dealers and traffickers.
5. Community Strategies - citizens and local community groups fighting against drugs.
   a. Law enforcement type efforts - block watches, cooperative police-community efforts, and citizen patrols.
   b. Civil justice system - to harass offenders.
   c. Community-based treatment efforts - citizen volunteers participate in self-help support programs like NA or Cocaine Anonymous.
   d. Activities to enhance the quality of life improve interpersonal relationships and upgrade the neighborhood's physical environment.
6. Drug-Testing Programs - employees, government workers and criminal offenders is believed to deter substance abuse.
7. Treatment Strategies
   a. Treatment Programs
   b. Detoxification Units
   c. Therapeutic Programs
8. Employment Programs - research indicates that abusers who obtain and keep employment will end or reduce the incidence of their substance abuse.
9. Legalization - or decriminalization of restricted drugs.
   a. The government would control price and distribution.
10. The Consequences of Legalization
    a. The short-term effect would reduce the association of drug use and crime.
    b. Might increase the nation's rate of drug usage.
    c. Drug users might increase their daily intake.

VIII. Summary

Key Terms

Public Order Crime - Acts that are considered illegal because they threaten the general well-being of society and challenge its accepted moral principles. Prostitution, drug use, and the sale of pornography are considered public order crimes.

Victimless Crime - Crimes that violate the moral order but in which there is no actual victim or target. In these crimes, which include drug abuse and sex offenses, it is society as a whole and not an individual who is considered the victim.

Moral Crusades - Efforts by interest-group members to stamp out behavior they find objectionable. Typically, moral crusades are directed at public order crimes, such as drug abuse or pornography.

Moral Entrepreneurs - Interest groups that attempt to control social life and the legal order in order to promote their own personal set of moral values. People who use their influence to shape the legal process in ways they see fit.

Gay Bashing - Violent acts directed at people because of their sexual orientation.

Homosexuality - Refers to erotic interest in members of one's own sex.

Sodomy - Illegal sexual intercourse. Sodomy has no single definition, and acts included within its scope are usually defined by state statute.

Paraphilias - Bizarre or abnormal sexual practices involving recurrent sexual urges focused on (1) nonhuman objects, (2) humiliation or the experience of receiving or giving pain or (3) children or others who cannot grant consent.

Prostitution - The act of publicly offering one's body for sale.

Brothels - Also known as bordellos, cathouses, sporting houses, and houses of ill repute, brothels flourished in the nineteenth and early twentieth centuries. They were large establishments, usually run by a madam and housed several prostitutes.

Madams - A woman who employs prostitutes, supervises their behavior, and receives a fee for her services; her cut is usually 40 to 60 percent of the prostitutes' earnings. The madam's role may include recruiting women into prostitution and socializing them into the trade.

Call Girls - The aristocrats of prostitution. They service upper-class customers and earn large sums of money.

Skeezers - Women who barter sex for drugs.

Massage Parlors - Base of some prostitutes. They may offer massage and some prostitution services for sale.

Mann Act - (1925) The Federal Act prohibited bringing women into the country or transporting them across state lines for the purposes of prostitution. Often called the "white slave act".

Pornography - Derives from the Greek porne, meaning "prostitute," and graphein, meaning "to write." Material that is used to provide sexual titillation and excitement for paying customers.

256

Obscenity - According to current legal theory, sexually explicit material that lacks a serious purpose and appeals solely to the prurient interest of the viewer.

Temperance Movement - An effort to prohibit the sale of liquor in the United States that resulted in the passage of the Eighteenth Amendment to the Constitution in 1919, which prohibited the sale of alcoholic beverages.

Crack - Processed street cocaine.

Addict - A person with an overpowering physical and psychological need to continue taking a particular substance or drug by any means possible.

Discussion Exercise

Look at the statutes concerning various drugs. Have the class debate the issue of legalizing any or all types of drugs. Are the penalties currently in place appropriate? Why or why not?

InfoTrac Assignment

GETTING STARTED: Search term words for subject guide: Morality, Homosexuality, Paraphilias, Prostitution, Pornography, Substance Abuse, Alcohol, Drugs.

CRITICAL THINKING PROJECT: Using the search term "Prostitution," find relevant articles.

Here are three articles:

Keire, Mara L. "The Vice Trust: A Reinterpretation of the White Slavery Scare in the United States." *Journal of Social History*.

Re, Richard "A Persisting Evil: The Global Problem of Slavery." *Harvard International Review*.

O'Beiren, Kate "Of Human Bondage: U.S. Policy and International Sex Trafficking." *National Review*.

Test Bank

Essay Questions

1. What are the current views on moral crimes? Describe morality crimes. How would you handle these types of crimes: legal or illegal?
2. What is the correct definition of homosexuality? What is the origin and history of homosexuality? Describe the various attitudes towards homosexuality in our society.
3. Who are paraphilias? What are the various crimes that fall under the category of paraphilia? How should policy makers handle these types of crimes?
4. Define prostitution. What is the origin and history of prostitution? Debate the various aspects of legalizing prostitution.
5. What is pornography? What are the dangers of pornography? Does pornography cause violence in our society?

Fill In The Blank

1. Interest groups that attempt to control social life and the legal order to promote their own personal set of moral values are referred to as **Moral Entrepreneurs.**

2. **Obscenity** is sexually explicit material that lacks a serious purpose and appeals solely to the interest of the viewer.

3. **Paraphilias** are bizarre or abnormal sexual practices involving recurrent sexual urges.

4. **Pornography** is material that is used to provide sexual titillation and excitement for paying customers.

5. **Prostitution** is the act of publicly offering one's body for sale.

6. Acts that are considered illegal because they threaten the general well-being of society and challenge its accepted moral principles are known as **Public Order Crimes**.

7. Women who barter sex for drugs are called **Skeezers.**

8. Illegal sexual intercourse is called **Sodomy.**

9. The **Temperance Movement** was an effort to prohibit the sale of liquor in the United States that resulted in the passage of the 18th Amendment to the Constitution in 1919.

10. **Victimless Crimes** are crimes that violate the moral order but in which there is no actual victim or target.

11. **Homophobia** is an extremely negative overreaction to homosexuals.

12. **Transvestite Fetishism** is wearing clothes normally worn by the opposite sex.

13. **Frotteurism** involves rubbing against or touching a nonconsenting person in a crowd, elevator, or other public area.

14. Obtaining sexual pleasure from spying on a stranger while he or she disrobes or engages in sexual behavior with another is known as **Voyeurism**.

15. **Exhibitionism** is deriving sexual pleasure from exposing the genitals to surprises or shock a stranger.

Multiple Choice

1. A person with an overpowering physical and psychological need to continue taking a particular substance or drug by any means possible is known as a(n):
   a. Addict
   b. Prostitute
   c. Skeezer
   d. Call girl
   (Answer = a)

2. Large establishments, usually run by a madam and houses several prostitutes is known as:
   a. Massage parlor
   b. Therapeutic program
   c. Employment program
   (Answer = d)

3. Prostitutes who service upper-class customers and earn large sums of money are known as:
   a. Streetwalkers
   b. Call girls
   c. Skeezers
   d. Drug addicts
   (Answer = b)

4. Processed street cocaine is known as:
   a. Heroin
   b. Marijuana
   c. Crack
   d. Pot
   (Answer = c)

5. Violent acts directed at people because of their sexual orientation are known as:
   a. Gay bashing
   b. Corporate Crime
   c. Insider trading
   d. Tying arrangement
   (Answer = a)

6. Erotic interest in members of one's own sex is known as:
   a. Prostitution
   b. Pornography
   c. Obscenity
   d. Homosexuality
   (Answer = d)

7. A woman who employs prostitutes, supervises their behavior and receives a fee for her services is known as a:
   a. Prostitute
   b. Madam
   c. Call girl
   d. Skeezer
   (Answer = b)

8. The 1925 Federal Act which prohibited bringing women into the country or transporting them across state lines for the purposes of prostitution is known as:
   a. Mann act
   b. Temperance movement
   c. Moral crusades
   d. Sherman antitrust act
   (Answer = a)

9. Base of some prostitutes where they offer massage and some prostitution services for sale is known as:
   a. Street corners
   b. Brothels
   c. Massage parlors
   d. None of the above
   (Answer = c)

10. Efforts by interest-group members to stamp out behavior they find objectionable is known as:
    a. Gay bashing
    b. Moral crusades
    c. Obscenity
    d. Temperance movement
    (Answer = b)

11. Interest groups that attempt to control social life and the legal order in order to promote their own personal set of moral values are known as:
    a. Addicts
    b. Call girls
    c. Skeezers
    d. Moral entrepreneurs
    (Answer = d)

12. According to current legal theory, sexually explicit material that lacks a serious purpose and appeals solely to the interest of the viewer is known as:
    a. Obscenity
    b. Homosexuality
    c. Mann act
    d. Sherman antitrust act
    (Answer = a)

13. Bizarre or abnormal sexual practices involving recurrent sexual urges are known as:
    a. Homosexuals
    b. Paraphilias
    c. Call girls
    d. Prostitution
    (Answer = b)

14. Material that is used to provide sexual titillation and excitement for paying customers is known as:
    a. Homosexuality
    b. Sodomy
    c. Paraphilias
    d. Pornography
    (Answer = d)

15. The act of publicly offering one's body for sale is known as:
    a. Homosexuality
    b. Sodomy
    c. Paraphilias
    d. Prostitution
    (Answer = d)

16. Acts that are considered illegal because they threaten the general well-being of society and challenge its accepted moral principles are known as:
   a. Obscenity
   b. Larency
   c. Burglary
   d. Public order crimes
   (Answer = d)

17. Which of the following are public-order crimes?
   a. prostitution
   b. drug use
   c. all of the above
   d. none of the above
   (Answer = c)

18. Women who barter sex for drugs are known as:
   a. call girls
   b. madams
   c. skeezers
   d. streetwalkers
   (Answer = c)

19. Illegal sexual intercourse is known as:
   a. sodomy
   b. obscenity
   c. pornography
   d. skeezers
   (Answer = a)

20. An effort to prohibit the sale of liquor in the United States that resulted in the passage of the 18th Amendment to the Constitution in 1919 is known as:
   a. War on Drugs
   b. Rehabilitation Movement
   c. Vietnam Era
   d. Temperance Movement
   (Answer = d)

21. Crimes that violate the moral order but in which there is no actual victim or target are known as:
   a. Victimless crimes
   b. Moral crusades
   c. Larceny
   d. Burglary
   (Answer = a)

22.Extremely negative overreaction to homosexuals is referred to as:
   a. Homosexuality
   b. Racism
   c. Sexism
   d. Homophobia
   (Answer = d)

23.Wearing clothing normally worn by the opposite sex is known as:
   a. Asphyxiophilia
   b. Transvestite fetishism
   c. Frotteurism
   d. Voyeurism
   (Answer = b)

24.Using something to induce oxygen deprivation to the brain to enhance sexual gratification is known as:
   a. Transvestite fetishism
   b. Frotteurism
   c. Asphyxiophilia
   d. Voyeurism
   (Answer = c)

25.Obtaining sexual pleasure from spying on a stranger while he or she disrobes or engages in sexual behavior with another is known as:
   a. Transvestite fetishism
   b. Frotteurism
   c. Asphyxiophilia
   d. Voyeurism
   (Answer = d)

26.Deriving sexual pleasure from exposing the genitals to surprise or shock a strangers is known as:
   a. Transvestite fetishism
   b. Asphyxiophilia
   c. Voyeurism
   d. Exhibitionism
   (Answer = d)

27. Deriving pleasure from receiving pain or inflicting pain on another is known as:
   a. Transvestite fetishism
   b. Voyeurism
   c. Sadomasochism
   d. Pedophila
   (Answer = c)

28. Attaining sexual pleasure through sexual activity with prepubescent children is known as:
    a. Transvestite fetishism
    b. Voyeurism
    c. Sadomasochism
    d. Pedophila
    (Answer = d)

29. Sex that involves unwilling or underage victims is known as:
    a. Voyeurism
    b. Sadomasochism
    c. Pedophila
    d. Paraphilia
    (Answer = d)

30. Streetwalkers are also referred to as:
    a. Hustlers
    b. Hookers
    c. All of the above
    d. None of the above
    (Answer = c)

31. Prostitutes who work the streets in plain sight of police, citizens and customers are referred to as:
    a. Streetwalkers
    b. Hustlers
    c. Hookers
    d. All of the above
    (Answer = d)

32. Girls who spend their time in bars, drinking and waiting to be picked up by customers are referred to as:
    a. Streetwalkers
    b. Hustlers
    c. Bar girls
    d. Hookers
    (Answer = c)

33. Large establishments usually run by a madam that houses several prostitutes is known as a:
    a. Brothel
    b. Bordello
    c. Cathouse
    d. All of the above
    (Answer = d)

34. A woman who employs prostitutes is called:
    a. Madam
    b. Hooker
    c. Hustler
    d. Bar girl
    (Answer = a)

35. The aristocrats of prostitution are called:
    a. Madams
    b. Skeezers
    c. Call girls
    d. Bar girls
    (Answer = c)

36. Prostitutes who move around in groups of two or three to lumber, labor and agricultural camps are called:
    a. Bar girls
    b. Call girls
    c. Circuit travelers
    d. Skeezers
    (Answer = c)

37. Women who barter drugs for sex are known as:
    a. Bar girls
    b. Circuit travelers
    c. Skeezers
    d. Call girls
    (Answer = c)

38. Research indicates that each year, approximately how many children are subject to some form of sexual exploitation?
    a. 500
    b. 5000
    c. 2500
    d. 25000
    (Answer = d)

39. Bringing women into the country or transporting them across state lines for the purposes of prostitution is prohibited under the:
    a. Federal Mann Act
    b. Sherman Antitrust Act
    c. Declaration of Independence
    d. None of the above
    (Answer = a)

40. The Federal Mann Act is also known as:
   a.   The trade act
   b.   The anti-abortion act
   c.   The working act
   d.   The white slave act
   (Answer = d)

True/False

T   1.   Despite long-standing biases, it is illegal to deprive gay men and women of due process of law.

F   2.   The military does not ban openly gay people from serving.

F   3.   Asphyxiophilia is the wearing of clothes normally worn by the opposite sex.

T   4.   Frotteurism is the rubbing against or touching a nonconsenting person in a crowd, elevator, or other public place.

T   5.   Voyeurism is obtaining sexual pleasure from spying on a stranger while he or she disrobes or engages in sexual behavior with another.

F   6.   Prostitutes who work the streets in plain sight of police are called call girls.

F   7.   Girls who spend their time in bars, drinking and waiting to be picked up by customers are called streetwalkers.

T   8.   Brothels are large establishments, usually run by madams that house several prostitutes.

T   9.   Prostitutes known as circuit travelers move around in-groups of two or three to lumber, labor, and agricultural camps.

F   10. Women who barter drugs for sex are called teasers.

T   11. Tranquilizers relieve uncomfortable emotional feelings by reducing levels of anxiety; they ease tension and promote a state of relaxation.

T   12. Amphetamines are synthetic drugs that stimulate action in the central nervous system.

F   13. Cocaine is produced from the leaves of Cannabis sativa, a plant grown throughout the world.

T   14.   Hallucinogens are drugs, either natural or synthetic, that produce vivid distortions of the senses without greatly disturbing the viewer's consciousness.

T   15.   Freebase is a chemical produced from street cocaine.

Chapter Fifteen

Overview of the Criminal Justice System

Summary

Chapter Fifteen examines the Criminal Justice System. The chapter begins with the origins of the Criminal Justice System and its development into the system that is operating today. The various components of the Criminal Justice System are described and the process of going through the system is outlined in detail. An analysis of Samuel Walker's "Wedding Cake" model is offered. An analysis of criminal justice and the rule of law are explained in detail. The various models of justice are explained and chapter fifteen concludes with the concepts of justice today.

Learning Objectives

After reading this chapter the student should be able to:
- Develop an understanding of the origins of criminal justice.
- Describe crime and justice in the 20th Century.
- Understand the various components of the criminal justice system.
- Develop an understanding of the Process of Justice.
- Understand Procedural Laws.
- Explore the Exclusionary Rule.
- Define the Crime Control Model.
- Understand the Justice Model.
- Develop an understanding of the Due Process Model
- Explain the Rehabilitation Model.
- Describe the concepts of justice today.

Chapter Overview

Introduction
Origins of Criminal Justice

Chapter Outline

I. **Introduction**
II. **Origins of American Justice**
   A. Early Origins of American Justice
      1. Vigilantes - After Civil War, towns set up "vigilance committees" and asked members to keep order and go after badmen.
      2. Common criminal justice agencies have existed for about 150 years.
      3. Institutions operated independently until 1919 a unified criminal justice system gained recognition.
      4. 1919 - Chicago Crime Commission - professional association created to act as a citizens' advocacy group and to keep track of activities of local justice agencies.
      5. 1931 - President Hoover appointed National Commission of Law Observance and Enforcement, known today as Wickersham Commission.
         a. Analyzes the American justice system
         b. Helped usher in era of treatment of rehabilitation.
   B. The Modern Era of Justice

1. American Bar Association explored some of the hidden or low-visibility processes of justice operations.
    a. Showed how informal decision-making and use of discretion are essential to the justice process.
    b. 1967 - President's Commission on Law Enforcement and Administration of Justice - published report titled The Challenge of Crime in a Free Society.
        1. Resulted in Congress passing the Safe Streets and Crime Control Act of 1968 - provided federal funds for state and local crime control.
        2. Funded the Law Enforcement Assistance Administration - agency that provides money to local and state agencies.
III. **What is the Criminal Justice System?** - Agencies of government charged with enforcing law, adjudicating crime, and correcting criminal conduct. An instrument of social control.
    A. Police and Law Enforcement
        1. Origin early 19th century in Britain.
        2. Tradition police:
            a. Maintained order through patrol
            b. Responded to calls for assistance
            c. Investigated crimes
            d. Identified crime suspects
        3. Expanded roles include:
            a. Preventing youth crime
            b. Diverting juvenile offenders
            c. Resolving family conflicts
            d. Facilitating the movement of people and vehicles
            e. Preserving civil order during emergencies
            f. Providing emergency medical care
            g. Improving police-community relations
        4. Most visible agents of the justice process.
        5. Carefully scrutinized in the news media.
            a. On-going problems:
                1. Racial Profiling - selecting suspects on the basis of their ethnic or racial background.
                2. Tremendous discretion
                3. Internal corruption
                4. Police brutality
    B. The Criminal Courts - the core element in the administration of criminal justice.
        1. Expected to try, convict and sentence those who commit crimes.
        2. Formally required to seek the truth, obtain justice and maintain the integrity of the government's rule of law.
        3. Rights of individuals protected by constitutional mandates, statutes and case law.

a. Right to an attorney
b. Right to a jury trial
c. Right to a speedy trial
d. Right to due process
e. Right to be treated with fundamental fairness
f. Right to be present at trial
g. Right to be notified of charges
h. Right to confront hostile witnesses
i. Right to have favorable witnesses appear
4. Objective, fairness and equal rights rarely achieved.
a. Court dockets are too crowded.
b. Funds too scare to grant defendant's full share of justice.
c. Plea-bargaining has developed.
1. Defendants asked to plead guilty in return for leniency or mercy.
2. Occurs in more than 90% of all criminal trials.
C. Corrections - administer the postjudicatory care given to offenders.
1. Probation - disposition that lets the offender remain in the community, subject to conditions imposed by court order under the supervision of a probation officer.
2. Incarceration - offender confined to a correctional institution for a specified period of time.
a. Jails or houses of correction - hold offenders convicted of misdemeanors and those awaiting trial or other proceedings.
b. Prisons or penitentiaries - state and federal correctional facilities that hold felony offenders sentenced by the courts.
c. Parole - when inmate is selected for early release and serves the remainder of the sentence in the community under the supervision of a parole officer.
IV. **The Process of Justice** - Series of decision points through which offenders' flow.
A. Initial Contact - Police may observe a crime or conduct an investigation where the offender comes into conduct with the justice system through the police.
B. Investigation - After a crime, police gather sufficient facts or evidence to identify the perpetrator justify an arrest and bring the offender to trial.
C. Arrest - Police take a person into custody for allegedly committing a crime. Arrests are legal when:
1. Officer believes there is sufficient evidence (probable cause) that a crime has been committed and the suspect committed the crime;
2. Officer deprives the individual of freedom and
3. Suspect believes to be in custody of police and cannot voluntarily leave.
D. Custody - after arrest, suspect remains in police custody.
1. Taken to police station.
2. Booking - Fingerprinted, photographed and personal information recorded.
3. Identification by witnesses in a lineup.

4. Interrogation by police.

E. Complaint/charging - With sufficient evidence, police turn case to prosecutor. Decision made to file complaint for court to have authority over case. Prosecutor determines the charges.

F. Preliminary hearing-grand jury - Constitution mandates that before standing trial for a serious crime, the state must prove probable cause that the accused committed the criminal act.

1. Grand jury - group of citizens brought together to consider the case in a closed hearing where the prosecutor presents evidence. With sufficient evidence, grand jury issues a "true bill of indictment" - the accused must stand trial.

2. Preliminary hearing - or probable cause hearing - prosecutor files a charging document called an information - hearing is then held to determine if there is sufficient evidence to actually try the case.

G. Arraignment - the accused is brought for the first time where they are informed of the charges against them, informed of their constitutional rights, have their bail considered and have their trial date set.

H. Bail or detention - a money bond, the amount of which is set by judicial authority; intended to ensure the defendant appears at trial while allowing freedom until that time.

I. Plea Bargaining - After arraignment, prosecution may offer the defense a possible guilty arrangement. The defendant agrees to plead guilty for reduced charges, a lenient sentence or another consideration.

J. Trial/Adjudication - With no plea-bargain, defendant goes to trial. A full-scale inquiry into the facts of the case before a judge, a jury or both. Defendant will be found either:

1. Guilty

2. Not Guilty

3. Hung Jury - when the jury fails to reach a decision; the case is then unresolved and open for possible retrial.

K. Disposition - Guilty defendants are sentenced by the presiding judge. Dispositions may include a fine, community service, probation, incarceration, or death.

L. Postconviction Remedies - After disposition, defendants may appeal if they feel they were treated unfairly. If the court agrees, the defendant may be granted a new trial or possible release.

M. Correctional Treatment - Offenders who are found guilty and are formally sentenced come under the jurisdiction of correction authorities.

N. Release - At the end of the correctional sentence, offenders are released into society.

O. Postrelease/aftercare - Some offenders are released to community correctional centers - to bridge the gap between a secure treatment facility an absolute freedom.

P. Going Through The Process

1. Every stage of the process decisions are made whether to send the case further down the line.
2. Decisions transform identifies of individuals from an accused, to a defendant, to a convicted criminal, to an inmate to an ex-con.
3. Decision-making and discretion mark each stage of the system.

Q. The "Wedding Cake" Model - Samuel Walker, justice historian, suggests criminal justice process is best conceived as a 4-layer cake.
   1. Celebrated Cases - First layer
      a. Receive a great deal of attention
      b. Cases receive the full panoply of criminal justice procedures
      c. Do not truly represent how the system works.
   2. Serious Felonies - Second layer
      a. Likely to be prosecuted to the full extent of the law
      b. If convicted, receive lengthy prison sentences
   3. Less Serious Felonies - Third layer
      a. Less money or damage involved than second layer
      b. Usually receive dismissal, plea bargain, reduction in charges or a probationary sentence
   4. Misdemeanors - Fourth layer
      a. Handled by lower criminal courts in assembly-line fashion.
      b. Few defendants exercise their constitutional rights
      c. Penalty is usually a small fine.
   5. Is There a Criminal Justice Wedding Cake?
      a. Outcome of cases is a function of how they are evaluated by decision-makers.
      b. High degree of consistency.
      c. Public opinion is often formed on what happens in a few celebrated cases.
      d. Process dominated by judges, prosecutors, and defense attorneys working in concert to get cases processed.

V. Criminal Justice and the Rule of Law
A. 1960's - under Chief Justice Earl Warren, U.S. Supreme Court became more active in the affairs of the justice system.
B. Law of Criminal Procedure - sets out and guarantees citizens certain rights and privileges when accused of a crime.
C. Procedural laws - control the actions of the agencies of justice and define the rights of criminal defendants.
D. Most important sources is the U.S. Constitution, specifically the first 10 amendments called the Bill of Rights.
E. 14TH Amendment - 1868 - made the first 10 amendments binding on the state governments.
F. 1963 - U.S. Supreme Court interpreted 6th Amendment to mean that all persons accused of felonies are entitled to legal counsel at trial.
G. If Supreme Court has ruled on a procedural issue, lower court must follow; if not, lower court are free to interpret the Constitution.

VI. **Concepts of Justice**
    A. Crime Control Model - crime rates trend upwards when criminals do not sufficiently fear apprehension and punishment.
        1. If justice became efficient, then the criminal law would be toughened, and crime rates would decline.
        2. Expensive
        3. Purpose of justice:
            a. Protect the public
            b. Deter criminal behavior
            c. Incapacitate known criminals
        4. Emphasizes protected society
        5. Compensating victims.
        6. Crime Control Policies
            a. Became dominant in 1960s and 1970s.
            b. Some states have recently enacted stiffer penalties for crimes.
            c. Research indicates some offenders reoffend even with stiffer penalties.
    B. Justice Model
        1. Most concerned about the presence of unequal treatment in the justice system.
        2. Concerned with racism and discrimination - which causes sentencing disparity and unequal treatment before the law.
        3. Calls for the adoption of sentencing policies, which require all offenders who commit the same type of crime, receive the same sentence.
        4. "Truth in Sentencing Laws" - requires offenders to serve a substantial portion of their prison sentence behind bars limiting their eligibility for early release on parole.
    C. Due Process Model
        1. Civil rights of the accused should be protected at all times.
        2. Requires practices such as strict scrutiny of police search and interrogation practices.
        3. Competent defense counsel, jury trials and other procedural safeguards be offered to every criminal defendant.
    D. Rehabilitation Model
        1. Believes that given proper care and treatment, criminals can be changed into productive, law-abiding citizens.
        2. Believes people commit crimes because they are victims of social injustice, poverty, and racism.
        3. Favors programs to help disadvantaged people who commit crime.
        4. Rehabilitation within the System
            a. Efforts should be made to treat criminals, rather than punish them.
            b. Also known as Medical Model - view of dispensing "treatment" to needy "patients".
            c. Effective treatment can make a significant difference in reducing offender recidivism.
    E. Nonintervention Model

1. When possible, justice agencies should limit their involvement with criminal defendants.
2. Noninterventionists are fearful of the harmful effects of stigma and negative labels.
3. Want to decriminalize (reduce penalties) and/or legalize non-serious victimless crimes such as small amounts of marijuana, public drunkenness and vagrancy.
4. Want non-violent offenders removed from the correctional system - deinstitutionalization.
5. Want first offenders of minor crimes to be placed in informal, community-based treatment programs - pretrial diversion.
6. Limiting government intrusion into the lives of people in trouble.

F. Restorative Justice Perspective
1. Belief that the purpose of the criminal justice system is to promote a peaceful, just society.
2. Advocate peacemaking, not punishment.
3. Believe that the efforts to punish and control encourage crime.
4. Restorative Justice Programs:
   a. Police officer-citizen dispute mediation programs
   b. Mediation and conflict resolution programs
   c. Community service restitution programs

VII. Concepts of Justice Today
A. Today, crime control and justice models have the support of the public and legislatures.

VIII. Summary

Key Terms

Chicago Crime Commission - A professional organization funded by private contributions. Created in 1919, this organization acted as a citizens' advocacy group and keeps track of the ongoing activities of local justice agencies.

Wickersham Commission - National study group appointed by President Herbert Hoover in 1931. Formerly called the National Commission of Law Observance and Enforcement, this national study group analyzed the American justice system in detail and helped usher in the era of treatment and rehabilitation.

Criminal Justice - Refers to the agencies of government charged with law enforcement, adjudicating crime and correcting criminal conduct.

Social Control - Laws which outlaw dangerous and destructive behavior and enforced by the Criminal Justice System. Other methods of social control include family, school and church designed to deal with moral behavior.

Sheriff's Department - Local county law enforcement agency.

Criminal Court - The core element in the administration of criminal justice. Expected to try, convict and sentence those who commit crimes while ensuring that the falsely accused are freed without any consequence or burden.

Due Process - Rights of the defendant are protected at all times by federal and state constitutional mandates, statutes, and case law.

Fundamental Fairness - The 5th and 14th Amendments of the U.S. Constitution guarantees the right of due process.

Plea Bargaining - Defendants are asked to plead guilty as charged in return for consideration for leniency or mercy.

Probation - The most common correctional treatment. A legal disposition that allows the convicted offender to remain in the community, subject to conditions imposed by court order under the supervision of a probation officer.

Jail - houses of correction which hold offenders convicted of misdemeanors and those awaiting trial or involved in other proceedings, such as grand jury deliberations, arraignments, or preliminary hearings.

Prison - State and federally operated correctional facilities that receive felony offenders sentenced by the criminal courts. Also known as penitentiaries.

Penitentiary - See prisons.

Parole - A process whereby an inmate is selected for early release and serves the remainder of the sentence in the community under the supervision of parole officer.

Arrest - Occurs when the police take a person into custody for allegedly committing a criminal act.

Probable Cause - Sufficient evidence that a crime has been committed and that the suspect committed the crime.

Lineup - Witnesses brought in to pick out the suspect from a group of individuals.

Complaint - Charges issued by the prosecutor's office against the defendant.

Information - Charging document filed by the prosecutor.

Indictment - With sufficient evidence, the grand jury issues a "true bill of indictment" which means the accused must stand trial.

Grand Jury - Group of citizens brought together to consider the case in a closed hearing in which only the prosecutor presents evidence. If the evidence is sufficient, the grand jury will issue "a true bill of indictment" which means that the accused must stand trial.

Preliminary Hearing - Held to determine if there is sufficient evidence to warrant a trial.

Probable Cause Hearing - See Preliminary Hearing.

Arraignment - The accused defendant is brought before the court and told of formal charges, informed of Constitutional Rights, has bail considered and trial date set.

Bail - Money bond set by judicial authority to ensure the presence of suspects at trial while allowing them their freedom until that time.

Hung Jury - When a jury fails to reach a decision, thereby leaving the case unresolved.

Disposition - Sentence that a defendant receives after being found guilty at trial. Sentence could be a fine, community service, probation, incarceration, or a combination of these up to the death penalty.

Bill of Rights - First 10 Amendments of the U.S. Constitution which are guarantees of freedom.

Exclusionary Rule - All evidence obtained by illegal searches and seizures is inadmissible in criminal trials; it also excludes the use of illegal confessions under the 5th Amendment.

Determinate Sentencing - A type of prison sentence in which the court has determined the exact length of imprisonment and parole supervision is fixed within statutory limits by the legislature.

Widening The Net - The view that diversion programs are designed to remove offenders from the justice system actually maintain their involvement in the system.

Discussion Exercise

Divide the class into four groups. Assign each group one of the criminal justice wedding cake layers. Have the group present their layer to the class with familiar cases that reflect their layer of the wedding cake.

InfoTrac Assignment

GETTING STARTED: Search term words for subject guide: Police, Law Enforcement, Criminal Courts, Corrections, Procedural Laws, Due Process, Exclusionary Rule, Crime Control, Justice, Rehabilitation Model.

CRITICAL THINKING PROJECT: Using the search term "Due Process," find relevant articles.

Here are three articles:

Kaye, D.H. "The Constitutionality of DNA Sampling on Arrest." *Cornell Journal of Law and Public Policy.*

Fisher, Barry J. "Judicial Suicide or Constitutional Autonomy? A Capital Defendant's Right to Plead Guilty." *Albany Law Review.*

Erickson, Kris "Constitutional Law: Use of Force by Mental Health Workers Violated Due Process." *Journal of Law, Medicine & Ethics.*

Test Bank

Essay Questions

1. Trace the origin of criminal justice. Compare and contrast the early origins of American Justice with today's era of justice.
2. Define and describe the Criminal Justice System. What are the various components and how do they interact with one another?
3. Explain Samuel Walker's Wedding Cake Model of Criminal Justice. Is this a realistic model of Criminal Justice in our society?
4. Trace the process of justice. Examine the various steps that a criminal defendant goes through as they are processed through the Criminal Justice system.
5. What is the role of the Criminal Courts? Which models of justice are being most used in our Criminal Courts?

Fill In The Blank

1. The charging document filed by the prosecutor is an **Information**.

2. Charges issued by the prosecutor's office against the defendant are known as a **Complaint**.

3. A **Lineup** consists of witnesses that are brought in to pick out the suspect from a group of individuals.

4. **Probable Cause** is sufficient evidence that a crime has been committed and that the suspect committed the crime.

5. Another name for a prison is a **Penitentiary.**

6. **Parole** is a process whereby an inmate is selected for early release and serves the remainder of the sentence in the community under the supervision of an officer.

7. **Arrest** occurs when the police take a person into custody for allegedly committing a criminal act.

8. An **Indictment** is the document issued by the Grand Jury when there is sufficient evidence for the accused to stand trial.

9. **Jails** are houses of correction, which hold offenders convicted of misdemeanors and those awaiting trial or involved in other proceedings, such as grand jury deliberations, arraignments, or preliminary hearings.

10. When defendants are asked to plead guilty as charged in return for consideration for leniency or mercy, they are offered a **Plea Bargain**.

11. **Prisons** are state and federally operated correctional facilities that receive felony offenders sentenced by the criminal courts.

12. **Probation** is a legal disposition that allows the convicted offender to remain in the community, subject to conditions imposed by court order under the supervision of a probation officer.

13. The local county law enforcement agency is known as the **Sheriff's Department**.

14. **Due Process** is where the rights of defendant are protected at all times by federal and state constitutional mandates, statutes and case law.

15. A **Hung Jury** is when a jury fails to reach a decision, thereby leaving the case unresolved.

Multiple Choice

1. A group of citizens brought together to consider the case in a closed hearing in which only the prosecutor presents evidence is called:
   a. Grand Jury
   b. Petit Jury
   c. Probable Cause Hearing
   d. Preliminary Hearing
   (Answer = a)

2. A hearing held to determine if there is sufficient evidence to warrant a trial is known as:
   a. Probable Cause Hearing
   b. Preliminary Hearing
   c. All of the above
   d. None of the above
   (Answer = c)

3. When the accused defendant is brought before the court and told of formal charges, informed of Constitutional Rights, has bail considered and the trial date is set, this is known as:
   a. Grand Jury
   b. Arraignment
   c. Probable Cause Hearing
   d. Preliminary Hearing
   (Answer = b)

4. Money bond set by judicial authority to ensure the presence of suspects at trial while allowing them their freedom until that time is known as:
   a. Jail
   b. Probation
   c. Parole
   d. Bail
   (Answer = d)

5. When a jury fails to reach a decision, thereby leaving the case unresolved, it is known as:
   a. Hung Jury
   b. Grand Jury
   c. Petit Jury
   d. All of the above
   (Answer = a)

6. A sentence that a defendant receives after being found guilty at trial is called a:
   a. Arraignment
   b. Probable Cause Hearing
   c. Exclusionary Rule
   d. Disposition
   (Answer = d)

7. The first 10 amendments of the U.S. Constitution which are guarantees of freedom are known as:
   a. The Exclusionary Rule
   b. The Bill of Rights
   c. The Declaration of Independence
   d. The Magna Carta
   (Answer = b)

8. All evidence obtained by illegal searches and seizures is inadmissible in criminal trials according to the:
    a. Exclusionary Rule
    b. Bill of Rights
    c. The Declaration of Independence
    d. Grand Jury
    (Answer = a)

9. A type of prison sentence in which the court has determined the exact length of imprisonment and parole supervision is fixed within statutory limits by the legislature is called:
    a. Indeterminate sentence
    b. Death sentence
    c. Determinate sentence
    d. Probation sentence
    (Answer = c)

10. The view that diversion programs are designed to remove offenders from the justice system when they actually maintain the offenders involvement in the system is known as:
    a. Determinate sentencing
    b. Widening the net
    c. Probable cause
    d. Disposition
    (Answer = b)

11. With sufficient evidence, the Grand Jury issues an:
    a. Information
    b. Arrest
    c. Arraignment
    d. Indictment
    (Answer = d)

12. The charging document filed by the prosecutor is known as an:
    a. Information
    b. Arrest
    c. Arraignment
    d. Indictment
    (Answer = a)

13. Charges issued by the prosecutor's office against the defendant are known as:
    a. complaint
    b. indictment
    c. information
    d. lineup
    (Answer = b)

14. Witnesses brought in to pick out the suspect from a group of individuals are known as:
    a. lineup
    b. backup
    c. Drift
    d. Social control
    (Answer = d)

15. Sufficient evidence that a crime has been committed by the suspect is known as:
    a. Reasonable belief
    b. Beyond a reasonable doubt
    c. Fundamental fairness
    d. Probable cause
    (Answer = d)

16. This occurs when the police take a person into custody for allegedly committing a criminal act:
    a. Investigation
    b. Hung jury
    c. Job offers
    d. Arrest
    (Answer = d)

17. A process whereby an inmate is selected for early release and serves the remainder of the sentence in the community under the supervision of a parole officer is known as:
    a. Probation
    b. Parole
    c. Incarceration
    d. Arrest
    (Answer = b)

18. Another name for prisons is:
    a. Parole
    b. Probation
    c. Penitentiary
    d. Jail
    (Answer = c)

19. State and federally operated correctional facilities that receive felony offenders sentenced by the criminal courts are known as:
    a. Prisons
    b. Parole
    c. Probation
    d. Jails
    (Answer = a)

20. Houses of correction that hold offenders convicted of misdemeanors and those awaiting trial or involved in other proceedings are known as:
    a. Prisons
    b. Jails
    c. Penitentiaries
    d. Probation
    (Answer = b)

21. A legal disposition that allows the convicted offender to remain in the community, subject to conditions imposed by court order under the supervision of an officer is known as:
    a. Prison
    b. Jail
    c. Parole
    d. Probation
    (Answer = d)

22. When defendants are asked to plead guilty as charged in return for consideration for leniency or mercy, this is known as:
    a. Probation
    b. Parole
    c. Prison
    d. Plea bargaining
    (Answer = d)

23. The element of criminal justice which is expected to try, convict, and sentence those who commit crimes while ensuring that the falsely accused are freed without any consequence or burden is known as:
    a. Civil court
    b. Criminal court
    c. Probation
    d. Parole
    (Answer = b)

24. The local county law enforcement agency is called the:
    a. Probation department
    b. Parole department
    c. Sheriff's department
    d. Jail
    (Answer = c)

25. The agencies of government charged with law enforcement, adjudicating crime and correcting criminal behavior are known as:
    a. Due process
    b. Probation
    c. Sheriff's department
    d. Criminal Justice
    (Answer = d)

26. The contemporary criminal justice system consists of _____ public agencies.
    a. 55
    b. 550
    c. 550
    d. 55000
    (Answer = d)

27. The justice system today employs approximately how many people?
    a. 100,000
    b. 1 million
    c. 2 million
    d. 10 million
    (Answer = c)

28. How much does it cost to build a prison cell?
    a. $70,000
    b. $7000
    c. $700
    d. $7
    (Answer = a)

29. In 2001, what percentage of the nation's adult population were incarcerated or on probation or on parole?
    a. 30%
    b. 50%
    c. 5%
    d. 3%
    (Answer = d)

30. The major components of the criminal justice system are:
    a. Courts
    b. Corrections
    c. Law Enforcement
    d. All of the Above
    (Answer = d)

31. When police select suspects on the basis of their ethnic or racial background, this is known as:
    a. Disposition
    b. Due process
    c. Racial profiling
    d. determinate sentencing
    (Answer = c)

32. The courts are formally required to:
    a. Seek the truth
    b. Obtain justice
    c. Maintain the integrity of the government's rule of law
    d. All of the above
    (Answer = c)

33. Prisons may be which of the following?
    a. Maximum security
    b. Medium security
    c. Minimum security
    d. All of the above
    (Answer = d)

34. A form of executive clemency is known as a:
    a. Pardon
    b. Probation
    c. Parole
    d. Prison
    (Answer = a)

35. The philosophy where the state acts in the best interests of children in trouble is known as:
    a. Parental control
    b. Due process
    c. Crime control model
    d. Parens patriae
    (Answer = d)

36. Juveniles who commit crimes are called:
    a. Status offenders
    b. Criminals
    c. Delinquents
    d. Adults
    (Answer = c)

37. Juveniles who are incorrigible, truants, runaways or unmanageable are called:
    a. Criminals
    b. Delinquents
    c. Status offenders
    d. Adults
    (Answer = c)

38. The initial contact an offender has with the justice system is usually with:
    a. The courts
    b. The police
    c. The congress
    d. The prison
    (Answer = b)

39. After a crime is recognized, police officers will gather facts, or evidence to identify the perpetrator, justify an arrest and bring the offender to trial and this is known as:
    a. Investigation
    b. Arrest
    c. Arraignment
    d. Grand jury
    (Answer = a)

40. When the police take a person into custody for allegedly committing a criminal act, it is known as:
    a. Investigation
    b. Arrest
    c. Arraignment
    d. Grand jury
    (Answer = b)

True/False

T   1. Each year about 8,000 kids are "waived" to the adult system to face long prison sentences and even the death penalty.

F   2. The initial contact an offender has with the justice system is usually with the correctional agency.

F   3. After a crime is recognized, police officers will conduct an arrest to gather sufficient facts, or evidence, to identify the perpetrator, justify an arrest, and bring the offender to trial.

T   4. An arrest occurs when the police take a person into custody for allegedly committing a criminal act.

286

T   5. Arrests can be made at the scene of a crime or after a warrant is issued by a magistrate.

F   6. If sufficient evidence is gathered, the police will turn the case over to the Judge's office.

F   7. Because it is a tremendous personal and financial burden, the Declaration of Independence mandates that before a person is forced to stand trial for a serious crime, the state must first prove there is at least reasonable belief that the accused committed the act.

T   8. Bail is a money bond, the amount of which is set by judicial authority.

T   9. After a criminal trial, a defendant who is found guilty as charged is sentenced by the presiding judge.

F   10. Offenders who are found not guilty and are formally sentenced come under the jurisdiction of correctional authorities.

T   11. At the end of the correctional sentence, the offender is released into the community.

T   12. Samuel Walker, a justice historian, suggests that the criminal justice process is best conceived of as a four-layer cake.

F   13. People in the first layer of the criminal justice wedding cake receive a great deal of public attention, because they are charged with misdemeanors.

T   14. The second and third layers of the cake are made up of those serious felonies encountered daily in urban jurisdictions such as robberies, burglaries, rapes and homicides.

T   15. Procedural laws control the actions of the agencies of justice and define the rights of criminal defendants.

Chapter Sixteen

Police and Law Enforcement System

Summary

Chapter Sixteen examines Police and the Law Enforcement System. Police history is traced from the London Police to the advent of professionalism. The different levels of law enforcement are introduced with the various police functions being detailed. How the police are changing with the advent of Community-Oriented Policing and Problem-Oriented Policing is discussed with the various rules of law that directly affect policing. Chapter Sixteen concludes with various issues in policing, such as discretion, women and minority officers and violence.

Learning Objectives

After reading this chapter the student should be able to:
- Trace the history of police.
- Develop an understanding of the London Police.
- Describe policing in early America.
- Understand the advent of police professionalism.
- Develop an understanding of the law enforcement agencies of today.
- Understand the various functions of the police.
- Explore the how the role of policing is changing.
- Define custodial interrogation.
- Understand Search and Seizure.
- Develop an understanding of discretion.
- Explain the role of women and minority officers.
- Understand the police and violence.

Chapter Overview

Introduction

History of Police
> The London Police
> Policing the American Colonies
> Early American Police Agencies
> Reform Movements
> The Advent of Professionalism

Law Enforcement Agencies Today
> Federal Law Enforcement
> County Law Enforcement
> State Police
> Metropolitan Police

Police Functions
> Patrol Function
> Investigation Function
> Other Police Functions

Changing the Police Role
> Community-Oriented Policing (COP)
> Problem-Oriented Policing
> Does Community Policing Work?

Police and the Rule of Law
> Custodial Interrogation
> Search and Seizure

Issues in Policing
> Police Personality and Subculture
> Discretion
> Women and Minority Police Officers
> The Police and Violence

Summary

Chapter Outline

I.   Introduction

    A. Police - gatekeepers of the Criminal Justice system.

        1. Initiate contact with law violators.

        2. Decide whether to formally arrest or settle informally.

        3. Most visible members of the Criminal Justice system.

II.   History of Police

    A. U.S. police agencies can be traced to early English society.

        1. Before Norman conquest, no regular police force.

        2. Pledge System - every man was responsible for aiding his neighbors and protecting the settlement from thieves and marauders.

3. Tithing - people grouped into a collective of 10 families.
4. Hundred - ten tithings
5. Constable - dealt with more serious breaches of the law.
6. Watch System - Watchmen that protect cities and towns by patrolling at night and protecting against robberies, fires and disturbances.
7. Shire reeve - forerunner of today's sheriff; appointed by the crown to supervise a certain territory and assure the local nobleman that order would be kept.
8. Justice of the Peace - Created in 1326 to assist the shire reeve in controlling the county.

B. The London Police
1. Sir Robert Peele -England's home secretary - 1829 - had Parliament to pass an "Act for Improving the Police In and Near the Metropolis."
2. Act established the first organized police in London.
3. Composed of 1000 men, along military lines.
4. Members wore a distinctive uniform.
5. Led by 2 magistrates, later known as commissioner.

C. Policing the American Colonies
1. Law Enforcement paralleled the British model.
2. County sheriff became the most important law enforcement agent.
    a. Peacekeeping and crime fighting
    b. Collected taxes
    c. Supervised elections
    d. Reacted to citizen's complaints
    e. Investigated crimes that already occurred.
    f. Paid by the fee system; given a fixed amount for every arrest made, subpoena served, or court appearance made.
3. Town marshal policed cities.
    a. Aided often unwillingly by constables, night watchmen, police justices and city council members.
    b. Offered rewards for the capture of felons.
4. After revolution, larger cities had elected or appointed leaders.
    a. Nightwatchmen - called leatherheads, because of their leather helmets, patrolled the streets calling the hour.

D. Early American Police Agencies
1. 19th century - urban mob violence led to modern police departments.
2. Boston - 1st formal police department - 1838.
3. New York - 1844.
4. Philadelphia - 1854.
5. Politics dominated the departments.
6. Mid-19th century - detective bureau set up in Boston police.
7. Police in 19th century - incompetent, corrupt, and disliked.

E. Reform Movements
1. Uniforms introduced in 1853 in New York.
2. Late 1850's - precincts linked to central headquarters by telegraph.

3. Call boxes - allowed patrol officers to communicate with commanders.
4. Nonpolice functions abandoned after civil war.
5. Efforts to prevent police corruption, but not very successful.
6. Boston Police Strike of 1914
   a. Dissatisfaction with the status of police officers in society.
   b. Police unionized, held a strike and lost public support.
   c. Striking officers were fired and replaced.
   d. Ended police unionism for decades.
F. The Advent of Professionalism
   1. 1920's - August Vollmer
      a. Police Chief of Berkeley, CA
      b. Instituted university training as part of development of police officers.
      c. Helped develop School of Criminology at the University of California at Berkeley - the model for justice related programs around the country.
   2. Technological Breakthroughs
      a. Communications - telegraph call boxes installed in 1867
      b. Transportation
         1. Bicycles - 1897
         2. Automobiles - 1910
   3. 1960's - efforts to promote understanding between police and community
      a. Reduce police brutality
      b. Recognize the stresses of police work.

III. **Law Enforcement Agencies Today**
A. Federal Law Enforcement - about 50 different organizations
   1. The Federal Bureau of Investigation
      a. 1870 - Attorney General - hired investigators to enforce the Mann Act.
      b. 1908 - Investigators formally made into the Bureau of Investigation.
      c. 1930's - Reorganized under J. Edgar Hoover into FBI.
      d. Today, an investigative agency with jurisdiction over all matters in which the U.S. is or may be an interested party.
      e. Jurisdiction limited to federal matters.
         1. Espionage
         2. Sabotage
         3. Treason
         3. Civil Rights Violations
         4. Murder and Assault of Federal Officers
         5. Mail Fraud
         6. Robbery and Burglary of Federally Insured Banks
         7. Kidnapping
         8. Interstate transportation of stolen vehicles and property.
      f. Offers services to local law enforcement agencies.
      g. Vast fingerprint file
      h. Sophisticated crime laboratory.

  i. FBI National Crime Information Center - computerized network to local police departments by terminals.

  2. Other Federal Agencies

   a. Drug Enforcement Administration - investigate illegal drug use; conduct independent surveillance and enforcement to control the importation of narcotics.

   b. U.S. Marshals - court officers who implement federal court rulings, transport prisoners, and enforce court orders.

   c. Immigration and Naturalization Service - administer immigration laws, deport illegal aliens and naturalize lawful aliens in the U.S. Also patrol borders.

   d. Alcohol, Tobacco, and Firearms (ATF) Bureau - Has jurisdiction over the sale and distribution of firearms, explosives, alcohol and tobacco products.

   e. Internal Revenue Service - established 1862 - enforces violations of income, excise, stamp and other tax laws. Pursues gamblers, narcotics dealers, and other violators who do not report illegal financial gains as income.

   f. Customs Bureau - Guards points of entry into U.S. and prevents smuggling of contraband in or out of the country.

   g. Secret Service - of the Treasury Department, originally enforced counterfeiting; today, also protects the president, vice-president and their families, presidential candidates, and former presidents.

B. County Law Enforcement

  1. Independent agency

  2. Senior officer - Sheriff - usually elected

  3. Evolved from early Shire reeve

  4. Today, nearly 3,100 sheriffs' offices nationwide

  5. Employs over 290,000 full-time employees

  6. About 186,000 sworn personnel

  7. Provides:

   a. Routine patrol

   b. Respond to citizen calls

   c. Investigate crimes

  8. Keepers of the county jail

  9. Court Attendants

  10. Executors of criminal and Civil Processes

C. State Police

  1. Texas Rangers - 1835 - considered the first state police force.

  2. Pennsylvania lead State Policing in 20th century

  3. State Police gave governor's powerful enforcement arm under their personal control and not of city politicians.

  4. Today about 55,000 full-time state police officers

  5. Major role

   a. Controlling traffic on the highway system

   b. Tracing stolen automobiles
   c. Aiding in disturbances
   d. Crowd control
  D. Metropolitan Police
   1. Today, estimated 556,631 full-time law enforcement employees
   2. About 436,000 sworn personnel
   3. 46 departments employ 1,000 or more officers
   4. About 800 departments employ just 1 officer.
   5. Larger, urban departments operate without specific administrative control from any higher governmental authority.
    a. Common for mayor to control hiring and firing of police chief.
   6. Duties include:
    a. Identifying criminal suspects.
    b. Investigating crimes.
    c. Apprehending offenders and participating in their trials.
    d. Deterring crime through patrol.
    e. Aiding individuals in danger or in need of assistance; providing emergency services.
    f. Resolving conflict and keeping the peace.
    g. Maintaining a sense of community security.
    h. Keeping vehicular and pedestrian movement efficient.
    i. Promoting civil order.
    j. Operating and administering the police department.

IV. **Police Functions**
  A. Patrol Function
   1. Involves police visible presence
   2. Purpose:
    a. Deter crime
    b. Maintain order
    c. Enforce Laws
    d. Aid in Service Functions
   3. Techniques
    a. Foot Patrol - officer walk the area, or beat, assigned
    b. Aggressive Preventive Patrol - designed to deter crime
     1. Stop-and-frisk techniques
   4. How Effective is Patrol?
    a. May have a direct deterrent effect.
    b. Increased community perception that police arrest offenders.
    c. Aggressive police arrest more suspects.
    d. Fewer criminals produce lower crime rates.
    e. More study needs to be done.
  B. Investigation Function
   1. Detective - established by the London Metropolitan Police - 1841
    a. Morals or Vice Squads - specialize in victimless crimes such as prostitution or gambling.

b. Usually enter a case after it has been reported to police.

c. Use various investigator techniques.

d. Use sting type operations to solve some cases.

2. Are Investigations Effective?

a. Rand Corporation - 1975 study of 153 detective bureaus

1. Found much of detectives' time was spent on unproductive work.

2. That investigative expertise did little to help solve cases.

3. Estimated that half of detectives could be removed without reducing clearance rates.

V. **Changing the Police Role**

A. Community-Oriented Policing (COP)

1. Wilson and Kelling article, "Broken Windows: The Police and Neighborhood Safety" called for a return to 19th century community policing.

a. Police should get out of their cars.

b. Deploy police on the basis of crime rates or where citizens make the most calls.

c. Elicit citizen cooperation.

d. Community preservation.

e. Public safety.

f. Order Maintenance.

g. Play an active role in the community.

h. Identify neighborhood problems and needs.

i. Set a course of action for an effective response.

2. Implementing COP

a. Foot patrol implemented.

b. Foot patrol has little effect on crime, but improves citizen attitudes toward police.

c. Neighborhood Watch

d. Community newsletters

e. Other devices to bring the police and the community together.

3. Community Policing in Action

a. Implemented in large cities, suburban areas and rural communities.

b. Some assign officers to neighborhoods.

c. Organize training programs for community leaders

d. Feature a bottom-up approach to dealing with community problems.

4. Neighborhood Policing

a. Policing must be flexible and adaptive.

b. Allocate resources to meet needs of various neighborhoods.

c. Neighborhood initiatives ideal way to fight crime.

d. Citizens provide information in crime investigations.

B. Does Community Policing Work?

1. Many have embraced community policing as revolutionary.

2. Credited with reducing crime rates in large cities such as Boston and New York.

3. Most professional and highly motivated will support COPS.
4. Critics say return to old style of policing is negative.
5. Difficult to retrain officers from their traditional roles.
6. Some consider the roles of COPS in conflict with effective law enforcement.
7. Some administrators consider law enforcement as their top priority; community service not necessarily a significant police role.
8. Research indicates that COP programs improve community relations, upgrade police image, and reduce levels of community fear.

C. Problem-Oriented Policing (POP)
1. Police play an active role in identifying particular community problems.
   a. Police develop strategies to counteract the problems.
   b. Encourages new solutions to old problems.
2. Crackdowns and Hot spots
   a. Crackdowns - POP strategy, which involves a particular problem area in a city and is the target of, increased police resources.
   b. Hot spot - A significant portion of all police calls emanate from relatively few locations such as bars, malls, the bus depot, hotels, and certain apartment buildings.
   c. Diffusion of Benefits - research indicates that by allocating resources that unintended crime benefits were recorded.
3. COPPS
   a. Community-Oriented, Problem-Solving Approach
   b. To identify, assess, and address crime-related community issues.

VI.   Police and the Rule of Law
A. Custodial Interrogation
1. Miranda v. Arizona (1966) - Court created objective standards for questioning by police after defendant taken into custody.
2. Miranda Warning - Officers must inform individual of the 5th Amendment to be free from self-incrimination.
   a. Right to remain silent.
   b. If they make a statement, it can be used against them in court.
   c. Right to call attorney and have attorney present at interrogation.
   d. If they cannot afford attorney, state will appoint one.
3. If Miranda is not issued, then interrogation cannot be admitted at trial.
4. The Miranda Rule Today
   a. Defendant's perjured testimony allows government to use illegal evidence to impeach testimony.
   b. Witnesses are allowed even if their revealed identity was in violation of Miranda.
   c. Miranda only applies to attorneys; not priest or probation officers.
   d. Inevitable discovery rule - information of evidence provided by suspect permissible if evidence would have been obtained anyway.
   e. Public Safety Doctrine - admissible evidence can be obtained without Miranda if the information sought is needed for public safety.

f. Initial errors do not make subsequent statements inadmissible; just give the Miranda warning.

g. Suspects do not have to understand the outcomes of waiving their Miranda rights.

h. Mentally impaired defendants admissions can be admitted if police acted properly and defendant understood Miranda.

i. Attorney's request to see defendant does not affect the validity of the right to counsel.

j. Mentally ill schizophrenia people may voluntarily confess and waive their Miranda rights.

k. Once Miranda rights invoked, police cannot reinitiate interrogation.

l. Admitting a coerced confession to trial can result in overturning a conviction.

m. Ambiguous statements about attorneys is not protected under Miranda.

B. Search and Seizure

1. Search Warrant - judicial order, based on probable cause, allowing police officers to search for evidence in a particular place, seize that evidence and carry it away. Evidence seized with a valid warrant, can be used at trial.

2. Under certain circumstances, search may be conducted without warrant:

a. Search Incident to Arrest

b. Threshold inquiry (stop-and-frisk) - reasonable belief; frisking is limited to a pat down of the outer clothing for a weapon.

c. Automobile Search - may be searched if believed to have been involved in a crime.

d. Motorist Search - if danger is perceived, then officer can order drivers and passengers from car during routine traffic stop and conduct limited search.

e. Consent Search - if people consent, they and their vehicle may be searched.

f. Plain View - contraband can be seized when it is in plain view.

g. Seizure of Nonphysical Evidence - such as conversation, police can seize if individuals had no reason to expect privacy.

VII. Issues in Policing

A. Police Personality and Subculture

1. Thought to be authoritarian

a. Suspicious

b. Racist

c. Hostile

d. Insecure

e. Conservative

f. Cynical

g. Secretive

h. Isolated from the rest of society

2. The Police Subculture
   a. William Westly argued that officers develop into cynics.
   b. Learn to mistrust citizens.
   c. Come to believe that people or out to break the law and harm officers.
   d. Most officers ban together in clannishness, secrecy and insulation from others in society.
3. The Myths of Police Work
   a. Frustrated by a criminal justice system that seems to favor the rights of criminals.
   b. Perceived lack of support from government officials and the public.
   c. Less likely to embrace community policing ideas.
   d. Resistance to change.
   e. Mistrust of the police they serve.
B. Discretion - crucial force in all law enforcement decision-making.
   1. Environmental and Community Factors
      a. Community crime levels
      b. Informal rules
      c. Social climate
      d. Community attitudes
      e. Treatment facilities
      f. Alternatives
   2. Departmental Factors
      a. Departmental norms
      b. Peers
      c. Directives
      d. Supervisors
   3. Situational Influences
      a. Demeanor
      b. Crime Scene
      c. Witness
      d. Backup
   4. Legal Factors
      a. Type of crime
      b. Seriousness of crime
   5. Extralegal Factors
      a. Income
      b. Race
      c. Gender
   6. Limiting Police Discretion
      a. Police administrators have tried to establish guidelines for officer behavior.
      b. Develop civilian review boards that monitor police behavior and investigate civilian behavior.
C. Diversity in Policing
   1. Minority Officers

297

a. First African-American officer - Chicago - 1872
b. Still underrepresented, but pressure to increase the numbers.
c. Black officers suffer double marginality - deal with the expectation they will give members of their own race a break and experience overt racism from police colleagues.
d. Findings show that black officers are often tougher on black offenders to prove lack of bias.

2. Female Police Officers
a. First female officer - 1845 - New York - matron - restricted to handling females in custody.
b. 1910 - Los Angeles - first woman to have title of police officer and full arrest powers.
c. 1972 - Title VII of the Civil Rights Act - police departments began to hire females and assign regular patrol duties.

3. How Effective Are Female Police Officers?
a. Evaluations show them to be equal or superior to male officers.
b. Likely to receive community support.
c. Less likely to be charged with police misconduct.
d. Have not received support from colleagues.
e. Struggling for acceptance.
f. Common to be sexually harassed by coworkers.

4. Black Female Police
a. Account for 2% of police officers.
b. Perceive significantly more racial discrimination than either other female or black male officers.
c. Other threatened they will replace them.
d. Little unity among female officers.

D. The Police and Violence
1. How Common is the Use of Force Today?
a. 1999 - of 43 million police-citizen interactions, 1% or 422,000 involved the use or threatened use of force.
b. Use of weapons is rare.

2. Race and Force
a. Minorities more likely to perceive that police will hassle them.
b. Minorities more likely to know one mistreated by police.

3. Deadly Force - actions of a police officer that shoots and kills a suspect either fleeing from arrest, assaulting a victim, or attacking the officer.
a. Estimates that police now kill 250 and 1,000 citizens each year.
b. The following are related to police violence:
   1. Exposure to threat and stress
   2. Police workload
   3. Firearm availability
   4. Population type and density
   5. Race and class discrimination

4. Controlling Force
   a. Tennessee v. Garner - 1985 - Court banned the shooting of unarmed or nondangerous fleeing felons.
   b. Developing administrative policies that limit the use of deadly force and contain armed offenders until trained backup teams arrive.
5. Killing Police
   a. The police are killing fewer people.
   b. Fewer police are being killed in the line of duty.
   c. 2000 - 51 law enforcement officers killed in the line of duty.
   d. About half of slain officers killed while making an arrest or conducting a traffic stop.
6. Nonlethal Weapons
   a. Wood, rubber or polyurethane bullets
   b. Pepper spray and tasers
   c. Other nonlethal weapons are still in development
      1. Guns that shoot nets.
      2. Guns that squirt sticky glue.
      3. Lights that temporarily blind a suspect.

VIII. Summary

Key Terms

Gatekeepers - In criminal justice, police are the most visible and have the most contact with the public. Police initiate contact with law violators, decide whether to arrest or settle an issue informally or take no action at all.

Mollen Commission - The commission investigating corruption among New York City police officers that found some officers actively involved in violence and drug dealing.

Knapp Commission - The commission that investigated corruption among New York City police officers and concluded that most corrupt police officers are "grass eaters."

Pledge System - During the Middle Ages, every man living in the villages scattered throughout the countryside was responsible for aiding his neighbors and protecting the settlement from thieves and marauders.

Watch System - Created to watch cities and towns. Supervised by the constable, watchmen patrolled at night and helped protect against robberies, fires, and disturbances.

Justice of the Peace - Created in 1326 to assist the shire reeve in controlling the county. Eventually, they took on judicial functions in addition to their primary duty as peacekeeper.

Sir Robert Peel - In 1829, as England's home secretary, he guided through Parliament an "Act for Improving the Police In and Near the Metropolis." This act established the first police force in London.

August Vollmer - While serving as Police Chief of Berkeley, CA, Vollmer instituted university training as a part of police training. Also helped develop the School of Criminology at the University of California at Berkeley.

Sheriff - The most important law enforcement agent in colonial America. Duties included: peacekeeping, crime fighting, collecting taxes, supervising elections and handling other legal business.

Shire Reeve - Forerunner of today's sheriff; appointed by the crown to supervise a certain territory and assure the local nobleman that order would be kept.

Foot Patrol - Area, or beat, that officer walks. In early policing, foot patrol was exclusively used.

Aggressive Preventive Patrol - Method of patrol designed to deter crime. Examples include random stop-and-frisks and rousting teenagers who congregate on street corners.

Internal Affairs Division - Department which investigates the activities of law enforcement officers.

Morals Squad - See Vice Squad.

Vice Squad - Detectives assigned to investigating crimes of vice such as prostitution.

Mug Shots - Photographs of offenders taken by law enforcement for victims to use in identifying offenders.

Modus Operandi (MO) - The working methods of particular offenders.

Sting - An operation where police pose as fences with thieves interested in selling stolen merchandise.

Selective Enforcement - The policy of police officers to concentrate on some crimes, but handling the majority in an informal manner.

Community-Oriented Policing - (COP) Police should play an active role in the community, identify neighborhood problems and needs, and set a course of action for an effective response.

Neighborhood Policing - Policing designated for a specific neighborhood and done at that level rather than far away.

Problem-Oriented Policing - New, aggressive strategy where police play an active role in first identifying particular community problems - street-level drug dealers, prostitution rings, gang hangouts - and then developing strategies to counteract them.

Crackdown - POP strategy where a particular problem area in a city is the target of increased police resources.

Hot Spots - Areas where a significant portion of all police calls emanate from, such as bars, malls, the bus depot, hotels, and certain apartment buildings.

Inevitable Discovery Rule - Information that is provided by the suspect and leads to the seizure of incriminating evidence is permissible if the evidence would have been obtained anyway by other means or sources.

Search Warrant - A judicial order, based on probable cause, allowing police officers to search for evidence in a particular place, seize that evidence and carry it away.

Blue Curtain - Code of silence among police officers.

Deadly Force - The actions of a police officer who shoots and kills a suspect whom is either fleeing from arrest, assaulting a victim, or attacking the officer.

Discussion Exercise

Have class watch the 1973 movie, *Serpico*. After the movie, break the class up into discussion groups. Have the groups discuss topics such as Blue Curtain, Ethics, Internal Affairs, and Discretion.

InfoTrac Assignment

GETTING STARTED: Search term words for subject guide: London Police, Federal Law Enforcement, State Police, Patrol, Community-Oriented Policing, Custodial Interrogation, Searches, Seizures, Discretion.

CRITICAL THINKING PROJECT: Using the search term "Custodial Interrogation," find relevant articles.

Here are three articles:

Levenberg, Thomas O. "Fifth Amendment - Responding to Ambiguous Requests for Counsel During Custodial Interrogations." *Journal of Criminal Law and Criminology*.

Hendrie, Edward M. "Beyond 'Miranda'." *The FBI Law Enforcement Bulletin*.

Weisselberg, Charles D. "In The Stationhouse After Dickerson." *Michigan Law Review*.

Test Bank

Essay Questions

1. Trace the history of law enforcement. Where did policing begin and with whom?
2. What events cause the advent of professionalism in policing? Who would be considered directly responsible for introducing professionalism to policing?
3. Define Federal Law Enforcement. What are some of the various law enforcement organizations under the federal system?

4. Compare and contrast County Law Enforcement with Metropolitan Police. What are the distinguishing characteristics of each? Which, if either, has more power and why?

5. Define the Federal Bureau of Investigation. Trace the history of the bureau. What are the duties and jurisdiction of the FBI?

Fill In The Blank

1. In criminal justice, the police are the most visible and have the most contact with the public and would be considered **Gatekeepers**.

2. The commission investigating corruption among New York City police officers that found some officers actively involved in violence and drug dealing is known as the **Mollen Commission**.

3. The commission that investigated corruption among New York City police officers and concluded that most corrupt police officers are "grass eaters" is known as the **Knapp Commission**.

4. **Pledge System** operated during the Middle Ages where every man living in the villages scattered throughout the countryside was responsible for aiding his neighbors and protecting the settlement from thieves and marauders.

5. Supervised by the constable, the **Watch System** was created to watch cities and towns.

6. The **Justice of the Peace** was created in 1326 to assist the shire reeve in controlling the county.

7. **Sir Robert Peel** established the first police force in London.

8. **August Vollmer** instituted university training as part of police training at UC-Berkeley.

9. The **Sheriff** was the most important law enforcement agent in colonial America.

10. When police play an active role in the community, identify neighborhood problems and needs, and set a course of action for an effective response, this is known as **Community-Oriented Policing**.

11. **Neighborhood Policing** is policing designated for a specific neighborhood and done at that level rather than far away.

12. **Problem-Oriented Policing** is a new, aggressive strategy where police play an active role in first identifying particular community problems.

13. POP strategy where a particular problem area in a city is the target of increased police resources is known as a **Crackdown**.

14. **Hot Spots** are areas where a significant portion of all police calls emanate from, such as bars, malls, the bus depot, hotels, and certain apartment buildings.

15. A **Search Warrant** is a judicial order, based on probable cause, allowing police officers to search for evidence in a particular place, seize the evidence and carry it away.

Multiple Choice

1. The actions of a police officer who shoots and kills a suspect whom is either fleeing from arrest, assaulting a victim or attacking the officer is called:
   a. Deadly Force
   b. Blue Curtain
   c. Crackdown
   d. Search and Seizure
   (Answer = a)

2. The code of silence among police officers is known as:
   a. Green grass
   b. Red shoes
   c. Blue curtain
   d. Tan dungarees
   (Answer = c)

3. A judicial order, based on probable cause, allowing police officers to search for evidence in a particular place, seize that evidence and carry it away is known as:
   a. Waiver
   b. Search Warrant
   c. Arrest Warrant
   d. Evidence
   (Answer = b)

4. Information that is provided by the suspect and leads to the seizure of incriminating evidence is permissible if the evidence would have been obtained anyway by other means or sources is known as:
   a. Exclusionary Rule
   b. Fruits of the Poisonous Tree
   c. Miranda Warning
   d. Inevitable Discovery Rule
   (Answer = d)

6. Areas where a significant portion of all police calls emanate from, such as bars, malls, the bus depot, hotels, and certain apartment buildings are known as:

a. Hot Spots
b. Crackdowns
c. Patrol Cars
d. Courtrooms
(Answer = a)

6. POP strategy where a particular problem area in a city is the target of increased police resources is called a:
a. Hotspot
b. Blue curtain
c. Sting
d. Crackdown
(Answer = d)

7. A new, aggressive strategy where police play an active role in first identifying particular community problems is known as:
a. Community-oriented policing
b. Problem-oriented policing
c. Neighborhood policing
d. Knapp commission
(Answer = b)

8. Policing designated for a specific neighborhood and done at that level rather than far away is known as:
a. Neighborhood policing
b. Community-oriented policing
c. Problem-oriented policing
d. Knapp commission
(Answer = a)

9. View that police should play an active role in the community, identify neighborhood problems and needs, and set a course of action for an effective response is called:
a. Neighborhood policing
b. Problem-oriented policing
c. Community-oriented policing
d. Knapp commission
(Answer = c)

10. The policy of police officers to concentrate on some crimes, but handle the majority of them in an informal manner is known as:
a. Pledge system
b. Selective enforcement
c. Foot patrol
d. Aggressive preventive patrol
(Answer = b)

11. An operation where police pose as fences with thieves interested in selling stolen merchandise is known as:
    a. Selective enforcement
    b. Watch system
    c. Pledge system
    d. Sting
    (Answer = d)

12. The working methods of particular is known as an:
    a. Modus Operandi
    b. Corpus delicti
    c. Mens rae
    d. Actus reus
    (Answer = a)

13. Photographs of offenders taken by law enforcement for victims to use in identifying offenders are known as:
    a. Complaints
    b. Mug shots
    c. Search warrants
    d. Arrest warrants
    (Answer = b)

14. Detectives assigned to investigating crimes of vice such as prostitution are known as:
    a. Vice Squad
    b. Morals Squad.
    c. All of the above
    d. None of the above
    (Answer = c)

15. Department which investigates the activities of law enforcement officers known as:
    a. Patrol Unit
    b. Detectives
    c. Homicide Unit
    d. Internal Affairs Division
    (Answer = d)

16. Method of patrol designed to deter crime is known as:
    a. Foot Patrol
    b. Bike Patrol
    c. Community Policing
    d. Aggressive Preventive Patrol
    (Answer = d)

17. Area or beat that an officer walks is known as:

a. Bike Patrol
b. Foot Patrol
c. Aggressive Preventive Patrol
d. None of the above
(Answer = b)

18. Forerunner of today's sheriff is known as:
a. Justice of the peace
b. Watch system
c. Shire reeve
d. Pledge system
(Answer = c)

19. The most important law enforcement agent in colonial America was known as:
a. Sheriff
b. Justice of the peace
c. Watch system
d. Pledge system
(Answer = a)

20. While serving as Police Chief of Berkeley, CA, he instituted university training as a part of police training:
a. Sir Robert Peel
b. August Vollmer
c. Travis Hirschi
d. Edwin Sutherland
(Answer = b)

21. He established the first police force in London:
a. Edwin Sutherland
b. Travis Hirschi
c. August Vollmer
d. Sir Robert Peel
(Answer = d)

22. Created in 1326 to assist the shire reeve in controlling the county, he was known as:
a. Watch system
b. Pledge system
c. Shire reeve
d. Justice of the peace
(Answer = d)

23. Supervised by the constable, this group was created to watch cities and towns and was known as:
a. Pledge system

b. Watch system
c. Shire reeve
d. Justice of the peace
(Answer = b)

24. During the Middle Ages, every man living in the villages scattered throughout the countryside was responsible for aiding his neighbors and protecting the settlement from thieves and marauders is called the:
a. Watch system
b. Shire reeve
c. Pledge system
d. Justice of the peace
(Answer = c)

25. The commission that investigated corruption among New York City police officers and concluded that most corrupt police officers are "grass eaters" is known as:
a. Mollen Commission
b. Warren Commission
c. Wickersham Commission
d. Knapp Commission
(Answer = d)

26. The commission investigating corruption among New York City police officers that found some officers actively involved in violence and drug dealing is known as:
a. Warren Commission
b. Wickersham Commission
c. Knapp Commission
d. Mollen Commission
(Answer = d)

27. In criminal justice, the police are the most visible and have the most contact with the public and are known as:
a. Detectives
b. Vice squad
c. Gatekeepers
d. Morals squad
(Answer = c)

28. One who might be considered the first real police officer who dealt with more serious breaches of the law would be called:
a. Constable
b. Shire reeve
c. Justice of the peace
d. Watch system
(Answer = a)

29. People grouped into a collective of 10 families are called a:
    a. Watch system
    b. Pledge system
    c. Hundred
    d. Tithing
    (Answer = d)

30. Ten tithings were grouped into:
    a. Watch system
    b. Pledge system
    c. Tithing
    d. Hundred
    (Answer = d)

31. The nation's first formal police department was created in:
    a. New York
    b. Philadelphia
    c. Boston
    d. Miami
    (Answer = c)

32. The federal government maintains about how many organizations involved in law enforcement?
    a. 100
    b. 200
    c. 50
    d. 10
    (Answer = c)

33. Which act prohibited prostitution across state lines?
    a. Miranda
    b. Wickersham
    c. Knapp
    d. Mann
    (Answer = d)

34. Which division of the FBI serves as the national registry for fingerprints?
    a. The Criminal Justice Information Services Division
    b. Crime Laboratory
    c. The Child Abduction and Serial Killer Unit
    d. Combined DNA Index System
    (Answer = a)

35. Which division of the FBI is one of the largest and most comprehensive forensic laboratories in the world?

a. The Criminal Justice Information Services Division
b. The Child Abduction and Serial Killer Unit
c. Combined DNA Index System
d. Crime Laboratory
(Answer = d)

36. Which division of the FBI responds upon request from local law enforcement agencies to kidnappings and to serial killer cases?
a. The Criminal Justice Information Services Division
b. Combined DNA Index System
c. The Child Abduction and Serial Killer Unit
d. Crime Laboratory
(Answer = c)

37. Which division of the FBI is a national database of DNA profiles from convicted offenders?
a. The Criminal Justice Information Services Division
b. The Child Abduction and Serial Killer Unit
c. Combined DNA Index System
d. Crime Laboratory
(Answer = c)

38. Which division of the FBI is ready to assist law enforcement agencies in hostage-taking and barricade situations, terrorist activities and other critical incidents?
a. The Criminal Justice Information Services Division
b. The Critical Incident Response Group
c. The Child Abduction and Serial Killer Unit
d. Combined DNA Index System
(Answer = b)

39. Which division of the FBI is an annual compilation of crimes reported to local police agencies, arrests, police killed or wounded in action, and other information?
a. The Uniform Crime Report
b. The Criminal Justice Information Services Division
c. The Critical Incident Response Group
d. The Child Abduction and Serial Killer Unit
(Answer = a)

40. Which division of the FBI is a computerized network linked to local police departments that provides ready information on stolen vehicles, wanted persons, stolen guns, and other crime related material?
a. The Uniform Crime Report
b. National Crime Information Center
c. The Critical Incident Response Group
d. The Child Abduction and Serial Killer Unit
(Answer = b)

True/False

T   1. The U.S. Marshals are court officers who help implement federal court rulings, transport prisoners, and enforce court orders.

F   2. The Drug Enforcement Administration administers immigration laws, deports illegal aliens, and naturalizes aliens lawfully present in the United States.

F   3. The Immigration and Naturalization Service investigate illegal drug use and carry out independent surveillance and enforcement activities to control the importation of narcotics.

T   4. Alcohol, Tobacco, and Firearms Bureau has jurisdiction over the sales and distribution of firearms, explosives, alcohol and tobacco products.

T   5. The Internal Revenue Service, established in 1862, enforces violations of income, excise, stamp, and other tax laws.

F   6. The Secret Service guard points of entry into the United States and prevents smuggling of contraband into or out of the country.

F   7. The Customs Bureau was originally charged with enforcing laws against counterfeiting.

T   8. The county police department is an independent agency whose senior officer, the sheriff, is usually elected.

T   9. The Texas Rangers, organized in 1835, are considered the first state police force.

F   10. Investigation entails police officers' visible presence on the streets and public places of their jurisdiction.

T   11. Investigators must often enter a case after it has been reported to police and attempt to accumulate enough evidence to identify the perpetrator.

T   12. Traditional policing models were reactive, responding to calls for help rather than attempting to prevent crimes before they occurred.

F   13. The Fourth Amendment guarantees people the right to be free from self-incrimination.

T   14. A search warrant is a judicial order, based on probable cause, which allows police officers to search for evidence in a particular place, seize that evidence and carry it away.

T   15. A warrantless search is valid if it is made incident to a lawful arrest.

Chapter Seventeen

The Judicatory Process

Summary

Chapter Seventeen begins with a detailed explanation of the federal and state court structure. The actors in the Judicatory Process are examined and the pretrial procedures are explained. Plea-bargaining is discussed as well as the specifics of the criminal trial. Sentencing is distinguished from the criminal trial and chapter seventeen concludes with a discussion of the death penalty.

Learning Objectives

After reading this chapter the student should be able to:

- Develop an understanding of the court structure.
- Describe the State and Federal Courts.
- Understand the actors in the Judicatory Process.
- Develop an understanding of pretrial procedures.
- Understand plea-bargaining.
- Explore the Criminal Trial.
- Define sentencing.
- Understand how people are sentenced.
- Develop an understanding of the Death Penalty debate.
- Explain the legality of the Death Penalty.

Chapter Overview

Introduction
Court Structure
      State Courts
      Federal Courts

Chapter Outline

I. **Introduction**

II. **Court Structure** - 16,000 courts in U.S. organized on the municipal, county, state and federal levels.

    A. State Courts

        1. Lower courts - try misdemeanors; conduct preliminary processing of felony offenders.

        2. Superior courts - try felony cases.

        3. Appellate courts - review criminal procedure of trial court to determine whether offenders were treated fairly.

        4. Superior Appellate courts or State Supreme Courts - review lower court decisions.

    B. Federal Courts

        1. U.S. District Courts - trial courts; have jurisdiction over cases involving violations of federal law.

        2. Immediate Courts of Appeal - hear appeals from U.S. District Court

        3. U.S. Supreme Court - highest federal appeal court; court of last resort for all cases in federal and state courts.

           a. Composed of nine members.

           b. Appointed for life by the president and approved by Congress.

  c. Court selects cases they want to hear.
    1. Selection by a Writ of Certiorari - requests a transcript of the case proceedings for review.
  d. Court decisions become precedent - must be honored by all lower courts.
    1. These rulings are referred to as landmark decisions.
 C. Court Case Flow
  1. Annually, about 90 million new cases brought to the courts
  2. Annually, about 280,000 new appeals brought to the courts
  3. Since 1984 domestic violence cases have increased.

III. **Actors in the Judicatory Process**
 A. Prosecutors
  1. Represents the State in criminal matters before the court.
  2. State court prosecutor's' office employed about 71,000 attorneys, investigators and support staff.
  3. Types of Prosecutors
   a. Federal - chief prosecuting officer is the U.S. Attorney General
    1. Assistants are known as U.S. Attorneys - appointed by the president.
    2. Represent the government in federal district courts.
   b. State - District Attorney, County Attorney, Prosecuting Attorney, Commonwealth Attorney or State's Attorney
    1. Typically elected officials.
    2. Other staff attorneys and support personnel handle most criminal prosecution.
    3. Work is often specialized into felonies, misdemeanors, trial and appeal assignments.
  4. Prosecutorial Discretion
   a. The choice of acting on the information brought by the police or deciding not to file for an indictment.
   b. Can attempt to prosecute and then drop the case - nolle prosequi.
   c. Plea negotiations.
  5.Factors Influencing Decision Making
   a. Characteristics of the crime
   b. The criminal
   c. The victim
   d. Offender's prior criminal record.
   e. Victim cooperation.
   f. Victim's attitude
   g. The cost of prosecution to the criminal justice system.
   h. The possibility of undue harm to the suspect.
   i. The availability of alternative procedures.
   j. The availability of civil sanctions.
   k. The willingness of the suspect to cooperate with law enforcement authorities.

      1.   Case pressure.
B. Defense Attorneys - represent the accused in the criminal process.
    1. Public Defender - salaried staff of full or part-time attorneys that render indigent criminal defense services through a public or private nonprofit organization, or as direct government paid employees.
    2. Assigned Counsel - Appointment from a list of private bar members who accept cases on a judge-by-judge, court-by-court, or case-by-case basis.
    3. Contract - Nonsalaried private attorneys, bar associations, law firms, consortiums or groups of attorneys, or nonprofit corporations that contract with a funding source to provide court-appointed representation in a jurisdiction.
    4. Conflicts of Defense
        a. Officers of the Court - obligated to uphold the integrity of the legal profession and to observe the requirements of the Code of Professional Responsibility of the American Bar Association in the defense of a client.
        b. Defense Advocate
        c. Clients who perjure themselves.
C. Judge - senior officer in a court of criminal law.
    1. During trial, judges rule on the appropriateness of conduct.
    2. Settle questions of evidence and procedure.
    3. Guide the questioning of witnesses.
    4. After trial, judges must instruct jury members on which evidence can be examined and which should be ignored.
    5. Formally charges the jury by instruction on the points of law.
    6. If jury trial is waived, judge must decide for complainant or defendant.
    7. If defendant is found guilty, judge decides sentence.
    8. Has considerable control over service agencies of the court, such as probation.
    9. Judicial Selection
        a. Some states, the governor appoints judges.
        b. Other states, judicial recommendations must be confirmed by another group like the state senate.
        c. Popular election
        d. Missouri Plan
            1. a judicial nominating commission to nominate candidates for the bench
            2. an elected official to make appointments form the list submitted by the commission
            3. Subsequent nonpartisan, noncompetitive elections in which incumbent judges run on their records.
  10. Judicial Overload
        a. Little or no formal training to be a judge.
        b. An overwhelming amount of work that has risen over the years.
        c. Case pressure to move the cases.

IV. **Pretrial Procedures**
   A. Bail
      1. Money or security provided to the court to ensure the appearance of the defendant at trial.
      2. Amount of bail set by magistrate.
      3. Defendants denied or cannot afford bail or usually held in the county lockup or jail.
      4. Bail system dates back to English common law.
      5. In U.S. right to bail comes under the 8th Amendment of the Constitution.
      6. Bail Today
         a. Data indicates that most defendants (64%) made bail.
         b. Estimated 36% held until the courts disposed of case.
      7. Making Bail
         a. Preventive detention - Defendants who are detained because they cannot afford bail or the danger they present to the community.
         b. Drug and public order offenders likely to be bailed.
         c. Violent offenders more likely to be detained.
      8. The Problems of Bail
         a. Penalizes the indigent offender who cannot pay the bond.
         b. State must pay for the detention of offender.
         c. Increases punishment risk.
         d. Bailing and Bonding Agents have been accused of unscrupulous practices such as bribing officials.
      9. Bail Reform - Began in 1961 to alleviate problems associated with bail.
         a. Release on Recognizance (ROR) - begun by the Vera Foundation in New York and proved to be successful.
         b. Federal Bail Act of 1984 - made ROR an assumption unless the need for greater control can be shown in court.
         c. Abuse by bail bonding agents have prompted some states to start a system of defendants posting 10% with the court. The full amount is required if defendant fails to show for court.
         d. Encouraged the use of pretrial release .
         e. Most defendants return for court.
         f. Most bailees do not commit more crime while in the community.
      10. Preventive Detention
         a. 2 Million people are arrested annually for felony offenses.
         b. 65% or 1.3 million receive bail.
         c. Person who has not been convicted of a crime is incarcerated for an extended period of time without the chance to participate in their own defense.
         d. *United States v. Salerno*, the Supreme Court upheld the Bail Reform Act's preventive detention because it is for public safety; it is not excessive and it is does not have a punitive intent.
   B. Plea Bargaining
      1. About two-thirds of felony defendants plea bargain to settle their case.

2. Motivations for Plea Bargains
    a. Prosecutions strong case
    b. To Minimize sentence
    c. Avoid the harmful effects of a criminal conviction.
    d. To protect accomplices.
    e. Defense attorney may seek to limit his or her involvement in the case.
3. Plea Bargaining Issues
    a. Costs of prosecution are reduced.
    b. Efficiency of the courts is improved.
    c. Prosecution can spend more time on cases of greater seriousness and importance.
    d. Defendant may receive reduced sentence.
    e. Encourages defendants to waive their constitutional right to trial.
    f. Some feel it allows the defendant to best the system.
    g. Raises the danger that an innocent person will be convicted.
    h. Some feel it allows dangerous criminals to get off light.
    i. May undermine public confidence in the law.
4. Control of Plea Bargaining
    a. Doubtful it will be totally eliminated.
    b. Efforts to convert plea bargaining into a visible, understandable and fair process.
    c. Some states have abolished plea bargaining.

V. **The Criminal Trial**

A. Jury Selection - 1st stage in the trial process.
    1. Jurors selected randomly usually from voter registration lists with court jurisdiction.
    2. Venire - jury array or initial list of persons chosen capable of serving on the jury.
    3. Court clerk randomly selects enough names to supply the required number of jurors.
    4. Usually, criminal trial jury consists of 12 persons, with 2 alternate jurors.
    5. After jurors selected, the process of voir dire begins.
    6. Jurors are questioned by both the prosecution and the defense to determine their appropriateness to sit on the jury.
    7. Jurors with bias, relationship to defendant or a formed opinion are replaced - Challenge for Cause.
    8. Peremptory Challenge - either side can excuse jurors for no particular reason.
    9. *Batson v. Kentucky*, the Court held that the use of peremptory challenges to dismiss all black jurors violated the defendant's right to equal protection of the law.
    10. Impartial Juries
        a. *Ham v. South Carolina* (1973) - Court held the defense counsel of an African-American civil rights leader was entitled to question each juror on the issue of radical prejudice.

316

    b. *Turner v. Murray* - Court held that African-American defendants accused of murdering whites are entitled to have jurors questioned about their racial bias.

    c. *Taylor v. Louisiana* - Court overturned the conviction of a man by an all-male jury because a Louisiana statute allowed women but not men to exempt themselves from jury duty.

B. The Trial Process - formal process conducted in a specific, orderly fashion in accordance with rules of criminal law, procedure and evidence.

  1. Opening Statements
    a. Prosecution and defense address the jury and present their cases.
    b. Describe what they will attempt to prove.
    c. Describe the major facts of the case.
    d. Introduce witnesses.
    e. Defense begins to emphasize doubt about the guilt of the accused.

  2. The Prosecution's case
    a. After opening statement, the state presents evidence through witnesses.
    b. Direct examination - the prosecutor questions the witness to reveal the facts believed pertinent to the government case.

  3. Cross-examination - After prosecution's examination, the defense may question the prosecution's witness. (Same for the defense side of the trial).

  4. The Defense's case
    a. After prosecutor has presented all of its' case, defense may ask for a directed verdict.
      1. Judge directs the jury to acquit defendant, which ends the trial.
      2. Means prosecution did not present enough evidence to prove all crime elements.
      3. If granted, trial ends; defendant is found not guilty.
      4. If not granted, defense proceeds with trial.
    b. Defense calls witnesses like the prosecution.

  5. Rebuttal
    a. After defense, prosecution may present rebuttal evidence.
      1. Evidence that was not used during prosecution's presentation.

  6. Closing Arguments
    a. Attorneys review the facts and evidence of the case.

  7. Instructions to the Jury
    a. Judge charges or instructs the jury on the principles of law to guide and control the decision making of the defendant's innocence or guilt.
    b. Judge explains the level and burden of proof to find the defendant guilty.

  8. Verdict
    a. Jurors retire to deliberate on a verdict.
    b. In a criminal trial, verdict usually must be unanimous.
    c. If no verdict can be reached, trial may result in a hung jury.

  9. Sentence
    a. If found not guilty, defendant is released.

b. If convicted, judge may order a presentence investigation by probation department.

c. In felony cases, judge sets a sentencing date.

d. At sentencing, judge may consider other evidence that is relevant.

e. Criminal penalties include:

1. Fines
2. Community Supervision
3. Incarceration
4. Death Penalty

10. Appeal

a. After sentencing, defendants have a right to appeal.

b. If appeal is granted, new trial is ordered.

c. If appeal is sustained, convicted offender serves the sentence imposed.

C. Trials and the Rule of Law

1. Right to a Speedy Trial

a. 6th Amendment guarantees a defendant the right to a speedy trial.

b. Accused is entitled to be tried within a reasonable period.

c. Defendant can waive the right to a speedy trial.

d. Federal Speedy Trial Act of 1974 - mandates 30 days from arrest to indictment and 70 days from indictment to trial.

2. Right to a Jury Trial

a. *Duncan v. Louisiana* - Court guaranteed the right to a jury trial.

b. *Baldwin v. New York* - Court held that defendants are entitled to a jury trial if they face a prison sentence of more than 6 months.

c. *Williams v. Florida* - Court held that a 6 person jury fulfilled defendant's right to a trial by jury.

3. Right to be free from Double Jeopardy

a. 5th Amendment provides no person "shall be subject for the same offense to be twice put in jeopardy of life or limb".

b. However, a person tried in federal court can be tried in state court and vice versa.

c. Dual Sovereignty Doctrine - legal jurisdictions have the right to enforce their own laws and a single act can violate the laws of two separate jurisdictions.

4. Right to Legal Counsel

a. 6th Amendment provides the right to be represented by an attorney in criminal trials.

b. Most defendants are indigents.

c. *Powell v. Alabama* - Court held that an attorney was essential in capital cases where the defendant's life was at stake.

d. *Gideon v. Wainwright* - Court granted the absolute right to counsel in all felony cases.

e. *Argersinger v. Hamlin* - Defendant's right to counsel was established in misdemeanor cases.

5. Right to Confront Witnesses

VI. Sentencing - imposition of a criminal penalty

  A. Purposes of Sentencing

    1. Deterrence

    2. Incapacitation

    3. Rehabilitation

    4. Desert/retribution

    5. Equity/restitution

  B. Sentencing Dispositions

    1. Fines

    2. Probation

    3. Alternative or intermediate sanctions

    4. Incarceration

    5. Capital punishment

    6. Imposing the Sentence

      a. Sentencing authority is exercised by the jury, an administrative body, a group of judges or it may be mandated by statute.

      b. Sentencing is based on a variety of information available to the judge.

      c. Sometimes victim impact statements are allowed.

      d. Presentence investigation reports are often ordered by the judge.

        1. Prepared by the probation department.

        2. Social and personal history as well as an evaluation of the defendant.

      e. When accused is convicted of 2 or more charges, sentence must be issued on each charge.

        1. Concurrent sentence - both sentences served at the same time, and imprisonment is completed after the longest time has been served.

        2. Consecutive sentence - After completing one sentence, the other term of incarceration begins.

  C. Sentencing Structures - according to the statutes of the jurisdiction in which the crime was committed.

    1. The Indeterminate Sentence - sentences with brief minimums and very long maximums, allowing parole boards to release when rehabilitated.

    2. The Determinate Sentence - Fixed term issued by the judge that falls within the set statute.

    3. Structured Sentencing - Guidelines developed to control and structure the sentencing process and make it more "rational".

      a. Based on the seriousness of the crime.

      b. Based on the background of the offender.

    4. How Are Guidelines Used?

      a. Today 17 states and the Federal Government use a type of structured sentencing.

      b. Voluntary/advisory Sentencing Guidelines - Guidelines used merely to suggest rather than mandate sentencing.

      c. Prescriptive Guidelines - created by appointed sentencing commission, which determine an "ideal" sentence for a particular crime and offender.

5. Configuring Guidelines
    a. Grid method, see table 17.1
6. Future of Structured Sentencing
    a. Research indicates judges diverge from guidelines.
    b. Legislatures created loopholes in the guidelines.
    c. Some attorneys oppose structured sentencing because it results in longer sentences.
    d. Little evidence they relieve crime rates.
7. Mandatory Sentences
    a. Require the incarceration of all offenders convicted of specific crimes.
    b. Limits the judges' discretionary power.
    c. May supplement an indeterminate sentencing structure or is a feature of structured sentencing.
    d. Some say they are overly restrictive.
8. Truth in Sentencing
    a. Require offenders to serve a substantial portion of their prison sentences behind bars.
    b. Parole eligibility and good time credits are limited.
    c. Response to prison crowding.
    d. Violent Offender Incarceration and Truth-In-Sentencing Incentive Grants Program of the 1994 Crime Act
        1. Offered states funds to support the costs of longer sentences.
        2. States must require convicted violent felony offenders to serve not less than 85% of their prison sentences.
        3. 27 states and the District of Columbia met the criteria.
9. Three Strikes Law
    a. Life sentence for anyone convicted of a third offense.
    b. Enables a judge to treat a third offense as a felony for purposes of applying the mandatory sentencing provisions.
    c. Aimed at getting habitual offenders off the street.
    d. Federal Crime Bill of 1994 - adopted a Three Strikes provision.
    e. Being challenged legally and future is uncertain.

D. How People Are Sentenced
    1. Sentencing Disparity
        a. Common for people convicted of similar crimes to receive widely different sentences.
        b. Few defendants actually serve their entire sentence.
        c. Factors which influence sentencing:
            1. The severity of the offense.
            2. Offender's prior criminal record.
            3. Offender's use of violence.
            4. Offender's use of weapons.
            5. Whether the crime was committed for money.

6. Age, race, gender and economic status may also influence sentencing.

VII. The Death Penalty

A. In U.S. death penalty used in 38 states and the federal government.
   1. 2000 - 37 states and federal government held 3,539 men and 54 women on death row.
   2. 2000 - 14 states executed 85 prisoners - 83 men and 2 women.
   3. Average time on death row - 11 years and 5 months.
   4. 2000 - Texas executed 40 people, about half of all executions.
   5. 2001 - lethal injection the predominant method of execution.

B. The Death Penalty Debate
   1. Arguments for the Death Penalty
      a. Inherent in human nature.
      b. Favored by most Americans and used in 3/4's of the world.
      c. Bible describes methods of executing criminals.
      d. Death penalty is in keeping with exacting the harshest penalty for the most severe crime.
      e. The only real threat available to deter crime.
      f. The ultimate incapacitation.
      g. Cost-effective.
      h. Little racism; more whites are on death row.
   2. Arguments against the Death Penalty
      a. Little deterrent effect.
      b. Executions may increase the likelihood of murders being committed - referred to as the brutalization effect.
      c. Capital punishment may be tarnished by racial, gender, ethnic and other bias.
      d. Social vengeance by death is a primitive way of revenge.
      e. Research indicates that many accept the death penalty, but believe it should be used rarely.
      f. It precludes any possibility of rehabilitation.
      g. Death penalty is capricious; receiving death is similar to losing a lottery.
      h. Punishment has never proven to be a deterrent.

C. Legalities of the Death Penalty
   1. *Furman v. Georgia* - 1972 - Court held the discretionary imposition of the death penalty was cruel and unusual punishment under the 8th Amendment.
   2. *Gregg v. Georgia* - 1976 - Court found valid the Georgia statute that held a jury must find at least one "aggravating circumstance" before the death penalty can be imposed in murder cases.
   3. *Tison v. Arizona* - Court permitted executions of people who were major participants in a murder case and displayed reckless indifference to human life but did not actually kill anybody.

VIII. Summary

Key Terms

U.S. District Courts - Trial courts of the federal court system; they have jurisdiction over cases involving violations of federal law, such as interstate transportation of stolen vehicles and racketeering.

Federal Courts of Appeal - The courts that hear the first appeal in the federal system from the lower courts.

U.S. Supreme Court - The court of last resort for all cases tried in the various federal and state courts.

Writ of Certiorari - An order issued by the Supreme Court when it decides to hear a case. The writ actually requests a transcript of the case proceedings for review.

Precedent - Decision by the Supreme Court that must be honored by all lower courts.

Landmark Decision - A decision by the Supreme Court that becomes the law of the land and serves as a precedent for similar legal issues.

Prosecution - Represents the state in criminal matters that come before the courts.

Attorney List/Assigned Counsel System - Public defendant services provided mainly by local private attorneys appointed and paid by the court.

Public Defenders - A salaried staff of full-time or part-time attorneys that render indigent criminal defense services through a public or private nonprofit organization, or as direct government paid employees.

Adversarial Process - The procedure used to determine truth in the adjudication of guilt or innocence in which the defense is pitted against the prosecution, with the judge acting as arbiter of the legal rules.

Judge - The third major participant in the criminal trial. The senior officer in a court of criminal law that rules on the appropriateness of conduct, settles questions of evidence and procedure, and guides the questioning of witnesses.

Missouri Plan - Method of selecting judges currently adopted by 16 states. This three-part approach consists of (1) a judicial nominating commission, (2) an elected official to make appointments from the list selected by the commission and (3) subsequent nonpartisan, noncompetitive elections in which incumbent judges run on their records.

Bill of Indictment - A formal written criminal accusation given by a grand jury setting out the crimes for which the defendant is to stand trial.

Information - The written accusation of the prosecutor setting out the charges against a defendant and used in place of the indictment in some jurisdictions.

Complaint - A sworn written statement to a court by the police, prosecutor, or individual alleging that an individual has committed an offense and requesting indictment and prosecution.

Arraignment - The step at which the accused are read the charges against them, asked how they wish to plead, and advised of their rights.

Bail - Money or some other security provided to the court to ensure the appearance of the defendant at trial.

Preventive Detention - Some defendants are detained because they cannot afford to make bail; others are denied bail because of the danger they present to the community.

Bail Bonding Agent - Those who practice providing bail to indigent offenders, usually at high rates of interest.

Release on Recognizance - The defendant is released on a promise to appear, without any requirement of money bond.

Deposit Bail - The defendant deposits a percentage of the bail amount, typically 10%, with the court. When the defendant appears in court, the deposit is returned, sometimes minus an administrative fee.

Bail Guidelines - The federal Bail Reform Act of 1984 provides that federal offenders may be detained without bail if "no condition or combination of conditions (of bail) will reasonably assure...the safety of any other person and the community".

Plea Bargaining - The decision between the prosecutor and the defense attorney to have the defendant plead guilty in exchange for some concession (such as a lesser charge).

Venire - The list of jurors called for jury duty from which jury panels are selected.

Voir Dire - The process of jury selection by questioning the prospective panel members.

Peremptory Challenge - Either the prosecution and the defense can excuse jurors for no particular or undisclosed reason during the voir dire process.

Direct Examination - Initial questioning of a witness by the party who called the witness to obtain testimony regarding the case.

Cross-examination - Questioning of a witness by the party that did not call the witness to obtain testimony regarding the case.

Redirect Examination - Secondary questioning of a witness by the party who called the witness to obtain testimony regarding the case.

Directed Verdict - A verdict in a case where the judge removes the decision from the jury by either telling them what to do or by actually making the decision.

Rebuttal - After the defense concludes its case, the government may present evidence to counteract the case of the defense.

Hearsay Evidence - Testimony that is not firsthand but is relied by a second party.

Sentencing - The criminal sanction imposed by the court on a convicted defendant.

Mandatory Prison Term - A statutory requirement that a certain penalty will be set and carried out in all of those types of cases.

Concurrent Sentence - Both sentences are served at the same time, and the term of imprisonment is completed after the longest term has been served.

Consecutive Sentence - Upon completing one prison sentence, the other term begins.

Indeterminate Sentence - A type of prison sentence where the court has determined that the convicted person should be imprisoned, the exact length of imprisonment and parole supervision is fixed within statutory limits by a parole authority.

Determinate Sentence - A type of prison sentence where the court has determined that the convicted person should be imprisoned, the exact length of imprisonment and parole supervision is fixed within statutory limits by the legislature.

Guideline Sentences - Based on the seriousness of the crime and the background of an offender; the more serious the crime and the more extensive the offender's criminal background, the longer the prison term recommended by the guidelines.

Sentencing Disparity - People convicted of similar criminal acts to receive widely differently sentences.

Contextual Discrimination - The practices of judges in some jurisdictions who impose harsher sentences on African-Americans who victimize whites, or impose prison sentences on racial minorities in "borderline" cases for which whites get probation.

Discussion Exercise

Have students visit the local courts. Discuss their preconceived notions of court and their actual experience.

InfoTrac Assignment

GETTING STARTED: Search term words for subject guide: State Courts, Federal Courts, Prosecutor, Defense Attorney, Judge, Bail, Plea Bargain, Jury, Death Penalty.

CRITICAL THINKING PROJECT: Using the search term "Bail," find relevant articles.

Here are three articles:

Parenti, Christian "'I Hunt Men': Meet the Self-Ordained Officers of the Bail-Bond Industry." *The Progressive*.

"U.S. District Court: Alien Bail." *Corrections Caselaw Quarterly*.

Petee, Thomas A. "Recommended for Release on Recognizance: Factors Affecting Pretrial Release Recommendations." *The Journal of Social Psychology*.

Test Bank

Essay Questions

1. Compare and contrast Federal and State Courts. Differentiate some of the jurisdictional situations that may occur between the federal and state governments.
2. Describe the actors in the judicatory process. What are their roles? Who possesses

power and over what aspects of the criminal procedure?

3. Define bail. What are the different types of bail available to a defendant? When is bail available and when is it not available to a defendant?

4. Describe plea-bargaining. What is the purpose of this practice and what are the benefits?

5. What is the jury selection process? What are the various methods that a prospective juror may be excused from a trial?

Fill In The Blank

1. A verdict in a case where the judge removes the decision from the jury by either telling them what to do or by actually making the decision is known as a **Directed Verdict**.

2. Secondary questioning of a witness by a party who called the witness to obtain testimony regarding the case is known as **Redirect Examination**.

3. Questioning of a witness by the party that did not call the witness to obtain testimony regarding the case is known as **Cross-examination**.

4. **Direct Examination** is initial questioning of a witness by the party who called the witness to obtain testimony regarding the case.

5. A **Peremptory Challenge** is when either the prosecutor or the defense can excuse jurors for no particular or undisclosed reason during the voir dire process.

6. **Voir Dire** is the process of jury selection by questioning the prospective panel members.

7. **Venire** is the list of jurors called for jury duty from which jury panels are selected.

8. A **Plea Bargain** is the decision between the prosecutor and the defense attorney to have the defendant plead guilty in exchange for some concession.

9. **Release on Recognizance** is when the defendant is released on a promise to appear, without any requirement of money bond.

10. Those who practice providing bail to indigent offenders, usually at high rates of interest are known as **Bail Bonding Agents**.

11. **Bail** is money or some other security provided to the court to ensure the appearance of a defendant at trial.

12. **Arraignment** is the step at which the accused are read the charges against them,

asked how they wish to plead and advised of their rights.

13. A sworn written statement to a court by the police, prosecutor or individual alleging that an individual has committed an offense and requesting indictment and prosecution is known as a **Complaint**.

14. **Preventive Detention** is when some defendants are detained because they cannot afford to make bail.

15. A formal written criminal accusation given by a grand jury setting out the crimes for which the defendant is to stand trial is known as a **Bill of Indictment**.

Multiple Choice

1. A verdict in a case where the judge removes the decision from the jury by either telling them what to do or by actually making the decision is called:
   a. Directed Verdict
   b. Redirect Examination
   c. Bill of Indictment
   d. Complaint
   (Answer = a)

2. Secondary questioning of a witness by the party who called the witness to obtain testimony regarding the case is known as:
   a. Direct examination
   b. Cross-examination
   c. Redirect examination
   d. All of the above
   (Answer = c)

3. Questioning of a witness by the party that did not call the witness to obtain testimony regarding the case is known as:
   a. Direct examination
   b. Cross-examination
   c. Redirect examination
   d. All of the above
   (Answer = b)

4. Initial questioning of a witness by the party who called the witness to obtain testimony regarding the case is known as:
   a. Direct examination
   b. Cross-examination
   c. Redirect examination
   d. All of the above
   (Answer = a)

5. Either the prosecution or the defense can excuse jurors for no particular or undisclosed reason during the voir dire process is known as:
   a. Peremptory challenge
   b. Challenge for cause
   c. Direct examination
   d. Cross-examination
   (Answer = a)

6. The process of jury selection by questioning the prospective panel members is known as:
   a. Arraignment
   b. Probable Cause Hearing
   c. Venire
   d. Voir dire
   (Answer = d)

7. The list of jurors called for jury duty from which jury panels are selected is known as:
   a. Voir dire
   b. Venire
   c. Bail bondsmen
   d. Judges
   (Answer = b)

8. The decision between the prosecutor and the defense attorney to have the defendant plead guilty in exchange for some concession is known as:
   a. Plea bargaining
   b. Voir dire
   c. Venire
   d. Cross-examination
   (Answer = a)

9. The Federal Bail Reform Act of 1984 provides that federal offenders may be detained without bail under certain specifications and this is called:
   a. Guideline Sentences
   b. Contextual discrimination
   c. Bail guidelines
   d. Arraignment
   (Answer = c)

10. When the defendant offers a percentage of the bail amount, such as 10%, with the court, this is known as:
    a. Release on recognizance
    b. Deposit bail
    c. Voir dire
    d. Peremptory challenge
    (Answer = b)

11. When the defendant is released on a promise to appear, without any requirement of money bond, it is known as:
    a. Peremptory challenge
    b. Voir dire
    c. Deposit bail
    d. Release on recognizance
    (Answer = d)

12. Those who practice providing bail to indigent offenders, usually at high rates of interest are known as:
    a. Bail bonding agents
    b. Attorneys
    c. Judges
    d. Prosecutors
    (Answer = a)

13. When defendants are detained because they cannot afford to make bail or because of the danger they present to the community, this is known as:
    a. Direct examination
    b. Preventive detention
    c. Arraignment
    d. Peremptory challenge
    (Answer = b)

14. Money or some other security provided to the court to ensure the appearance of the defendant at trial is known as:
    a. Voir dire
    b. Information
    c. Complaint
    d. Bail
    (Answer = d)

15. The step at which the accused are read the charges against them, asked how they wish to plead, and are advised of their rights is known as:
    a. Grand jury
    b. Preliminary hearing
    c. First appearance
    d. Arraignment
    (Answer = d)

16. A sworn written statement to a court by the police, prosecutor, or individual alleging that an individual has committed an offense and requesting indictment and prosecution is known as:
    a. Information

b. Indictment
c. Warrant
d. Complaint
(Answer = d)

17. The written accusation of the prosecutor setting out the charges against a defendant and used in place of the indictment in some jurisdictions is known as:
a. Complaint
b. Information
c. Indictment
d. Warrant
(Answer = b)

18. A formal written criminal accusation given by a grand jury setting out the crimes for which the defendant is to stand trial is known as:
a. Information
b. Complaint
c. Bill of indictment
d. Warrant
(Answer = c)

19. A method of selecting judges with a three part approach is known as:
a. Missouri plan
b. Voir dire
c. Venire
d. Arraignment
(Answer = a)

20. The senior officer in a court of criminal law that rules on the appropriateness of conduct, settles questions of evidence and procedure, and guides the questioning of witnesses is known as:
a. Prosecutor
b. Judge
c. Jury
d. Witnesses
(Answer = b)

21. Trial courts of the federal court system are known as:
a. State courts
b. Supreme courts
c. Federal courts of appeal
d. U.S. District Courts
(Answer = d)

22. The courts that hear the first appeal in the federal system from the lower courts is known as:
    a. State courts
    b. Supreme courts
    c. U.S. District Courts
    d. Federal courts of appeal
    (Answer = d)

23. The court of last resort for all cases tried in the various federal and state courts is known as:
    a. State courts
    b. Supreme court
    c. U.S. District Courts
    d. Federal courts of appeal
    (Answer = b)

24. An order issued by the Supreme Court when it decides to hear a case is known as a:
    a. Warrant
    b. Complaint
    c. Writ of Certiorari
    d. Indictment
    (Answer = c)

25. Decision by the Supreme Court that must be honored by all lower courts is known as:
    a. Prosecution
    b. Indictment
    c. Information
    d. Precedent
    (Answer = d)

26. A decision by the Supreme Court that becomes the law of the land and serves as a precedent for similar legal issues is known as:
    a. Prosecution
    b. Indictment
    c. Information
    d. Landmark decision
    (Answer = d)

27. They represent the state in criminal matters that come before the courts:
    a. Judges
    b. Juries
    c. Prosecution
    d. Public defenders
    (Answer = c)

28. A salaried staff of full-time or part-time attorneys that render indigent criminal defense services through a public or private nonprofit organization, or as direct government paid employees are known as:
    a. Public defenders
    b. Prosecutors
    c. Judges
    d. Juries
    (Answer = a)

29. Public defendant services provided mainly by local private attorneys appointed and paid by the court are known as:
    a. Indigents
    b. Judges
    c. Bail bondsmen
    d. Assigned counsel system
    (Answer = d)

30. The procedure used to determine truth in the adjudication of guilt or innocence in which the defense is pitted against the prosecution, with the judge acting as arbiter of the legal rules is known as:
    a. Arraignment
    b. Indictment
    c. Sentencing
    d. Adversarial process
    (Answer = d)

31. After the defense concludes its case, the government may present evidence to counteract the case of the defense and this is known as:
    a. Hearsay evidence
    b. Indictment
    c. Rebuttal
    d. Sentencing
    (Answer = c)

32. Testimony that is not firsthand but is relied by a second party is known as:
    a. Indictment
    b. Rebuttal
    c. Hearsay evidence
    d. Sentencing
    (Answer = c)

33. The criminal sanction imposed by the court on a convicted defendant is known as:
    a. indictment
    b. rebuttal
    c. hearsay evidence

d. sentencing

(Answer = d)

34. A statutory requirement that a certain penalty will be set and carried out in all of those types of case is known as a:
   a. Mandatory Prison Term
   b. Concurrent Sentence
   c. Consecutive Sentence
   d. Rebuttal

(Answer = a)

35. When both sentences are served at the same time, and the term of imprisonment is completed after the longest term has been served is known as:
   a. Consecutive sentence
   b. Mandatory prison term
   c. Rebuttal
   d. Concurrent sentence

(Answer = d)

36. When a convicted offender completes one sentence and the other prison term begins is called:
   a. Mandatory prison term
   b. Rebuttal
   c. Consecutive sentence
   d. Concurrent sentence

(Answer = c)

37. A type of prison sentence where the court has determined that the convicted person should be imprisoned, the exact length of imprisonment and parole supervision is fixed within statutory limits by a parole authority is called:
   a. Concurrent sentence
   b. Consecutive sentence
   c. Indeterminate sentence
   d. Determinate sentence

(Answer = c)

38. A type of prison sentence where the court has determined that the convicted person should be imprisoned, the exact length of imprisonment and parole supervision is fixed within statutory limits by the legislatures is called:
   a. Indeterminate sentence
   b. Determinate sentence
   c. Concurrent sentence
   d. Consecutive sentence

(Answer = b)

39. Based on the seriousness of the crime and the background of an offender, the more serious the crime and the more extensive the offender's criminal background, the longer the prison term recommended is directed by:
   a. Guideline sentences
   b. Determinate sentences
   c. Indeterminate sentences
   d. Concurrent sentences
   (Answer = a)

40. When people convicted of similar criminal acts often receive widely different sentences, it is known as:
   a. Guideline sentences
   b. Sentencing disparity
   c. Concurrent sentences
   d. Consecutive sentences
   (Answer = b)

True/False

T   1. The nation's 16,000 courts are organized on the municipal, county, state and federal levels.

F   2. Most states employ a single tiered court structure.

F   3. A specialty court, Gun Court, has jurisdiction over the burgeoning number of cases involving substance abuse and trafficking.

T   4. By 1998, all but 17 states had family courts, that served some number of counties, districts or were statewide.

T   5. There are currently over 450 tribal justice forums among the 556 Federally recognized tribes in the United States.

F   6. The Supreme Court is composed of 18 members, appointed for life.

F   7. The public defenders represent the state in criminal matters that come before the courts.

T   8. The judge, the prosecutor, and the defense attorney are the key players in the adversary process.

T   9. In the federal system, the chief prosecuting officer is the U.S. attorney general.

F   10. Federal prosecutors are semiprofessional, unpaid, contract workers.

T   11. Prosecutors maintain broad discretion in the exercise of their duties.

T   12.   Case pressure is considered an important influence on prosecutorial discretion.

F   13. Judges have the easiest job on the planet.

T   14. Bail represents money or some other security provided to the court to ensure the appearance of the defendant at trial.

T   15. The bail system goes back to English common law.

Chapter Eighteen

Corrections

Summary

Chapter Eighteen examines the Corrections System of the Criminal Justice System. The chapter begins with the history of punishment and corrections from the Middle Ages to the modern era of today. The various types of punishment in the United States are explained and defined beginning with probation. The discussion continues with intermediate sanctions, jail and prisons. Chapter Eighteen concludes with an explanation of parole and the parolee.

Learning Objectives

After reading this chapter the student should be able to:

- Develop an understanding of the history of punishment and corrections.
- Describe punishment during the 17th, 18th, 19th, and 20th Century.
- Understand the various types of punishment in the United States today.
- Develop an understanding of Probation.
- Understand the various Intermediate Sanctions.
- Explore jail populations and jail conditions.
- Distinguish between jails and prisons.
- Understand prison life in the United States.
- Develop an understanding of the Parole System.
- Describe the parolee in the community.

Chapter Overview

Introduction
History of Punishment and Corrections
    The Middle Ages

Chapter Outline

I.   **Introduction**

II.   **History of Punishment and Corrections**
      A. The Middle Ages
         1. Little law or governmental control existed (5th to 11th century A.D.)

2. Offenses settled by blood feuds between families of injured parties.
3. After 11th century, forfeiture of land and property were common punishment for lawbreakers.
4. Wergild - Payment to the injured party.
5. Corporal punishment - whipping or branding as a substitute penalty for a fine.
6. Wealthy could buy their way out of punishment.
7. Poor subject to execution and mutilation.
8. Punishment became gruesome.
9. Punishment became a public spectacle.

B. Punishment in the Seventeenth and Eighteenth Centuries
  1. Major population growth in England and France.
  2. Labor shortage due to population growth.
  3. Punishment changed to meet demands of social conditions.
  4. Instead of capital and corporal punishment, offenders were forced to labor.
  5. Poor laws required poor, vagrants, and vagabonds work in public or private enterprise.
  6. Houses of correction developed to assign work details for petty offenders.
  7. Galley slaves - offenders forced into sea duty; loathsome punishment.
  8. Vagrancy Act of 1597 - legalized deportation of offenders.
  9. Transportation to colonies became popular as punishment.
    a. Labor
    b. Cheap
    c. Profitable for the government since owners paid for convict services.

C. Corrections in the Late Eighteenth and Nineteenth Centuries
  1. Population in America increased.
  2. Crime rate rose significantly.
  3. Return of physical punishment and the death penalty.
  4. William Penn - Pennsylvania - lead correctional reform
    a. Revised Pennsylvania's criminal code to forbid torture.
    b. Penalties of imprisonment at hard labor, flogging, fines and forfeiture of property were implemented.
    c. Instituted house of corrections, similar to today's jail.
    d. In effect until Penn's death in 1718 and code reverted back to earlier emphasis on open public punishment and harsh brutality.
  5. 1776 - Penn's code readopted.
  6. 1787 - Quaker, Dr. Benjamin Rush formed the Philadelphia Society for Alleviating the Miseries of Public Prisons.
    a. To bring humane and orderly treatment to the penal system.
    b. Led to limiting the death penalty by the legislature to cases of treason, murder, rape and arson.
  7. 1790 - Quakers called for renovation of Prison system
    a. Philadelphia's Walnut Street Prison
    b. Solitary confinement.
    c. No right to work.

d. Penitentiary House - quarters of Walnut Street Prison which housed solitary or separate cells.

8. The Auburn System - built in 1816 in New York
   a. Tier system - cells were built vertically on five floors of the structure.
   b. Referred to as congregate system - prisoners ate and worked in groups.
   c. 1819 - solitary cells for unruly prisoners.
   d. Three classes of inmates created.
      1. Solitary confinement for prison discipline
      2. Allowed labor as a form of recreation
      3. Largest class worked and ate together in the day and in seclusion in the nights.
   e. Philosophy - crime prevention through fear of punishment and silent confinement.
   f. Total isolation abolished in 1823 due to high rates of mental breakdown, suicide and self-mutilation.
   g. Hard work and silence became the foundation of Auburn system.

9. The New Pennsylvania System - 1818
   a. Single cell with no work.
   b. No classifications.
   c. Called the Western Penitentiary - unusual architectural design.
   d. Built in semicircle with cells along the circumference.
   e. Solitary confinement with an hour a day for exercise.
   f. 1820 - similar prison in Philadelphia called the Eastern Penitentiary.
   g. Supporters believed penitentiary to be a place to do penance.
      1. Removing the sinner from society
      2. Allowing prisoner isolation to reflect on evils of crime.
      3. Influence of religious philosophy on corrections.
      4. Depressed conditions; inmates treated harshly, routinely whipped or tortured.
      5. Corporal punishment moved behind doors and became more savage.

10. Post-Civil War Developments - late 19th century much like that of today.
    a. Prisons experienced overcrowding.
    b. Single cell principle often ignored.
    c. Prison became scene of political intrigue.
    d. Prison industry developed.
    e. Some prisons used contract system - officials sold inmate labor to private businesses.
    f. Convict-lease system - state leased its prisoners to business for fixed annuals fee and gave up supervision and control.
    g. State account system - prisoners produce goods in prison for state use.
    h. Prison industry led to abuse of inmates.
    i. Prisons manufactured clothes, shoes, boots, furniture and the like.
    j. 1880's - Trade union opposition sparked restrictions on interstate commerce of prison goods and ended profitability.

      k. Z.R. Brockway - Warden of Elmira Reformatory in New York

          1. Advocated individualized treatment, indeterminate sentences and parole

          2. Program included elementary education for illiterates

          3. Designated library hours

          4. Lectures by local college faculty members

          5. Vocational training shops.

D. Corrections in the Twentieth Century

    1. Mutual Welfare League led by Thomas Mott Osborne advocated reform.

      a. Proposed better treatment.

      b. End harsh corporal punishment.

      c. Creation of meaningful prison industry and education programs.

      d. Prisoners should not be isolated from society.

    2. Opposition included the conservative prison administrators and state officials.

      a. Believed stern discipline needed to control dangerous inmates.

      b. Solitary confinement in dark, bare cells was common.

    3. 1930's inmate suits changed from red and white stripe to nondescript gray.

      a. Code of Silence ended.

      b. Lockstep shuffle ended.

      c. Movies and radios appeared in prisons.

      d. Visiting policies and mail privileges were liberalized.

      e. Specialized prisons designed to treat different types of offenders.

      f. Prison industry evolved.

      g. Convict-lease system and forced inmate labor ended.

      h. Severe discipline, harsh rules and solitary confinement remained.

E. The Modern Era

    1. 1960 - 1980's - much inmate litigation seeking greater rights and privileges.

    2. Inmates received rights of freedom of religion, speech, medical care, due process and proper living conditions.

    3. Since 1980's - prisoners rights movement has slowed.

    4. Violence in correctional systems became national scandal

      a. Riot at New York's Attica Prison and New Mexico State Penitentiary.

    5. Failure of rehabilitation has prompted many to reconsider incarceration.

    6. Inability of prison to reduce recidivism.

    7. Corrections Today

      a. Community-Based Programs

          1. Probation - supervision under the control of the sentencing court.

          2. An array of intermediate sanctions.

      b. Secure confinement

          1. Jail - house misdemeanants (and some felons) serving their sentence, as well as those awaiting trial not released on bail.

          2. Parole - supervises prisoners given early release from their sentences.

III. **Probation** - Suspension of the offender's sentence in return for the promise of good behavior in the community under the supervision of the probation department.
   A. Probationary Sentences
      1. May be granted by state and federal district courts and state superior (felony) courts.
      2. Accepted, widely used for adult felons, misdemeanants and juvenile delinquents.
   B. Probation Organizations
      1. About 2,000 adult probation agencies nationwide.
      2. 2001- about 3,840,000 adults under Federal, State, or local probation.
      3. Over 52% convicted of committing a felony.
      4. 46% convicted of committing a misdemeanor.
      5. 2% convicted of committing other infractions.
   C. Probation Services
      1. After conviction, probation department investigates offender's case
      2. Probation submits presentence investigation to the sentencing judge.
      3. Judge sentences offender.
      4. If offender is sentenced to probation, the department assesses the their personality and treatment needs - offender classification.
      5. Minimal risks will be given little supervision - perhaps a monthly visit or phone call.
      6. Probationers are placed in treatment programs such as community mental health, substance abuse and family counseling clinics when available.
   D. Probation Rules and Revocation
      1. Probationers are given a set of rules to guide their behavior.
      2. Typical rules include:
         a. Maintaining steady employment.
         b. Making restitution for loss or damage.
         c. Cooperating with the probation officer.
         d. Obeying all laws.
         e. Meeting family responsibilities.
         f. Individualized rules tailored to offender's specific needs.
      3. If rules are violated, probation may be revoked by the court and the person may begin serving their active sentence.
   E. Success of Probation
      1. Studies indicate that probation is not as successful as hoped.
      2. National data shows 60% of probationers successfully complete probation.
      3. About 40% are re-arrested, violate rules of probation or abscond.
      4. Most probation violations are for technical violations.
      5. Recidivism rate is lower for probationers than prison inmates.
      6. Probation is the preferred sentence for about 1/3 of all felony cases.
IV. **Intermediate Sanctions**
   A. New form of corrections that falls between probation and incarceration.
      1. Alternative to incarceration.

2. Punishments that are fair, equitable and proportional.
3. Likely candidates are convicted offenders who would be sent to prison, have a low risk of recidivating, and pose little threat to society.
B. Fines
1. Monetary payments imposed on the offender as an intermediate punishment for criminal acts.
2. Can be used alone or with other punishments.
3. Often other monetary sanctions are added to fines, such as:
   a. Court costs
   b. Public defender fees
   c. Probation and treatment fees
   d. Victim restitution
   e. Day fines - fines geared to an offender's net daily income in an effort to make them more equitable.
C. Forfeiture
1. Financially based alternative sanction.
2. The seizure of goods and instrumentality's related to the commission or outcome of a criminal act.
3. Criminal forfeiture - targets criminal defendants and only follows a criminal conviction.
4. Civil forfeiture - targets property used in a crime and does not require that formal criminal proceedings be initiated against a person or that they be proven guilty of a crime.
5. Forfeiture evolved from the Middle Ages.
   a. Forfeiture of an estate was a mandatory result of felony convictions.
   b. Reintroduced to American law with the passage of the RICO and the Continuing Criminal Enterprises acts - allow the seizure of any property derived from illegal enterprises or conspiracies.
D. Restitution
1. Require offender to pay the victim (monetary restitution) or serve the community (community service restitution).
2. Offer convicted offenders a way to avoid jail, prison or lengthy probation.
3. Appears to benefit the victim, the offender, the criminal justice system and society.
4. Inexpensive avoids stigma and helps compensate crime victims.
5. Almost 90% of offenders successfully complete restitution and have a lower recidivism rate.
E. Shock Probation and Split Sentencing
1. Alternative sanctions that allow judges to grant offenders community release only after they have sampled prison life.
2. Split sentencing - jail term as condition of probation.
3. Shock probation - resentencing an offender after a short prison stay.
F. Intensive Probation Supervision
1. Implemented in about 45 states.
2. Involve small caseloads of 15 to 40 clients.

3. Kept under close supervision by probation officers.
4. Primary goal is diversion - keeping probationers from the overcrowded prisons.
5. Second goal - control: high-risk offenders kept under closer security.
6. Third goal - reintegration: offenders can maintain community ties and be reoriented toward a more productive life while avoiding imprisonment.
7. Most have criteria as to eligibility:
   a. Nature of the offense.
   b. Offender's criminal background.
   c. Some exclude violent offenders.
8. Failure rate is quite high.

G. Home Confinement/Electronic Monitoring
1. Called house arrest or home detention.
2. Requires convicted offenders to spend extended periods of time in their own homes as an alternative to incarceration.
3. No data yet as to crime deterrence.
4. Random calls and visits are used to insure compliance with the house arrest orders.
5. Electronic monitoring device - offenders wear devices attached to their ankles, wrists or necks that send signals back to the control office.
   a. If offender leaves designated area at unauthorized time, the signal is broken and failure recorded.
   b. Other systems use a variety of technologies to monitor the offender.
6. Being hailed as one of the most important developments in correctional policy.
7. Indicated that recidivism rates are lower than other probationer groups.
8. Juveniles respond better than adults.

H. Residential Community Corrections
1. Nonsecure building that is not a part of a prison or jail and house pretrial and adjudicated adults.
2. Residents depart for work, attend school and/or participate in community correction activities and programs.
3. Clients reestablish family and friendship ties.
4. Shock of sudden reentry into society is reduced.
5. Can provide intermediate sanctions as well as prerelease center for those about to be released from prison.
6. Can be used as a halfway house.

I. Boot Camps/Shock Incarceration
1. Typically involve youthful, first-time offenders.
2. Feature military discipline and physical training.
3. Short periods (90 to 180 days) of high-intensity exercise and work.
4. Designed to promote responsibility and improve decision-making skills, build self-confidence, and teach socialization skills.
5. Inmates treated with rough intensity by drillmasters.
6. Results are mixed as to success rate.

J. Can Alternatives Work?
1. Little evidence that alternatives prevent crime, reduce recidivism or work better than other programs.
2. Other studies indicate that alternative sanctions have met their goal of providing correctional alternatives.

V.   Jails
A. Secure institution used to:
1. Detain offenders before trial if they cannot afford or are not eligible for bail
2. House misdemeanants sentenced to terms of one year or less, as well as some nonserious felons.
B. Originated in Europe in 16th century.
1. Used to house those awaiting trial and punishment.
2. Did not house sentenced criminals because punishment was fine, corporal punishment or death.
C. Walnut Street Jail - 1st modern jail - built 1790.
D. Jail Population
1. Population steadily increasing.
   a. 2000 - 621,149 people in America's jails.
   b. About 3,500 jails in U.S. today.
2. Who Are Jail Inmates?
   a. Over 50,000 youth admitted to adult jails each year.
   b. Over 8,000 persons under age 18 in an adult jail on a given day.
   c. 90% of jail population are males.
   d. Majority of jail inmates are either black or Hispanic.
   e. White non-Hispanics make up 42% of jail population.
   f. Black non-Hispanics make up 41% of jail population.
   g. Hispanics make up 15% of jail population.
3. New Generation Jails
   a. Modern designs to improve effectiveness.
   b. Tradition jails constructed in linear/intermittent surveillance model.
   c. Two types of New Generation Jails
      1. Direct Supervision - cluster of cells where officer can interact with inmates in a direct method of supervision.
      2. Indirect Supervision - Correctional officer is outside of cells in a secure room.

VI.   The Prison System
A. Federal Bureau of Prison and every state government maintain closed correction facilities.
1. Vast and costly system.
2. Nationwide about $22 billion sent on prisons.
B. Types of Institutions
1. 2002 - Over 1,550 state public and private adult correctional facilities.
   a. 84 Federal facilities and 25 private facilities.
   b. Categorized according to level of security and inmate populations.

    c. Maximum-security prisons - surrounded by high walls, have elaborate security measures, armed guards and house potentially dangerous inmates.

    d. Medium-security prisons - similar to maximum but usually contain less violent offenders.

    e. Minimum-security prisons - operate without armed guards or walls; house the most trustworthy and least violent offenders.

2. Farms and Camps

    a. Found primarily in the South and the West.

    b. Farms - inmates produce dairy products, grain and vegetable crops used in state government facilities.

    c. Camps - Forestry camp inmates maintain state parks, fight forest fires and do reforestation work.

    d. Ranches - Usually in the West, employ inmates in cattle raising and horse breeding.

    e. Road gangs repair roads and state highways.

3. Private Prisons

    1. 1986 - U.S. Corrections Corporation - opened 1st private state prison in Marion, Kentucky - 300 bed minimum-security facility.

    2. Today, more than 20 companies run private prisons.

    3. For-profit incarceration.

C. Prisoners in the United States

1. 2001 - about 1.4 million prisoners under Federal or State jurisdiction.

2. Prison population increased substantially since 1990.

D. Profile of Prison Inmates

1. Reflect the same profiles of arrestees.

2. Predominantly poor

3. Young adult male

4. Less than high school education

5. Longer sentences have dictated an aging inmate population.

6. 1997 - median age inmate was 32.

7. Over 60% have never been incarcerated before.

8. Over 15% have 6 or more prior incarcerations.

9. Many inmates come from single-parent homes.

10. Over 80% have been substance abusers themselves.

11. Males and minorities are overrepresented in prisons.

12. 2001- 91,612 women in state and federal prisons (6.6 % of all inmates).

13. Females in prison are the fastest growing population.

14. Educational and vocational underachievers.

15. Over 40% never finished high school.

16. Less than 20% were never married.

E. Prison Life: Males

1. Inmates are cut off from families, friends and associates.

    a. Fathers become depressed about children.

    b. Families and friends have trouble visiting due to long distances.

c. Mail is censored and often destroyed.

d. Prison is total institution regulating dress, work, and sleep and eating.

e. Inmates must learn a new world in prison.

f. Losses include:
1. Goods and services
2. Heterosexual relationships
3. Autonomy
4. Security
5. Privacy

g. Those who obey rules are offered, choice work, privileges and educational opportunities.

h. Those who break rules may be segregated, locked in their cells or put in solitary confinement (the hole).

i. Inmates must deal with sexual exploitation and violence.

j. To avoid victimization, inmates must adapt to new lifestyle.

k. Some join gangs and cliques for protection.

l. Hustle - black market economy involving the sale of illegal commodities such as drugs, alcohol, weapons, and illegal food and supplies.

m. Inmates must deal with daily racial conflict.

2. Inmate Society

a. Inmate subculture - unique social code - unwritten guidelines that express the values, attitudes and types of behavior that the older inmates demand of younger inmates.

b. Prisonization process - inmate's assimilation into the prison culture through acceptance of its language, sexual code and norms of behavior.

3. The New Inmate Culture

a. Old inmate culture harmful due to values and norms insulated inmate from change efforts.

b. Old inmate culture created order and prevented violence.

c. Old inmate culture is dying or dead in most prisons.

d. Racial tension has created many divisions.

e. Predatory inmates victimize others without fear of retaliation.

f. New inmate culture is one of danger and chaos.

g. Prison life is more disorganized.

h. Gangs forming and engaging in ever-increasing violent confrontations.

F. Prison Life: Females

1. Usually housed in minimum-security institutions more like college dorms.

2. Women do not present the danger that men do in prison.

3. Women deal with a lot of fear and violence.

4. Violence in female prisons is common.

5. Many women undergo a process of socialization with danger and volatile situations.

6. Often experience severe anxiety and anger due to separation from families.
7. Females may resort to self-destructive acts to cope with their problems.
8. Females are more likely to be treated with mood-altering drugs and placed in psychiatric care.
9. Surrogate families develop in female prisons.
10. Health care is an issue.
11. Many institutions have inadequate facilities to deal with pregnancy, HIV and AIDS.
12. Female inmates are still being trained vocationally for women's roles.
13. Sexual Exploitation
    a. Numerous reports of female prisoners being sexually abused by male correctional officers.
14. Adapting to Prison
    a. Rigid, antiauthority inmate social code does not exist in female institutions.
    b. Female inmates more likely to mutilate their bodies and commit suicide.
G. Correctional Treatment
   1. Over 90% of inmates participate in a program or activity after admission.
   2. Medical Model of Treatment - rely heavily on counseling and clinical therapy.
   3. Reintegration - work release, vocational training, and educational opportunities.
   4. Self-Help programs
   5. Programs with a religious theme.
   6. Therapy and Counseling
      a. Counseling exists in almost every institution.
      b. Some stress individual therapy.
      c. Most have group session, due to resource limitations.
   7. Educational Programs
      a. First treatment programs.
      b. Prison school opened at the Walnut Street Prison in 1784.
      c. Most institutions provide some education.
   8. Vocational Rehabilitation
      a. Most prisons operate numerous vocational training programs to help inmates develop skills for employment in society.
      b. Work furlough programs in some prisons.
      c. Prerelease and postrelease employment services in some prisons.
   9. Private Industry in Prisons
      a. Can take many forms.
      b. Attractive on paper.
      c. Teaches inmates skills in desirable commercial areas.
      d. Increases employment opportunities on the outside.
   10. Inmate Self-Help

a. Inmates have organized self-help groups to prevent recidivism.

b. Alcoholics Anonymous

c. Boy Scout Troops

d. Racial and ethnic groups

e. Groups designed to help inmates find strength on the outside.

f. Fortune society

g. 7th Step organization

h. Prison Fellowship

11. Does Rehabilitation Work?

a. Some question the effectiveness of rehabilitation.

b. High-risk offenders are more likely to commit crimes after they have been placed in treatment programs.

c. Some view prisons as places of incapacitation and confinement; their purpose is punishment, not treatment.

d. Treatment more effective if matched with the needs of inmates.

H. Prison Violence

1. Fear of prison administrators.

2. Jails and prisons have a climate of violence.

3. Causes of prison violence

a. Inmates may suffer from personality disorders.

b. Prisons may convert people to violence by their inhumane conditions, overcrowding, depersonalization and threats of rape.

c. Mismanagement, lack of strong security, and inadequate control by officials.

d. Changing prison population to younger, more violent inmates.

I. Corrections and the Rule of Law

1. Freedom of press and speech - courts ruled inmates retain freedom of speech and press unless it interferes with institutional freedom.

2. Medical rights - Inmates are entitled to proper medical attention.

3. Cruel and Unusual Punishment and Overall Conditions - many rulings by the Court as to cruel and unusual punishment violating the 8th Amendment.

VII. **Parole** - the planned release and community supervision of incarcerated offenders before the expiration of their prison sentences.

A. Discretionary Parole

1. Some jurisdictions grant parole by a decision of a state parole board.

2. Board meet offender, reviews the information, and decides whether or not to grant parole.

3. Good time credits - reduce the minimum sentence and therefore hasten eligibility for parole.

4. Considerations include:

a. Inmate's offense

b. Time served

c. Evidence of adjustment

d. Opportunities on the outside.

B. Mandatory Parole
1. States with determinate sentencing statutes do not use parole boards, but release inmates at the conclusion of their pre-determined sentence less accumulated good time.
C. The Parolee in the Community
1. Offender supervised by trained parole officers to help readjust to the community.
2. Parolees subject to strict standardized or personalized rules that guide their behavior and limit their activities.
3. Parole can be revoked if offender commits another offense.
D. How Effective is Parole?
1. Surveys indicate more than half of parolees eventually return to prison.
2. Older parolees age 55 and up and females have higher success rates than younger and male parolees.

VIII. **Summary**

Key Terms

Capital Punishment - Execution by the government for a crime committed by the offender.

Corporal Punishment - Physical pain inflicted on the offender for the purposes of punishment.

Poor Laws - 17th century laws in England that bound out vagrants, abandoned and neglected children as indentured servants.

Walnut Street Prison - A wing of the Walnut Street Jail that became the prison for convicted felons as a result of pressure from the Quakers on the Pennsylvania State Legislature.

Auburn System - The prison system developed in New York during the nineteenth century that stressed congregate working conditions.

Contract System - System used to lease inmates out to private industry to work.

Convict-lease System - System used where the state leased inmates to a business for a fixed annual fee and the state gave up supervision and control.

State Account System - Prisoners produce goods in prison for state use.

Z.R. Brockway - Warden of the Elmira Reformatory in New York. He advocated individualized treatment, indeterminate sentences, and parole.

Probation - A sentence of release into the community under the supervision of the court subject to certain conditions.

Intermediate Sanction - Punishments falling between probation and prison including house arrest and intensive supervision.

Revoke - Judicial order by a court removing a person from parole or probation in response to a violation on the part of the parolee or probationer.

Offender Classification - Probation department diagnoses offender's personality and treatment needs.

Technical Violation - Violation of rules of probation or parole.

Day Fines - A fine geared to an offender's net daily income in an effort to make them more equitable.

Forfeiture - The seizure of personal property by the state as a civil or criminal penalty.

Monetary Restitution - A direct payment to the victim as a form of compensation.

Community Service Restitution - Work in the community by the offender in lieu of more severe criminal penalties.

Split Sentencing - Sentence which includes a jail term as a condition of probation.

Shock Probation - Sentence in which offenders serve a short prison term to impress them with the pains of imprisonment before they begin probation.

Intensive Probation Supervision - Type of immediate sanction involving small probation caseloads and strict monitoring.

Home Confinement - Requires convicted offenders to spend extended periods of time in their own homes as an alternative to incarceration.

Electronic Monitoring - Device convicted offender wears under the home confinement penalty.

Shock Incarceration - A short prison sentence served in boot-camp type facilities.

Boot Camps - A short-term military style correctional facility in which inmates undergo intensive physical conditioning and discipline.

Jail - A place to detain people awaiting trial, hold drunks and disorderly individuals, and confine convicted misdemeanants serving sentences of less than one year.

Prison - State or federal correctional institution for incarceration of felony offenders for terms of one year or more.

Penitentiary - Prisoner quarters that contained the solitary or separate cells.

The Hole - Solitary confinement of an inmate.

Inmate Subculture - The loosely defined culture in a prison that has its own norms, rules and language.

Social Code - The values of interpersonal relations within the prison.

Prisonization - Assimilation into the prison culture that has its own set of behaviors.

Importation Model - View that the violent prison culture reflects the criminal culture of the outside world.

Parole - Early release of a prisoner from prison with conditions set by a parole board.

Parole Grant Hearing - In states where discretionary parole is used, the release decision is made by a board that meets the convict, reviews the information and makes the decision whether or not to grant parole.

Discussion Exercise

Break class up into groups. Assign each group a correctional sanction. Have each group present to the class the positive and negative aspects of their correctional sanction. Cast votes as to which the group feels is most effective?

InfoTrac Assignment

GETTING STARTED: Search term words for subject guide: Punishment, Corrections, Probation, Fines, Forfeiture, Restitution, Boot Camps, Jail, Prisoners, Parole.

CRITICAL THINKING PROJECT: Using the search term "Forfeiture," find relevant articles.

Here are three articles:

O'Meara, Kelly Patricia "When Feds Say Seize and Desist." *Insight on the News*.

Hartman, Victor E. "Implementing An Asset Forfeiture Program." *The FBI Law Enforcement Bulletin*.

Zakhary, Joseph R. "Fraud & Abuse: Excessive Fines Clause of the Eighth Amendment -

United States v. Bajakajian." *American Journal of Law & Medicine*.

Test Bank

Essay Questions

1. Trace the history of punishment and corrections from the Middle Ages to our modern era. Which punishments were most effective?
2. Define probation. What are the various probation organizations and what types of services do they provide?
3. What are intermediate sanctions? Which intermediate sanctions are the most effective? Which intermediate sanctions are the least effective?

4. What is a jail? Describe the individuals who are incarcerated in our jails? What are the prerequisites for one being incarcerated in a jail?

5. Define prisons. What are the various types of prisons in the United States? Which types of inmates are sentenced to which classification of prison?

Fill In The Blank

1. Prisoner quarters that contained the solitary or separate cells are known as **Penitentiary**.

2. Solitary confinement of an inmate is also known as the **Hole**.

3. The loosely defined culture in a prison that has its own set of norms, rules and language is known as the **Inmate Subculture**.

4. The values of interpersonal relations within the prison are known as the **Social Code**.

5. **Prisonization** is the assimilation into the prison culture that has its own set of behaviors.

6. The **Importation Model** is the view that the violent prison culture reflects the criminal culture of the outside world.

7. **Parole** is the early release of a prisoner from prison with conditions set by a parole board.

8. In states where discretionary parole is used, the release decision is made by a board that meets the convict, reviews the information, and makes the decision whether or not to grant parole is known as a **Parole Grant Hearing**.

9. **Capital Punishment** is execution of a convicted criminal by the government for a crime committed by the offender.

10. A State or Federal correctional institution for incarceration of felony offenders for terms of one year or more is known as a **Prison**.

11. **Prisons** are state and federally operated correctional facilities that receive felony offenders sentenced by the criminal courts.

12. **Jails** detain people awaiting trial, hold drunks and disorderly individuals, and confine convicted misdemeanants serving sentences of less than one year.

13. A short-term military style correctional facility in which inmates undergo intensive physical conditioning and discipline are known as **Boot Camps**.

14. **Home Confinement** requires convicted offenders to spend extended periods of time in their own homes as an alternative to incarceration.

15. A type of immediate sanction involving small probation caseloads and strict monitoring is known as **Intensive Probation Supervision**.

Multiple Choice

1. State or federal correctional institution for incarceration of felony offenders for terms of one year or more is known as a:
    a. Prison
    b. Jail
    c. Boot camp
    d. Auburn system
    (Answer = a)

2. Execution by the government for a crime committed by the offender is known as:
    a. Corporal punishment
    b. Parole
    c. Capital punishment
    d. Probation
    (Answer = c)

3. Prisoner quarters that contain solitary or separate cells are known as:
    a. The hole
    b. Penitentiary
    c. Jail
    d. Boot camp
    (Answer = b)

4. Solitary confinement of an inmate is commonly called:
    a. Boot camp
    b. Jail
    c. Shock incarceration
    d. The hole
    (Answer = d)

5. The loosely defined culture n a prison that has its own norms, rules and language is known as:
    a. Inmate subculture
    b. Importation model
    c. Parole
    d. Segregation
    (Answer = a)

6. The values of interpersonal relations within the prison are known as:
   a. Importation model
   b. Parole
   c. Segregation
   d. Social code
   (Answer = d)

7. Assimilation into the prison culture that has its own set of behaviors is known as:
   a. Social code
   b. Prisonization
   c. Importation code
   d. Parole grant hearing
   (Answer = b)

8. The view that the violent prison culture reflects the criminal culture of the outside world is known as:
   a. Importation model
   b. Social code
   c. Prisonization
   d. Parole grant hearing
   (Answer = a)

9. The early release of a prisoner from prison with conditions set by a parole board is known as:
   a. Importation model
   b. Social code
   c. Parole
   d. Prisonization
   (Answer = c)

10. In states where discretionary parole is used, the release decision is made by a board that meets the convict, reviews the information and makes the decision whether or not to grant parole is known as:
   a. Importation model
   b. Parole grant hearing
   c. Social code
   d. Prisonization
   (Answer = b)

11. During the Middle Ages, payment made by the offender to the victim was called:
   a. Incarceration
   b. Probation
   c. Parole
   d. Wergild
   (Answer = d)

12. During the 18th century, this was a popular form of punishment, which banished offenders to the American colonies as a source of labor:
    a. Transportation
    b. Prison
    c. Parole
    d. Probation
    (Answer = a)

13. During the last part of the 18th century there were how many types of crimes in England punishable by death?
    a. 3
    b. 350
    c. 35
    d. 3500
    (Answer = b)

14. Correctional reform in the United States was first instituted in Pennsylvania under the leadership of:
    a. George Washington
    b. Thomas Jefferson
    c. Richard Petty
    d. William Penn
    (Answer = d)

15. During the Civil War era, prisons were major manufacturers of:
    a. Clothes
    b. Shoes
    c. Boots
    d. All of the above
    (Answer = d)

16. One of the worst prison riots in history occurred at:
    a. Attica Prison
    b. New Mexico State Penitentiary
    c. All of the above
    d. None of the above
    (Answer = c)

17. How many agencies nationwide list adult probation as their major function?
    a. 200
    b. 2000
    c. 200000
    d. 2 million
    (Answer = b)

18. As of 2001, approximately how many adults were under Federal, State or local probation?
    a. 3840
    b. 38400
    c. 3840000
    d. 3
    (Answer = c)

19. What percentage of probationers committed a felony?
    a. 52%
    b. 11%
    c. 5%
    d. 1%
    (Answer = a)

20. What percentages of probationers were convicted of committing a misdemeanor?
    a. 4%
    b. 46%
    c. 6%
    d. 64%
    (Answer = b)

21. Most probation agencies operate at what level?
    a. Federal
    b. Local
    c. Municipal
    d. State
    (Answer = d)

22. What percentages of probationers successfully complete probation?
    a. 6%
    b. 10%
    c. 100%
    d. 60%
    (Answer = d)

23. What percentage of eligible offenders successfully completes their restitution orders?
    a. 9%
    b. 90%
    c. 80%
    d. 8%
    (Answer = b)

24. Under current federal practices, what percentages of all convicted federal offenders receive some sort of split sentence?
    a. 2%
    b. 5%
    c. 25%
    d. 52%
    (Answer = c)

25. Intensive probation caseloads are usually what size?
    a. 5 to 10
    b. 5 to 20
    c. 20 to 40
    d. 15 to 40
    (Answer = d)

26. What is the failure rate of intensive supervision probation cases?
    a. 10%
    b. 20%
    c. 40%
    d. 50%
    (Answer = d)

27. The length of time offenders spend in boot camp is normally:
    a. 5 to 50 days
    b. 50 to 100 days
    c. 90 to 180 days
    d. 2 years
    (Answer = c)

28. In 2000 how many people were incarcerated in the U.S. jails?
    a. 621,149
    b. 62,149
    c. 6,214
    d. 621
    (Answer = a)

29. Male inmates make up what percentage of the local jail population?
    a. 10%
    b. 40%
    c. 60%
    d. 90%
    (Answer = d)

30. Jails being built today that use modern designs are referred to as:
    a. Linear Designs
    b. Campus Style
    c. Intermittent Surveillance
    d. New Generation
    (Answer = d)

31. As of 2002, there are more than how many public and private adult correctional facilities housing State prisoners?
    a. 150
    b. 155
    c. 1550
    d. 15550
    (Answer = c)

32. Prisons that are surrounded by high walls, have elaborate security measures and armed guards are referred to as:
    a. Minimum security
    b. Medium security
    c. Maximum security
    d. None of the above
    (Answer = c)

33. The first Federal maxi prison was located in:
    a. Raleigh, NC
    b. Las Cruces, NM
    c. Sacramento, CA
    d. Marion, Illinois
    (Answer = d)

34. Prisons that have less violent inmates, offer a variety of treatment and education programs and resemble maximum security prisons are known as:
    a. Medium security
    b. Minimum security
    c. Super maxi security
    d. None of the above
    (Answer = a)

35. Prisons which operate without armed guards or walls and are usually constructed in compounds surrounded by chain links are known as:
    a. Super maxi security
    b. Maximum security
    c. Medium security
    d. Minimum security
    (Answer = d)

36. As of 2001, how many prisoners were under Federal or State jurisdiction?
    a. 10 million
    b. 5 million
    c. 1.4 million
    d. 1 million
    (Answer = c)

37. What percentages of inmates have been incarcerated before?
    a. 1%
    b. 6%
    c. 60%
    d. 100%
    (Answer = c)

38. The first prison treatment programs were:
    a. Vocational
    b. Educational
    c. Religious
    d. Counseling
    (Answer = b)

39. On a given day, how many persons under age 18 are housed in adult jails?
    a. 8000
    b. 80000
    c. 800
    d. 8
    (Answer = a)

40. What percentage does white non-Hispanic constitutes of the jail population?
    a. 5%
    b. 42%
    c. 4%
    d. 52%
    (Answer = b)

True/False

T   1. In ancient times, the most common state-administered punishment was banishment or exile.

F   2. In both ancient Greece and Rome, interpersonal violence, even murder, was viewed as a public matter.

F   3. Heavy government control existed during the early Middle Ages.

T   4. Poor laws developed in the early seventeenth century required that the poor, vagrants, and vagabonds be put to work in public or private enterprise.

T   5. Transportation to the colonies waned as a method of punishment with the increase in colonial population, the further development of the land, and the increasing importation of African slaves in the eighteenth century.

F   6. Between the American Revolution in 1776 and the first decades of the nineteenth century, the population of Europe and America decreased rapidly.

F   7. During the last part of the twentieth century, 350 types of crime in England were punishable by death.

T   8. Correctional reform in the United States was first instituted in Pennsylvania under the leadership of William Penn.

T   9. In 1818 Pennsylvania took the radical step of establishing a prison that laced each inmate in a single cell with no work to do.

F   10. The congregate system eventually failed, however, and spread throughout the United States; many of its features are still used today.

T   11. Z.R. Brockway, warden at the Elmira Reformatory in New York advocated individualized treatment, indeterminate sentences, and parole.

T   12. Between 1960 and 1980, a great deal of litigation was brought by inmates seeking greater rights and privileges.

F   13. Since 1980, the "prisoners' rights" movement has increased as judicial activism waned during the Reagan-Bush era.

T   14. Correctional treatment can be divided today into community-based programs and secure confinement.

T   15. Jails house misdemeanants (and some felons) serving their sentences, as well as felons and misdemeanants awaiting trial who have not been released on bail.

Appendix A

WebTutor™ Integration Tips

Contents of the Appendix:

Tips for Integrating
WebTutor™on Blackboard from Thomson Learning

Feature	Description - Benefit
THOMSON PROVIDED CONTENT	
Summary Materials	Students will be able to view summary material tied directly to their course textbook. These can include, but are not limited to Chapter Outlines, Summaries, exercises, graphics, and special topics.
Quizzes	Allows students to practice what they have learned in the textbook. Quizzes are automatically graded so instructors can view results. Students can take quizzes multiple times, or if the instructor prefers, they can limit the number of times, set a time limit, or specify a specific time when the quiz is available.
Flashcards	Flashcards allow students to review key terms from the textbook. Because students learn in many ways, flashcards (w/audio) allow students to hear the pronunciation of the term and in some cases, the definition. Flashcards are especially beneficial to the ESL or Learning Disabled student.
Web Links	Web links help keep the course current for the instructor and provide numerous opportunities for students to do additional research or project-based activities right on the web. Each WebTutor product comes pre-loaded with web links designed to enhance the course.
Discussion Topics	Threaded Discussion or Bulletin Board systems allow students and instructors to engage in a lively, on going discussion, anytime or anywhere. All Thomson WebTutor products come pre-loaded with suggested discussion topics. Of course, instructors and students can add their own.
PowerPoint Presentations	Many WebTutor products include PowerPoint presentations keyed to the textbook.
COMMUNICATION TOOLS	
Integrated Calendar	An integrated calendar provides the ability to enter information at the institutional, course, and personal level. My Institution Page will show any entries available for that day.
Web Mail	Blackboard has third party software embedded in the product to seamlessly link to students existing email accounts.
Virtual Classroom	The Virtual Classroom allows for real-time, communication with the class and combines chat, whiteboard technology and a web browser into a synchronous learning tool. There are many possible uses for chat including virtual office hours, group study sessions or projects, and guest speakers. All chat sessions are logged for the instructor to view - even if they are not an active participant.
Threaded Discussion or Bulletin Board	Threaded Discussion or Bulletin Board systems allow students and instructors to engage in a lively, on going discussion, anytime or anywhere. This tool has many applications including discussion of course topics, debates, or general discussions about course issues. Instructors can create private discussion forums, or allow students to post anonymously. Instructors may assign a student moderator.
Group Pages	Group pages allow the instructor to create collaborative learning environment on-line for specific group of students. This is useful for group projects and presentations.
Announcements	An announcement feature allows instructors to post time sensitive information to their class.

STUDENT MANAGEMENT TOOLS	
Course Statistics	Instructors will receive reports on each student that allow them to identify students first and last login, a distribution of hits, percentage of content visited and a complete history of all pages visited. Instructors can use this tool to monitor students progress and identify problem areas in a timely manner.
Discussion Boards	Instructors will receive information about students participation in the discussion area including the number of items read, the number of original postings and the number of follow up postings. In an online environment, this is a great tool for instructors to measure a student's participation in class.
Online Gradebook	Allows instructors to view all students registered in the class and the results of their graded online quizzes and assignments.
Item Analysis	Allows instructors to see which students have accessed pages of content (from a path) - both the number of times and the time spent. Using this information, instructors can identify where students are spending their time and which areas of the course either need work, or additional reinforcement in class.
Recycle Course	Allows instructors to recycle their courses from term to term without losing their customization. Student rosters, Bulletin Boards, online gradebook, Virtual Classroom archives are reset in preparation for the next term.
CUSTOMIZATION OPTIONS	
Look and feel	Instructors have complete control over the look and feel of their course - they can change button names and colors, add text and images and their school logo if they choose.
Quizzes	All quizzes are fully editable. Instructors can also create their own quizzes, or banks of questions for additional study or exams. Additionally quizzes can be set up to prompt students for a password or require that a student is accessing the quiz from a certain IP address.
Content	Instructors can edit, delete or hide any content provided in the WebTutor product. They can also add their own content as well as re-sequencing the way the current content is presented.
Add additional Blackboard tools	Blackboard provides additional functionality for instructors wanting to take their course to the next level. Here are just a few: a student/instructor dropbox and an Electric Blackboard for notetaking.
HOSTING OPTIONS	
Centrally hosted	For schools that do not have Blackboard, we provide a hosted option (through Blackboard). All centrally hosted courses include technical support directly from Blackboard.
Locally Hosted	For schools that have Blackboard 5.0, Thomson will provide the school with an access key so that they can download the content cartridge to their local server. Blackboard provides additional technical support to supplement resources available on campus.

For additional information, including Frequently Asked Questions, tours, and downloadable Instructor and Student guides, visit us at http://webtutor.thomsonlearning.com

Tips for Integrating
WebTutor™ on WebCT from Thomson Learning

Feature	Description - Benefit
THOMSON PROVIDED CONTENT	
Summary Materials	Students will be able to view summary material tied directly to their course textbook. These can include, but are not limited to Chapter Outlines, Summaries, exercises, graphics, and special topics.
Quizzes	Allows students to practice what they have learned in the textbook. Quizzes are automatically graded so instructors can view results. Students can take quizzes multiple times, or if the instructor prefers, they can limit the number of times, set a time limit, or specify a specific time when the quiz is available.
Flashcards	Flashcards allow students to review key terms from the textbook. Because students learn in many ways, flashcards (w/audio) allow students to hear the pronunciation of the term and in some cases, the definition. Flashcards are especially beneficial to the ESL or Learning Disabled student.
Web Links	Web links help keep the course current for the instructor and provide numerous opportunities for students to do additional research or project-based activities right on the web. Each WebTutor product comes pre-loaded with web links designed to enhance the course.
Discussion Topics	Threaded Discussion or Bulletin Board systems allow students and instructors to engage in a lively, on going discussion, anytime or anywhere. All Thomson WebTutor products come pre-loaded with suggested discussion topics. Of course, instructors and students can add their own.
PowerPoint Presentations	Many WebTutor products include PowerPoint presentations keyed to the textbook.
COMMUNICATION TOOLS	
Integrated Calendar	An integrated calendar can serve as a syllabus tool for instructors and allows them to enter information and key dates for the course. A pop-up window will always notify students when NEW information is placed on the calendar. Instructors can also create a link that will take students directly to a content page (chapter summary, quiz, etc). Students (and instructors) can also use the compile feature to print all assignments for a selected date range. Private entries are also allowed.
e-mail	An integrated e-mail system automatically builds a directory for the course as students create accounts. Students are not required to have an external email account to use WebTutor.
Chat	Chat allows for real-time, synchronous communication with the class. There are many possible uses for chat including virtual office hours, group study sessions or projects, and guest speakers. All chat sessions are logged for the instructor to view - even if they are not an active participant.
Threaded Discussion or Bulletin Board	Threaded Discussion or Bulletin Board systems allow students and instructors to engage in a lively, on going discussion, anytime or anywhere. This tool has many applications including discussion of course topics, debates, or general discussions about course issues. Instructors can create private discussion forums, or allow students to post anonymously.
Whiteboard	A whiteboard provides a real time graphical interface to instructors wishing to display images, etc to students. The whiteboard allows instructors and students to draw to the board for all other users to see.

STUDENT MANAGEMENT TOOLS	
Progress Tracking	Instructors will receive reports on each student that allow them to identify students first and last login, a distribution of hits, percentage of content visited and a complete history of all pages visited. Instructors can use this tool to monitor students progress and identify problem areas in a timely manner.
Participation in Discussion	Instructors will receive information about students participation in the discussion area including the number of items read, the number of original postings and the number of follow up postings. In an online environment, this is a great tool for instructors to measure a student's participation in class.
Student Management	Allows instructors to view all students registered in the class and the results of their graded online quizzes and assignments.
Page Tracking	Allows instructors to see which students have accessed pages of content (from a path) - both the number of times and the time spent. Using this information, instructors can identify where students are spending their time and which areas of the course either need work, or additional reinforcement in class.
Grader Management	Allows the instructor to add graders to the course who have access to quiz information for assistance with grading.
Course RESET	Allows instructors to reset portions of their course for easy transition from term to term without losing their customization. Instructors can reset the student database, e-mail, Bulletin Boards, grader database, chat logs, the calendar tool, and the page-tracking tool.
Selective Release of Content	Instructors can choose to release content based on certain criteria such as date or time, to a selected group of students, or based on the result of quiz scores.
CUSTOMIZATION OPTIONS	
Look and feel	Instructors have complete control over the look and feel of their course - they can change screen colors, add text and images, counters and their school logo if they choose.
Quizzes	All quizzes are fully editable. Instructors can also create their own quizzes, or banks of questions for additional study or exams. Additionally quizzes can be set up to prompt students for a password or require that a student is accessing the quiz from a certain IP address.
Content	Instructors can edit, delete or hide any content provided in the WebTutor product. They can also add their own content as well as re-sequencing the way the current content is presented.
Add additional WebCT tools	WebCT provides additional functionality for instructors wanting to take their course to the next level. Here are just a few: an assignment dropbox, student presentation areas or homepages, image libraries, audio and video files, and more.
HOSTING OPTIONS	
Centrally hosted	For schools that do not have WebCT, we provide a hosted option (through WebCT). All centrally hosted courses include unlimited technical support directly from WebCT for both instructors and students.
Locally Hosted	For schools that have WebCT, Thomson will provide the school with a content cartridge that they can install on their local server. Instructors and students also receive technical support from WebCT as well as the resources they have available on campus.

**For additional information, including Frequently Asked Questions, tours, and
downloadable Instructor and Student guides, visit us at
http://webtutor.thomsonlearning.com**

Appendix B

InfoTrac® College Edition
User Guide for the Instructor

Contents of the Appendix:

INTRODUCTION

InfoTrac College Edition is a fully searchable online university library containing complete articles and their images. Its database gives you access to hundreds of scholarly and popular publications–all reliable sources, including journals, magazines, encyclopedias, and newsletters. Updated daily, the *InfoTrac College Edition* database also includes articles dating back as much as four years. And every article within the database can be easily printed for reading and reference purposes or quickly arranged into a bibliography.

24 Hours a Day

InfoTrac College Edition means anytime, anywhere Internet access to thousands of articles, from school or home. Student subscribers receive a personalized "account ID number" that gives them unlimited access to *InfoTrac College Edition* for four full months at any hour of the day, anywhere they happen to be. The 24-hour, four-month subscription will launch your students on a quest for knowledge for term papers, class assignments, and lab projects, and you can be rest assured that your students' Internet research will be complete and based exclusively on reliable published sources; what's more, it's not just abstracts!

Use it as Part of Your Course

InfoTrac College Edition also does something for you, the instructor. It gives you the flexibility to require outside readings–an online reader–without sinking your students' textbook budgets. *InfoTrac College Edition* can be integrated into your course syllabi. With your free subscription, you can use it to prepare lectures and assignments, or to build a reader from the database for your discipline.

QUICK TIPS FOR THE CLASSROOM

InfoTrac College Edition is an excellent tool to introduce students to researching subjects. You can use it to prepare lectures and outside assignments or to build a reader from the database for your discipline. Students will appreciate the ease of online research, especially when writing papers, preparing class presentations, or researching a key topic. Below are some suggestions on how to incorporate *ICE* in your classroom.

Writing Assignments
- Provide a topic to your students to research in *ICE*. Have them choose one article that interests them and have them write a thesis on that specific article and construct an outline.
- Point students to *ICE* as an excellent reference and information source when preparing their term papers.

Study Questions
- Prepare a list of study questions on a lecture topic and have the students research and answer them using *ICE*.
- Have students explore answers to the end-of-chapter study questions of the book using *ICE*.

Reading Assignments
- Select specific articles and assign them to your students for further reading.
- Use as a vehicle for critical thinking.

Classroom Activities
- Divide the classroom into groups and provide them with a topic to research and discuss for the next class. Have each group present their discoveries and summary of that topic.
- Set up classroom debates by providing a subject and assigning students to research a pro or con stance to discuss in class.

GETTING STARTED

Go to *http://www.infotrac-college.com*

Click "Enter InfoTrac College Edition."

Enter your passcode. **Keep your passcode card safe.** (We cannot replace it.) You will need it every time you log in to ICE.

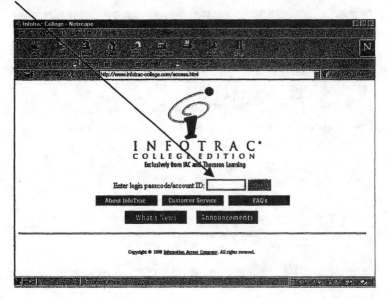

Registration

If you are using InfoTrac College Edition for the first time, you will need to complete the registration form. Any items in **bold** type must be completed before your account can be activated.

If required items are missing or invalid on the registration form, an error message from Customer Service describing the problem will appear. Simply click the "Back" button on your browser's toolbar to return to the registration form.

After the registration form is successfully completed, you will be asked to confirm that all information is accurate. Click on the "Submit" button to send your completed registration form.

Click **Submit/Agree to Terms/Subscribe** to complete the registration process, accept the licensing agreement, and begin using InfoTrac College Edition.

USING INFOTRAC COLLEGE EDITION

The Header Bar

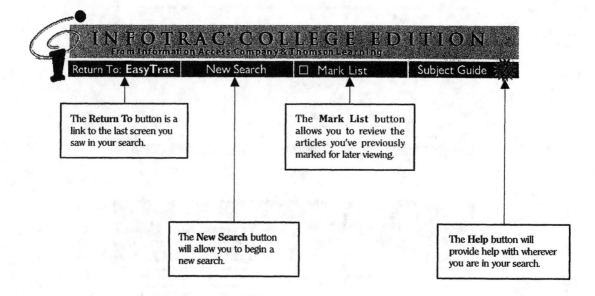

The **Return To** button is a link to the last screen you saw in your search.

The **Mark List** button allows you to review the articles you've previously marked for later viewing.

The **New Search** button will allow you to begin a new search.

The **Help** button will provide help with wherever you are in your search.

EasyTrac Searching

After signing in, the EasyTrac search screen will appear. EasyTrac is designed for basic research needs. You can research articles via Subject Guide or Key Words. Type in the topic you would like to research.

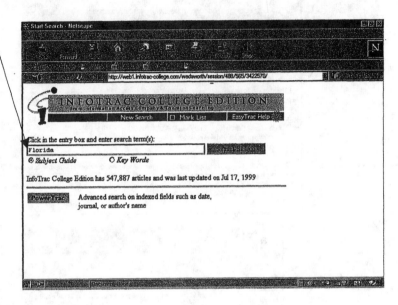

There are two ways to research your topic, by Subject Guide or Key Words.

<u>Subject Guide</u> allows you to do a broad search on a topic. The Subject Guide screen lists all headings containing your specific topic along with the number of articles/citations found with each heading. Clicking on the "View" link will take you to the specific articles/citations for that heading.

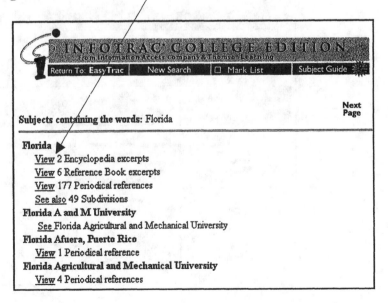

Key Word search is more effective when looking for a specific topic, title, author name, or product. The Key Word search will give you a list of articles containing the key word topic. Click on "View" to link to the article.

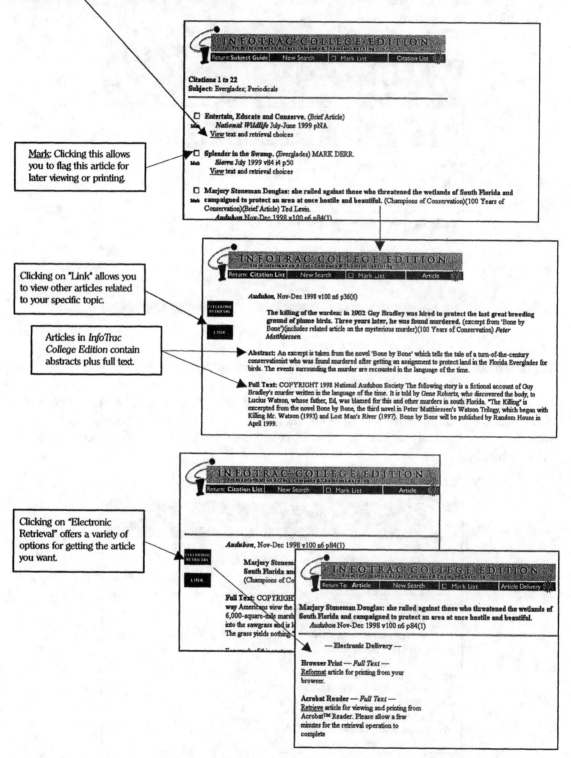

Mark: Clicking this allows you to flag this article for later viewing or printing.

Clicking on "Link" allows you to view other articles related to your specific topic.

Articles in *InfoTrac College Edition* contain abstracts plus full text.

Clicking on "Electronic Retrieval" offers a variety of options for getting the article you want.

PowerTrac Searching

To begin a more advanced search on a topic, click on "PowerTrac."

The PowerTrac search provides a variety of ways to search the database for articles. The "Choose Search Index" drop down box displays the indices available in this database.

For example, by clicking on "Journal Name" and typing the name of a specific journal, this will search the database for all articles pertaining to that journal. Simply click on "View" to see the complete list of articles.

What is an Index? Each article is indexed by certain variables. These indices include the article's author name, where and when it was published, etc. You can search the following indices by using their **Index Abbreviations** (listed in parenthesis below).

Indexes for Searching in PowerTrac:

Abstract (ab): Includes words from article abstracts as well as from any author's abstracts.

Author (au): Authors are indexed in surname/given name order; for example, "nelan bruce w." It's best to search in surname-first order. Enter a surname and, optionally, a given name.

Content (ac): Lets you locate all records with full text and eliminate those without. To search this index, enter the word "fulltext."

Date (da): The date the article was published.

Journal Name (jn): The name of the magazine or periodical.

Journal Name List (jn=): Provides a list of magazines or periodicals in which the search topic appears.

Key Word (ke): Words in article titles and authors, as well as subjects, people, companies, products, vocations, events, etc., featured in articles.

Record num. (rn): A full record always includes a unique record number. If you note a record number, you can easily find the record again with the record number index.

Source (so): Lets you search for records by the source from which they're taken (e.g., encyclopedia or newsletter).

Source List (so=): Lets you browse an alphabetical list of subjects that contain the word or words you type.

Subject (su): Lets you search for references by the topic under which they are indexed.

Subject List (su=): Provides a list of references by topic.

Text Word (tx): Composed of words from the body of articles and reports.

Title (ti): The title index is composed of all words in article, report or book titles.

Using Wildcards in PowerTrac Searches

At times, you might want to find more than just exact matches to a search term. For instance, you might want to find both the singular and plural forms of a word or variant spellings. Wildcards let you broaden your searches to match a pattern.

InfoTrac provides three wildcards:

- An asterisk (*) stands for any number of characters, including none. For example, **pigment*** matches "pigment," "pigments," "pigmentation," etc. The asterisk wildcard can also be used inside a word. For example, **colo*r** matches both "color" and "colour."
- A question mark (?) stands for exactly one character. Multiple question marks in a row stand for the same number of characters as there are question marks. For example, **psych????y** matches either "psychology" or "psychiatry" but not "psychotherapy."
- An exclamation point (!) stands for one or no characters. For example, **analog!!** matches "analog," "analogs" or "analogue" but not "analogous."

If you see a message about a search being invalid, you'll need to add at least one character before one of the wildcards.

Troubleshooting & Frequently Asked Questions

If you are experiencing any technical difficulties, you can send a form to Technical Support from the ICE Customer Service page, or you can send an e-mail to *wp-support@infotrac-college.com*.

Q: *What are the system requirements to run InfoTrac College Edition?*

A: Netscape Navigator v3.0 or later, Internet Explorer v3.0 or later.

Q: *If I have a problem, what information do I need to provide in my message to InfoTrac customer service? When will I receive a response? How do I submit information?*

A: Click on the Customer Service button on the welcome screen. You will be prompted for all necessary information.

Q: *How do I access the on-line help file?*

A: Each Screen has context sensitive help. Just click on the help button.

Q: *What if I lose or forget my passcode/account ID?*

A: Please keep your passcode/account ID card safe. We **cannot** replace lost passcodes/account IDs.

Q: *Will I be reminded or notified before my subscription expires?*

A: Yes.

Q: *Is that a 0 (zero) or an O (oh) in my passcode/account ID?*

A: Passcodes/account IDs contain no vowels. It's a 0 (zero).

Q: *How often is the database updated?*

A: InfoTrac SearchBank databases are updated every business day. Daily publications such as newspapers are indexed on a daily basis. Weekly publications as well as those with time-sensitive content are indexed and abstracted within the same day or within 1-3 days of receipt.

QUICK GUIDE FOR YOUR STUDENTS

The following pages may be duplicated and distributed to your students.

INFOTRAC® COLLEGE EDITION

Quick Start Guide

InfoTrac College Edition is a fully searchable online university library containing complete articles and their images. Its database gives you access to hundreds of scholarly and popular publications–including magazines, journals, encyclopedias, and newsletters. Updated daily, the *InfoTrac College Edition* database also includes articles dating back as much as four years. And every article within the database can be easily printed for reading and reference purposes or quickly arranged into a bibliography.

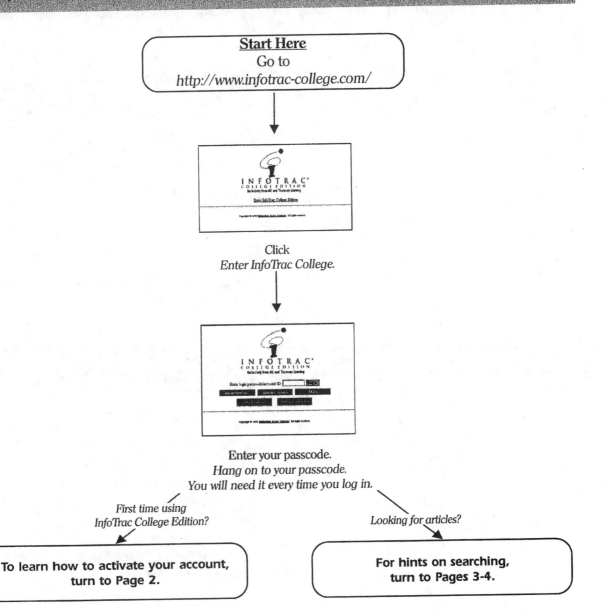

Start Here
Go to
http://www.infotrac-college.com/

Click
Enter InfoTrac College.

Enter your passcode.
*Hang on to your passcode.
You will need it every time you log in.*

*First time using
InfoTrac College Edition?*

Looking for articles?

**To learn how to activate your account,
turn to Page 2.**

**For hints on searching,
turn to Pages 3-4.**

Activating Your Account

If you are using *InfoTrac College Edition* for the first time, you will need to complete the registration form. Any items in **bold** type must be completed before your account can be activated. *(see Figure 1)*

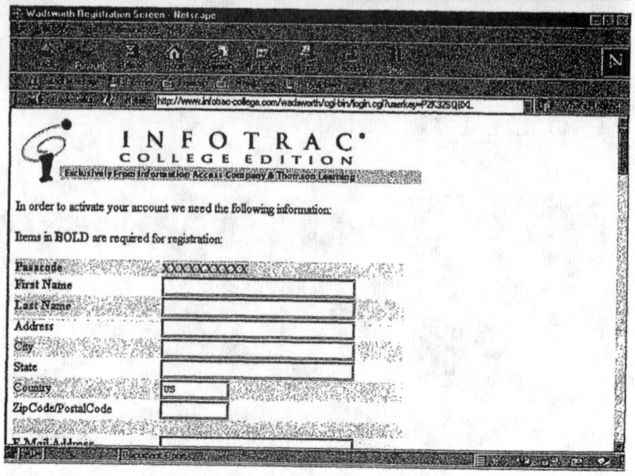

Figure 1. *Registration Screen*

If required items are missing or invalid on the registration form, an error message from Customer Service describing the problem will appear. Simply click the "Back" button on your browser's toolbar to return to the registration form. *(see Figure 2)*

Figure 2. *Error message*

After the registration form is successfully completed, you will be asked to confirm that all information is accurate. Click on the "Submit" button to send in your completed registration form. *(see Figure 3)*

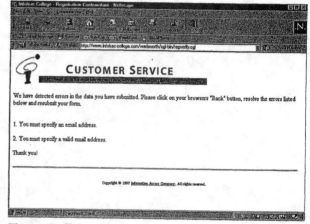

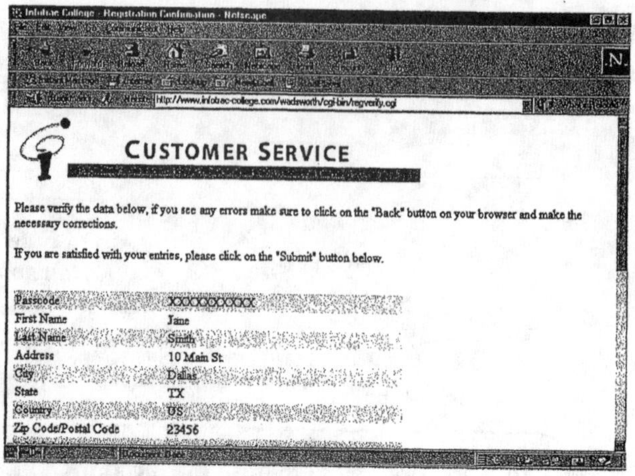

Figure 3. *Confirmation Screen*

Searching the *InfoTrac College Edition* Database

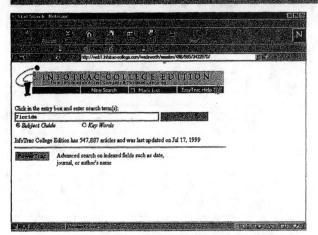

Figure 4. *Search Screen*

After signing in, the search screen will appear. Type in the topic you would like to research. Select "Subject Guide" or "Key Words" and click the "Submit Search" button. *(see Figure 4)*

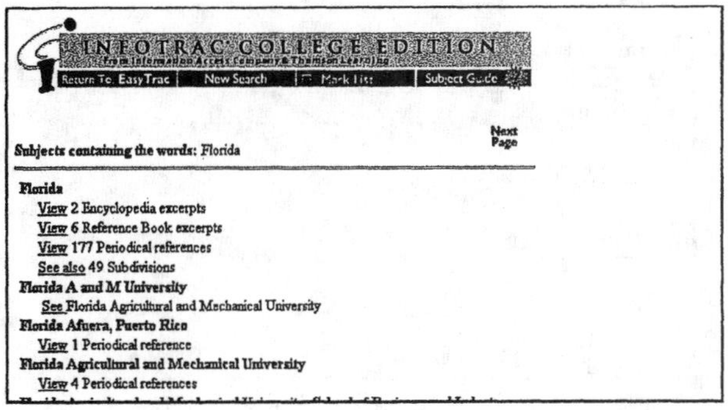

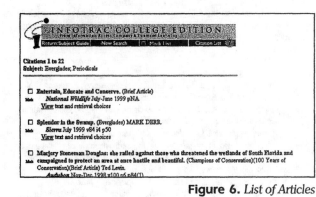

Figure 5. *Subject Screen*

Subject Guide Search

If your search words do not match the Subject Guide database, a list of similar and related subjects will come up on the screen. Simply select the subject that most closely matches your topic.

Once a subject has been selected from the database, a screen will appear with links to Periodical References, Subdivisions, and Related Subjects. *(see Figure 5)*

Periodical References will list the title, author and publications for articles available on your subject.

Subdivisions will list subcategories of articles in your subject.

Related Subjects will list topics closely associated to your subject.

Figure 6. *List of Articles*

A list will appear on the screen containing bibliographic information for each article in your search to a maximum of 20 articles per page. *(see Figure 6)*

To select an article, check the "Mark" box by clicking on it with your mouse.

To read your selected articles, click on the "View text and retrieval choices" link.

Your marked articles will have the bibliographic information at the top of the article followed by an abstract (when available) and the full text of the article. To browse through your articles, click on the **Prev. Next ◀◀Record▶▶** link. Articles can also be printed. *(see Figure 7)*

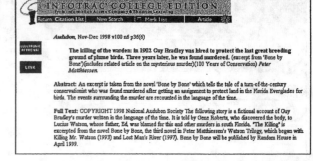

Figure 7. *Sample Article*

With PowerTrac, a more complex search can be conducted. Click on the ▣ on the "Select an Index" listbox, choose the type of criteria you want to search for. The code for your criteria will appear in the entry box. Type your criteria in the entry box after the code. *(see Figure 8)*

If you want to search by multiple criterion, simply repeat the process with an operator between them (see list below).

Logical operators (and/or/not) specify inclusive or exclusive relationships between search terms or result sets.

Proximity operators (Wn, Nn) specify that two search terms must be within a specified distance (in words) of each other. Proximity operators work only with free text indexes such as keywords, abstracts, text and titles.

Range operators (since, before, etc.) specify upper bounds, lower bounds or both in searches for numeric data. Numeric indexes include publication dates, number of employees and annual sales.

Nesting operators determine the order in which operators are evaluated.

Indexes for Searching in PowerTrac

Abstract (ab): Includes words from article abstracts as well as from any author's abstracts.

Author (au): Authors are indexed in surname/given name order; for example, "nelan bruce w." It's best to search in surname-first order. Enter a surname and, optionally, a given name.

Content (ac): Lets you locate all records with full text and eliminate those without. To search this index, enter the word "fulltext."

Date (da): The date the article was published.

Journal Name (jn): The name of the magazine or periodical.

Journal Name List (jn=): Provides a list of magazines or periodicals in which the search topic appears.

Key Word (ke): Words in article titles and authors, as well as subjects, people, companies, products, vocations, events, etc., featured in articles.

Record Number (rn): A full record always includes a unique record number. If you note a record number, you can easily find the record again with the record number index.

Source (so): Lets you search for records by the source from which they're taken (e.g., encyclopedia or newsletter).

Source List (so=): Lets you browse an alphabetical list of subjects that contain the word or words you type.

Subject (su): Lets you search for references by the topic under which they are indexed.

Subject List (su=): Provides a list of references by topic.

Figure 8. *PowerTrac Search Screen*

Text Word (tx): Composed of words from the body of articles and reports.

Title (ti): The title index is composed of all words in article, report or book titles.

Using Wildcards in PowerTrac Searches

At times, you might want to find more than just exact matches to a search term. For instance, you might want to find both the singular and plural forms of a word or variant spellings. Wildcards let you broaden your searches to match a pattern.

InfoTrac provides three wildcards:

* An asterisk (*) stands for any number of characters, including none. For example, **pigment*** matches "pigment," "pigments," "pigmentation," etc. The asterisk wildcard can also be used inside a word. For example, **colo*r** matches both "color" and "colour."

* A question mark (?) stands for exactly one character. Multiple question marks in a row stand for the same number of characters as there are question marks. For example, **psych????y** matches either "psychology" or "psychiatry" but not "psychotherapy."

* An exclamation point (!) stands for one or no characters. For example, **analog!!** matches "analog," "analogs" or "analogue" but not "analogous."

If you see a message about a search being invalid, you'll need to add at least one character before one of the wildcards.